Making All Things New

CATHOLICITY IN AN EVOLVING UNIVERSE

Making All Things New

Catholicity, Cosmology, Consciousness

to Thomas,
Blessings & peace,

ILIA DELIO, OSF

ORBIS BOOKS

Maryknoll, New York 10545

Second Printing, November 2015

Founded in 1970, Orbis Books endeavors to publish works that enlighten the mind, nourish the spirit, and challenge the conscience. The publishing arm of the Maryknoll Fathers and Brothers, Orbis seeks to explore the global dimensions of the Christian faith and mission, to invite dialogue with diverse cultures and religious traditions, and to serve the cause of reconciliation and peace. The books published reflect the views of their authors and do not represent the official position of the Maryknoll Society. To learn more about Maryknoll and Orbis Books, please visit our website at www.maryknollsociety.org.

Library of Congress Cataloging-in-Publication Data

Delio, Ilia.
   Making all things new : catholicity, cosmology, consciousness / Ilia Delio, OSF.
      pages cm. — (Catholicity in an evolving universe)
   Includes bibliographical references and index.
   ISBN 978-1-62698-136-2
   1. Church—Catholicity. 2. Cosmology. I. Title.
BV601.3.D45 2015
261.5'5—dc23

                                                    2015005857

Glorious Lord Christ:

*The divine influence secretly diffused and active
in the depths of matter,*

*And the dazzling center where all the innumberable fibres
of the manifold meet;*

Power as implacable as the world and as warm as life;

You whose forehead is of the whiteness of snow,

Whose eyes are of fire,

And whose feet are brighter than molten gold;

You whose hands imprison the stars;

You who are the first and the last,

The living and the dead and the risen again;

*You who gather into your exuberant unity every mode
of existence;*

*It is you to whom my being cries out with a desire
as vast as the universe:*

In truth you are my Lord and my God.

—Pierre Teihard de Chardin, S.J.
Hymn of the Universe

Pick a flower on Earth and you move the farthest star.

—Paul Dirac
Nobel Prize 1933

Contents

Introduction

This is a book about catholicity. I hope you will not put it down too quickly if you are not Catholic, because it is not exactly about the Catholic Church but about *catholicity* or awareness of how sun, moon, stars, Kepler, Saturn, maple trees, muddy rivers, amoeba, bacteria, and all peoples of the earth form a whole. *Catholicity* is from a Greek word, *katholikos*, which means "of the whole" or "a sense of wholeness." It is the orientation of all life toward making wholes and thus toward universality or turning together as one. So, by way of introduction, this book is about wholeness and wholemaking that emerges from the nexus of catholicity, cosmology, and consciousness. The early Greeks coined the word *catholic* to describe attunement to the physical order, so that *catholicity* meant living in harmony with the stars. To live in catholicity was to have a sense of the cosmos or the whole order of things, including physical and spiritual things.

The word *whole* today is alluring—whole foods, holistic health, whole body workouts. it is a word that has become embedded in our cultural consciousness, despite our radically divided world. The longing for wholeness today speaks to something deep within the human person and nature itself. Are we whole by nature? Does wholeness emerge with the development of life, or is life an unfolding of an already existing wholeness? Today, physics speaks of a quantum whole and systems biology tells us that living organisms emerge as complex wholes. Modern science, therefore, suggests that we do not invent a whole; rather, the whole exists prior to anything else. We are to awaken to the whole we already are and deepen it by becoming more whole and unified through creativity, convergence, and consciousness.

Interestingly, the priestly author of Genesis had an implicit sense of catholicity even before the word was coined. "In the beginning God created heaven and earth," he writes, "and the earth was a formless void" (Gn 1:1). This same sense would eventually be taken up by Christians for whom God and humanity, Alpha and Omega, are united in the person of Jesus Christ. The early Christians adopted the word *catholic* to describe the Church as disciples gathered in the name of Jesus Christ. To have a sense of the whole was to have a consciousness of Christ and to gather into community as one in Christ. Over time, the significance of catholicity shifted from wholeness to orthodoxy, especially as the Church grew into a major intellectual and cultural force in the Western world. Christians came to believe that catholicity meant expansion of the institutional Church throughout the world. Jean Maalouf writes:

> Indeed, for a long period of time, Christians were thought to believe that Catholicity meant the extension of the institutional Church to entire Christianity, and perhaps beyond. The hierarchy of the Church was not only a model but also a solid foundation for political power in the world. Universalism meant the extension of political, cultural and religious particularism. This was believed to be the more or less perfect image of the Kingdom of God on earth, whose center was out of this world.[1]

Although catholicity began as a consciousness of the whole order of things (cosmos), over time it became detached from cosmology and conflated with the pope, Rome, and the institutional Church. Catholic universalism became equivalent to power, authority, and moral order. But as Maalouf writes: "The truth is that Catholicity is not an abstract concept, and it does not mean the universalization of one culture, but the universalization of the human being."[2] Catholicity does not mean that everyone is to become Catholic; rather, to be catholic is to be aware of belonging to a whole and to act according to the whole, including the galaxies and stars, earth, animals, plants, and human life. To paraphrase Saint Augustine: "You have made us for wholeness,

---

[1] Jean Maalouf, "*The Divine Milieu*: A Spiritual Classic for Today and Tomorrow," *Teilhard Studies* 38 (1999): 15.

[2] Ibid.

O Lord, and our hearts are restless until they find their wholeness in You."[3]

While there are a number of outstanding theologians of the
modern period who have written on catholicity, only a few have
reconciled the dynamic of catholicity with the physical world, as
science describes it today. In this respect Pierre Teilhard de Chardin, SJ, stands out as a voice of catholicity in the wilderness. In *The
Divine Milieu*, Teilhard disclosed a new catholicity, a new awareness, which was both shocking and exuberant with life. By bringing together Christianity and evolution, he renewed catholicity in
its deep cosmic roots. Sister Catherine R. O'Connor, CSJ, writes:

> The sense of the sacredness of the earth and of man's
> rootedness in it could be, in conjunction with ritual and
> sacrament, a rich source of nourishment for the human
> spirit. Teilhard's particular thrust in the area of the im-
> portance of human action and passion in making 'contact'
> with God through the earth would add a new dimension
> to an approach to Christianity that still tends to be merely
> legal and moral.[4]

Catholicity, as a consciousness of the sacred earth, of the universal spirit, and our longing for completion, is at the core of
evolution. Teilhard had a sense of "deep catholicity," an intrinsic
wholeness at the heart of life yearning to become more whole in
and through the human person. He described this wholeness as
"Omega," a oneness already within and yet ahead of us, drawing
us onward toward greater unity in love. For Teilhard, modern
science awakens us to a new sense of catholicity and empowers us to participate in evolution as co-creators of the emerging
whole. Can we connect catholicity and cosmology in a way that
revitalizes Christianity in an evolutionary universe? The answer

---

[3] Augustine, *The Confessions of St. Augustine*, trans. John K. Ryan
(New York: Image Books, 1960), 43. In the opening paragraph of his
Confessions Augustine proclaims: "You have made us for yourself, and
our heart is restless until it rests in you."

[4] Sister Catherine R. O'Connor, CSJ, *Woman and Cosmos: The
Feminine in the Thought of Teilhard de Chardin* (Englewood Cliffs, NJ:
Prentice-Hall, 1971), 150.

to this question is essentially the basis of this book, which spearheads a new book series called *Catholicity in an Evolving Universe* by Orbis Books. This series will explore the dimensions of catholicity in an evolving universe with particular emphasis on theology, spirituality, science, the arts, the economy, and the environment. Catholicity reflects divine incarnational energy at the heart of cosmic evolution. The series seeks to illuminate the meaning and purpose of an unfinished universe, the role of human life in evolution, and the significance of Christogenesis (literally, "Christ birthing") or the emerging, personalizing union of God, human, and cosmos.

My explorations in this book begin with certain premises: First, Catholicity is first and foremost linked with cosmology. It arises with the introduction of space into the physical order creating a "cosmos," an orderly connectedness of reality. Catholicity, therefore, is based on the Greek understanding of cosmos as a three-dimensional sphere rather than a two-dimensional flat earth. Second, Catholicity is a function of consciousness. The rise of catholicity and cosmology takes place in the axial period in which the human person emerges as individual subject. Catholicity is awareness of the one amid the many through the human person whose consciousness "catholicizes" or unifies the many parts. Third, Catholicity is consciousness of the whole, an orientation *toward* universality or turning together as one. In this respect catholicity and universality are *not* equivalent although they are deeply connected. Although the Church identifies catholicity with universality, a more fruitful relationship between catholicity and universality begins with reorienting these within a wider cosmological and evolutionary framework.

I became aware of revisiting catholicity in light of an evolving universe through my friendship and collaboration with John Haughey, SJ, whose book, *Where Is Knowing Going*, awakened me to catholicity in a wider narrative. However, the work of French philosopher Rémi Brague enabled me to understand catholicity in its relation to cosmology, as the Greeks first conceived this idea. To this end I examine catholicity on four different levels: (1) catholicity in nature, including Big Bang cosmology and quantum consciousness; (2) catholicity and the human person; (3) catholicity and Jesus; and (4) the institutionalization of catholicity or the Catholic Church.

Chapter 1 examines Brague's principal thesis, namely, that we have lost the wisdom of the world because we have forgotten how to read the stars. I look at the emergence of the word *cosmos* in the work of Plato and the significance of cosmology for anthropology, as ancient cultures conceived it. Since the word *catholic* was adopted by the early Christians to define their understanding of church, I briefly explore its early usage by Ignatius of Antioch and Irenaeus of Lyons. I then look at the mutation of catholicity, as Christianity became a politicized religion under Constantine the Great, and catholicity was defined as orthodoxy, especially in light of the Arian crisis. Chapter 2 looks at catholicity in the medieval synthesis of microcosm and macrocosm and the loss of this synthesis with the rise of modern science. The powerful influence of Newtonian science on culture shifted the emphasis of catholicity from a cosmological whole to mechanistic lawfulness. I discuss the shift in catholicity from wholemaking to lawfulness, especially with the development of manual theology and the effects of mechanistic Catholicism on the alienation of the Church from the world.

The discoveries of twentieth-century science ushered in a new vision of the cosmos and the relationship of the human person to the cosmos. Insights from modern science, therefore, provide new ground to explore catholicity for twenty-first-century life. Chapter 3 develops catholicity as an intrinsic aspect of nature itself. Beginning with Big Bang cosmology, the primacy of energy, and quantum consciousness, catholicity in nature is viewed as the impulse in evolution toward greater wholeness. The term *emergence* best describes the unfolding of life from simple to complex life marked by a rise of consciousness. Hence, I speak of "Big Bang catholicity" insofar as the physical cosmos bears witness to an unyielding wholeness within it.

Chapter 4 focuses, more specifically, on quantum consciousness with a view toward understanding consciousness based on quantum physics. In the midst of the twentieth century Jesuit scientist Pierre Teilhard de Chardin described evolution as the rise of consciousness, indicating that mind is in matter from the beginning of the universe. Today, scientists and philosophers are supporting this insight, realizing that mind is more than the human brain and consciousness is more than the human mind. These ideas are explored in such a way that we begin to understand the connection between nature's inner propensity for wholeness and the rise of consciousness. In other words, there is an intrinsic relationship between catholicity and consciousness. The rise of consciousness and complex wholeness simultaneously in nature undergirds the profound role consciousness plays in realizing wholeness on the human level. If nature bears within it what we might call an intrinsic catholicity, why is wholeness so difficult on the human level? I explore this question in terms of the complex human brain with its divided right and left hemispheres, conscious self-reflection, and language, which distinguishes the human species. The mark of the human person is verbal language and communication, and thus the freedom to express oneself. The human person is one of desire and decision. How we think, what we think, what enters or leaves our minds, where we focus our minds—all shape our actions and, in turn, our world. On the human level where there is free will and intellect, the whole is not a given; it is a choice in relation to God, neighbor, and earth community. For the Christian the choice for wholeness is embedded in the gospel life, following the words of Jesus: "I have come so that you may have life and have it to the full" (Jn 10:10). We are to focus our minds on the whole and choose the whole for the sake of abundant life.

Understanding catholicity in its organic and cosmological context sheds new light on the person of Jesus Christ and the significance of his life for the emergence of the Catholic Church. Chapter 5 examines the spirit of creative wholeness that marks the life of Jesus in his public ministry. To better understand this creative wholeness, I use Teilhard de Chardin's paradigm of Christogenesis, or the evolutionary emergence of Christ. Teilhard identified Omega with Christ and posited a third or organic nature of Christ, meaning that God is incarnate from the beginning of the universe. If Christ Omega is the goal of evolution (following the Pauline notion of "all things in Christ") then the goal is already present in the unfolding process of life. Christ the evolver (or Christ *in* evolution) and Christ Omega (Christ as goal of evolution) are one and same and come to explicit consciousness in the person of Jesus of Nazareth. I look at the ministry of Jesus in terms of catholicity and discuss the sacraments of baptism and Eucharist as new forms of relatedness with Christ in an expanding field of compassionate love.

The diminishment of catholicity by institutionalization and alienation from worldly affairs relates to the development of Catholicism's teaching on the four last things: heaven, hell, death, and final judgment.[5] Chapter 6 revisits these four quadrants of Catholic belief in the wider framework of evolution and Christogenesis. In particular, Teilhard's emphasis on Christianity as an evolutionary, world-affirming religion is highlighted, and his "mysticism of action" is discussed. I look at the constraints of institutional catholicity against the backdrop of a wider cultural catholicity, exploring jazz fests, social media, and baseball as cultural ritual events where catholicity is vibrant. My particular interest in computer technology and its impact on the shape of humankind is then examined in light of the four last things. The rapid development of computer technology today is seeking to fill a religious void, extending the religious self into the cyber world so that the last four things no longer seem to constrain human destiny.

The advantage of exploring catholicity within a wider cosmological and cultural framework is that it provides new language and new paradigms to explore the catholicity of the institutional church. Chapter 7 examines the Church as an open system, since the Church is an organizational system, and the dynamics of its organization affects its function and outreach to the world. The term *open system* comes from the biological sciences and refers to openness of the system to the environment and, as such, its capacity to self-organize. Using Teilhard's notion of the Church as a new phylum of christified persons in evolution, I creatively imagine what an open-systems Church might look like from the point of administrative organization to the development of theology as open-systems theology. I explore briefly the significance of open-systems theology for the discovery of truth in an evolutionary world.

Since my aim is to kindle a new consciousness of catholicity for an evolutionary age, I seek to discover a deeper mean-

---

[5] It is important to point out here that I am distinguishing catholicity (with a lowercase "c") from Catholicism (with an uppercase "C") insofar as catholicity or orientation toward wholeness is intrinsic to nature and organic consciousness, whereas I see the institutionalization of catholicity expressed (or thwarted) in Catholicism.

ing of this consciousness for the Church and the world today. Chapter 8 takes up Saint Paul's injunction to "put on the mind of Christ" and considers what this means in terms of quantum consciousness and spirituality. Here I focus more specifically on training the mind for unified consciousness. Insights from the Buddhist nun Tenzin Palmo are helpful, as well as the writings of Etty Hillesum, who died at a young age in a Nazi concentration camp. Etty's bridge between inner world and outer world through a unified consciousness in God illuminates the inner capacity of the human person to think widely and deeply even in the midst of suffering and violence. She also shows us how expansion of the mind-soul can influence the world around us. Centuries before Etty, Francis of Assisi came to similar insights through a deep, christic mindfulness, and I briefly explore his path to a "uni-verse" through the centrality of love and the poverty of letting go into a wider embrace of life.

Finally, after searching the lines of catholicity from the Big Bang to quantum consciousness and evolution, to the life of Jesus and the emergence of church from the patristic era to the postmodern age, Chapter 9 revisits the meaning of catholicity in light of scientific insights and cosmology and asks, What are we called to today, as citizens of the universe, as followers of Jesus Christ and as members of the institutional Church? The final chapter seeks to clarify the meaning of catholicity in its various levels (nature, person, Jesus, and Church) and to examine briefly models of catholicity in our current age. Of the four models discussed in this chapter (Pope Francis, Barbara Marx Hubbard, the Dalai Lama, and the Leadership Conference of Women Religious), I want to highlight the spirit of Pope Francis. Elected to the papacy following the resignation of Pope Benedict XVI, Pope Francis (Jose Maria Bergoglio), in his late seventies, brings a new spirit to the Church that reflects a consciousness of catholicity that we explore here. His is an inner spirit of freedom grounded in the love of God, guided by the gospel message of the new kingdom at hand, and open to a world of change. He desires a Church on the margins, where the poor and the forgotten can be brought into a new unity; a Church that advocates life at all costs and promotes peaceful life in a war-torn and violent world; a Church that models justice in an age of greed, consumerism, and power; a Church centered on the risen Christ, empowering a consciousness of the whole. This is a church leader who desperately wants to breathe a new spirit of catholicity into a world dying for wholeness and unity.

But the numbers speak otherwise. Mark Gray of the Center for Research in the Apostolate (CARA-Georgetown) states that at the end of 2014, "about 28.9 million people in the U.S. who were baptized and raised Catholic . . . no longer self-identify as Catholic." This is equivalent to more than 900,000 people each year and is slightly larger than the number the Church added in baptisms and receptions into full communion in 2012.[6] Gray's statistics on all levels of Catholic life show downward trends and no signs of improvement. So while Pope Francis is seeking to expand the Church's presence in the world, catholicity seems to be diminishing due, in part, to a growing irrelevance of institutional religion.

There is an urgency today to reconnect cosmology and catholicity, not as abstract concepts, but as the reconciliation of modern science and religion. The Catholic Church, with its core incarnational foundation, can play a major role in this renewal. "Science develops best," Saint John Paul II wrote, "when its concepts and conclusions can be integrated into the wider human culture and its concerns for ultimate meaning and value."[7] Religion, too, develops best when its doctrines are not abstract and fixed in an ancient past but integrated into the wider stream

---

[6] Mark Gray, "1964–CARA." Available online. Also, *The Economist* reported that Naci Mocan and Luiza Pogorelova of the National Bureau of Economic Research examined the relationship between religiosity and the length of time spent in school and concluded that "just one extra year of schooling makes someone 10% less likely to attend a church, mosque, or temple, pray alone or describe himself as religious." The authors felt "reasonably certain that extra schooling actually caused religiosity to fall, rather than merely being correlated with the decline. During those extra years mathematics and science classes typically become more rigorous, points out Naci Mocan, one of the authors—and increased exposure to analytical thinking may weaken the tendency to believe" ("Falling Away: How Education Makes People Less Religious—and Less Superstitious too," *The Economist* [October 11, 2014]).

[7] "Letter of His Holiness John Paul II to Reverend George Coyne, SJ, Director of the Vatican Observatory," available on the vatican.va website.

of life. Albert Einstein once said that "science without religion is lame and religion without science is blind."[8] So too, John Paul II wrote: "Science can purify religion from error and superstition; religion can purify science from idolatry and false absolutes. Each can draw the other into a wider world, a world in which both can flourish."[9] Teilhard de Chardin saw that dialogue alone between the disciplines is insufficient; what we need is a new synthesis of science and religion, drawing insights from each discipline into a new unity. In a remarkable letter to the director of the Vatican Observatory, John Paul II wrote:

> The church does not propose that science should become religion or religion science. On the contrary, unity always presupposes the diversity and integrity of its elements. Each of these members should become not less itself but more itself in a dynamic interchange, for a unity in which one of the elements is reduced to the other is destructive, false in its promises of harmony, and ruinous of the integrity of its components. We are asked to become one. We are not asked to become each other. . . . Unity involves the drive of the human mind towards understanding and the desire of the human spirit for love. When human beings seek to understand the multiplicities that surround them, when they seek to make sense of experience, they do so by bringing many factors into a common vision. Understanding is achieved when many data are unified by a common structure. The one illuminates the many: it makes sense of the whole. . . . We move towards unity as we move towards meaning in our lives. Unity is also the consequence of love. If love is genuine, it moves not towards the assimilation of the other but towards union with the other. Human community begins in desire when that union has not been achieved, and it is completed in joy when those who have been apart are now united.[10]

---

[8] Albert Einstein, "Science and Religion," Princeton Theological Seminary, May 19, 1939.

[9] "Letter of His Holiness John Paul II to Reverend George Coyne, SJ, Director of the Vatican Observatory."

[10] Ibid.

The words of the late pope highlight the core of catholicity: consciousness of belonging to a whole and unity as a consequence of love. Yet, our world is divided, and the divisions are not abstract; they are real and deepening. They are the heart-wrenching divisions of religious wars, economic gaps, racial hatred, fears of terrorism—division upon division—to the extent that our only hope is another world, whether it is the otherworldliness of heaven or the cyber world of virtual reality. Nature reminds us, however, that in our cosmic roots we are already one. Can we learn from nature how to create a unified world? Can religion inspire an evolution toward unity? Can we reimagine Christian life in an evolving universe? The world is not a given but a gift to create. Catholicity invites us to wake up, open our eyes, and reach for the stars to create a new world together by becoming a new community of life.

Chapter 1

Catholicity and Cosmos

The Wisdom of the World

We are meaning makers and storytellers. The stories we tell one another shape the meaning of our lives. Every religion tells a story in a way that combines beliefs, images, events, and divinity in a coherent, meaningful form. Despite the modern privatization of religion or the outright dismissal of it, religion won't go away—ever—because religion is about the deep-rooted energies of the spirit yearning for ultimate meaning and fulfillment. The word *religion* means literally "to be bound" or "to be bound back" (*re-ligare*) just as a ligament binds two bones together. Religion undergirds the unyielding longing to be bound to an ultimate source. Catholicity is not about religion per se, but it is complementary to religion because it is about wholemaking. In its Greek origin, the word *catholicity* is a composite of the preposition *kata* (according to) and the noun *holos* (whole), so that *kath' holou* can be an adverb meaning "wholly" or *katholikos*, a substantive that is best rendered in English as "catholicity."[1] My understanding of *catholicity*, therefore, is a "sense of the whole" or "according to the whole." The whole, however, is not a given; rather, it flows from my human consciousness and attention. The word *attention* means "to extend or reach out a hand." Imagine extending your hand to reach for the stars: you see the stars,

[1] John C. Haughey, SJ, *Where Is Knowing Going? The Horizons of the Knowing Subject* (Washington, DC: Georgetown University Press, 2009), 40.

you feel connected to them, and you long to touch them. That is the type of attention or consciousness that marks catholicity.

Catholicity, like consciousness itself, is not static; it is not a fixed ideal. Rather, it is an outflow of human awareness in relation to the surrounding world; it is like a connecting thread between the human person and the cosmos. Catholicity undergirds these questions: Are we aware of belonging to a whole? What are the wholes we are making through our own self-conscious acts? Walter Ong, SJ, likened catholicity to the parable of the yeast (Lk 13:20–21), that small, invisible power that spreads throughout the whole of the dough and catalyzes movement toward a unified loaf of bread.[2] To *catalyze* (a word borrowed from modern science) means to initiate or accelerate a process of transformation. In physical nature catalytic elements are essential to chemical, biochemical, and environmental processes. The catalyst both accelerates the rate of transformation and lowers the activation energy needed for the transition state so that the process of transformation takes place more efficiently. In a similar way catholicity catalyzes the movement *toward* wholeness or universality by way of consciousness. Whereas universality undergirds oneness or unified wholeness, catholicity is the dynamic consciousness of the whole that makes oneness possible. In this respect *catholicity* is not a noun; it does not define anything. Rather, *catholicity* is an adjective or, better yet, a verb; it is what moves (catalyzes) a person to think, move, and orient his or her life toward making wholes from the partials of experience. Catholicity depends on how we see the world. To appreciate the relationship between catholicity and cosmos, I would like to explore catholicity in three different periods: pre-axial religious consciousness, axial-period consciousness, and Christianity.

Pre-Axial Religions

In his fascinating book *The Wisdom of the World*, Rémi Brague develops a historical link between wisdom and cosmos. He begins his study by exploring the cultures of ancient Mesopotamia and

---

[2] Walter Ong, "Yeast, A Parable for Catholic Higher Education," *America* (April 7, 1990): 347.

Egypt where a word that encompassed not only the human sphere but also the heavens and the realm of the gods was conspicuously absent. Instead, the cultures of ancient Mesopotamia and Egypt used lists such as *the heavens and the earth* or collective words such as *everything* and *all,* which, Brague argues, are not quite the same as *world.*[3] These ancient civilizations tended to look at the physical and human worlds as interdependent. An imbalance in one sphere could result in an imbalance in the other. The dominant form of pre-axial consciousness was cosmic, collective, tribal, mythic, and ritualistic. Cultures were intimately related to the cosmos and to the fertility cycles of nature. Thus, there was established a rich and creative harmony between primal peoples and the world of nature, a harmony which was explored, expressed, and celebrated in myth and ritual. Just as they felt themselves part of nature, so they experienced themselves as part of the tribe. It was precisely the web of interrelationships within the tribe that sustained them psychologically, energizing all aspects of their lives. To be separated from the tribe threatened them with death, not only physical but also psychological. However, their relation to the collectivity usually did not extend beyond their own tribe, for they often looked upon other tribes as hostile. Yet within their tribe they felt organically related to their group as a whole, to the lifecycles of birth and death, and to nature and the cosmos. The order of the natural cosmos followed the order in the social cosmos. That is, human activity in the public sphere had an influence on the cosmic order. Lack of order in the cosmos, for example, in the realm of plants, such as infertility, could only be repaired if one began by reestablishing the human social order. Justice among humans contributed to maintaining the world in movement. People believed that human action was required to maintain the order of the universe, and they conducted rituals and sacrifices to renew and restore it.[4]

One well-known example of a pre-axial culture is the Noble Ones (Aryans), the Indo-Iranian peoples of the Central Asian steppes who lived a nomadic tribal life (c. 1000–900 BCE). They

---

[3] Rémi Brague, *The Wisdom of the World: The Human Experience of the Universe in Western Thought,* trans. Teresa Lavendar Fagan (Chicago: The University of Chicago Press, 2003), 15.

[4] Ibid., 16.

led peaceful, fairly static, simple lives. They had their gods; their beliefs about the nature of the world; and their rituals to help them understand and influence these gods, which they identified with natural and cosmic forces: the god of the sun, the gods of the earth, the moon, and the winds. Fire, water, and the "soul of the bull" were gods associated with ritual practices and, as such, were particularly venerated. They also venerated trees, especially by rivers or streams, probably because these often had healing properties. In addition they had a class of gods called Ahuras, associated with oaths and promise-keeping. The Ahuras originally included a divine power to enforce oaths that later became the responsibility of three main Ahuras: Varuna, the guardian of order; Mithra, the god of storm, thunder, and rain; and Mazda, the lord of justice and wisdom. The Noble Ones were guided by a realm of intermediate deities, everything from speech to binding oaths, chanting, and the act of listening to a sacred text, all were guided by supernatural forces that brought them nearer to the gods. Daily religious ritual and sacrifice to the gods helped them maintain productivity, harmony, and a cosmic order against disorder. According to their sacred texts, the earth was created in seven stages. First, the sky came into being—this was an inverted bowl of beautiful stone. Second, the water was created at the bottom of the sky shell, and then third, the earth that floated on water. To this the gods added one plant, one animal, and a bull, and then in the sixth stage, man. Fire was added in the seventh stage, pervading the entire world and residing in seen and unseen places. As a final act of creation the gods assembled and performed the first sacrifice. The primordial plant, the bull, and the man were crushed and from them the vegetable, animal, and human realms were created and populated the earth. New life and death were created, and the world was set in motion.[5]

---

[5] John Grim describes similar practices for the Teotihuacanos peoples of Mexico (c. 700–200 BCE) for whom spirituality meant a connectedness between the human body, the local bioregion, and the celestial forces. See John Grim, "Apocalyptic Spirituality in the Old and New Worlds: The Rivisioning of History and Matter," *Teilhard Studies* 27 (1992): 9–10.

The Noble Ones performed rituals that reenacted this primordial sacrifice to maintain cosmic order and ensure the continuation of the lifecycle. Libations were performed in the home, for example, of water or fire to return these vital elements to the gods to support them, and a perpetual fire was kept burning. The Indo-Iranians revered life, and like all pre-axial peoples, they felt a strong affinity between themselves and animals. They ate only consecrated animal flesh that had been offered to the gods with prayers to ensure the animal's safe return to the soul of the bull. They believed the soul of the bull was the life energy of the animal world, whose spirit was energized through their sacrifice of animal blood. This nourished the deity and helped the gods look after the animal world and ensured plenty.[6] The "catholicity" of the Noble Ones, like that of many of the pre-axial religions, was a consciousness of connectivity to the plants, the animals, the sky, and to the whole of nature. They believed gods or spirits in nature influenced human action, and in turn, human action (and ritual) had its effects on nature. Their sense of the whole was a sense of belonging to a web of life guided by supernatural forces or deities. All things shared the same breadth of life—animals, trees, humans. All things were bound together.

The Axial Age and Catholicity

In 1949 German philosopher Karl Theodor Jaspers coined the term *Achsenzeit* (Axial Age or Axis Age in English) to describe a time between approximately 900 and 200 BCE when the spiritual foundations of modern humanity were established. It was a pivotal time in early human history when human beings began to reflect for the first time about individual existence and the meaning of life and death. Increasing urban civilization, initially brought about under the leadership of a priestly ruling class, encouraged trade and brought different societies closer together. But as urban life accelerated and expanded, it disrupted the old sense of order. This new way of living generated unprecedented social and political conflict and an increase in

---

[6] "The Human Journey," www.humanjourney.us.

violence and aggression. Old customs could no longer be taken for granted. People began to question their own beliefs once they came into contact with others whose beliefs were different. They were challenged to look at themselves in different ways and entertain new ideas or cling steadfastly to their old ones. With a rise in population and the mixing of cultures, more people were exposed to the realities of life, such as sickness, greed, suffering, inhumanity, and social injustice. As a result, people began to experience themselves as separate from others for the very first time. In this new age, Jaspers claimed, man became conscious of being as a whole, of himself and his limitations. He experiences the tension of the world and his own powerlessness. He asks radical questions. Face to face with the void, he strives for liberation and redemption. By consciously recognizing his limits, he sets himself the highest goals. He experiences absoluteness in the depths of self-hood and in the lucidity of transcendence.[7] William Thompson states that "what makes this period the 'axis' of human history, even our own history today, is the fact that humans emerged as 'individuals' in the proper sense."[8]

Axial consciousness generated a new self-awareness that included awareness of autonomy and a new sense of individuality. The human person as *subject* emerged. The awareness of the self in the present brought with it awareness of the self after death. People began searching for more comprehensive religious and ethical concepts and to formulate a more enlightened morality where each person was responsible for his or her own destiny. During the Axial Age a new mode of thinking developed almost simultaneously in four major areas of the world: China, India, the Middle East, and Northern Mediterranean Europe. Whereas primal consciousness was tribal, axial consciousness was individual. "Know thyself" became the watchword of Greece; the Upanishads identified the atman, the transcendent center of the self. The Buddha charted the way of individual enlightenment;

---

[7] Karl Jaspers, *The Origin and Goal of History*, trans. Michael Bullock (New Haven, CT: Yale University Press, 1953), 1, 2, 23, 27.

[8] William M. Thompson, *Christ and Consciousness: Exploring Christ's Contribution to Human Consciousness* (New York: Paulist, 1977), 21.

the Jewish prophets awakened individual moral responsibility.[9] This sense of individual identity, as distinct from the tribe and nature, is the most characteristic mark of axial consciousness. This new consciousness was distinguished from pre-axial consciousness of interdependence; axial consciousness was self-reflective, analytic, and could be applied to nature in the form of scientific theories, to society in the form of social critique, to knowledge in the form of philosophy, and to religion in the form of mapping an individual spiritual journey. This self-reflective, analytic, critical consciousness stood in sharp contrast to primal mythic and ritualistic consciousness. Although axial consciousness brought many benefits, it involved loss as well. It severed the harmony with nature and the tribe. Axial persons were in possession of their own identity, it is true, but they had lost their organic relation to nature and community. They now ran the risk of being alienated from the matrix of being and life. With their new powers they could criticize the social structure and by analysis discover the abstract laws of science and metaphysics, but they might find themselves mere spectators of a drama of which in reality they were an integral part.[10]

It is in the Axial Age that the word *cosmos* emerged. Beginning in the Hellenic Ages, the universe came to be seen existing apart from human action and possessing a kind of wisdom that humanity did not have. The word *cosmos* arose among the Greeks and referred to the "whole" or that which makes the world a "world." The pre-Socratic philosopher Heraclitus of Ephesus (c. 540–c. 480 BCE) referred to *ta panta* (all things), which another pre-Socratic, Empedocles (c. 490–430 BCE), transformed into the singular *to pan* (the all). The Greeks' most innovative step was the formulation of a special word for the world. The word they chose was *kosmos,* first used in Homer's *Iliad* to mean "in good order" or the order that gives rise to

---

[9] Ewert H. Cousins, *Christ of the Twenty-first Century* (Rockport, MA: Element Books, 1992), 6; idem, "Teilhard's Concept of Religion and the Religious Phenomenon of Our Time," *Teilhard Studies* 49 (Fall 2004): 10–11.

[10] Ewert Cousins, "The World Religions: Facing Modernity Together," globalethic.org.

beauty, such as an ornament (hence, the word *cosmos* is related to "cosmetics").[11]

The separation of human from world allowed the ancient Greeks to discover a cosmos that could provide humans with models of perfection to gaze upon (cosmology) and natural spaces to define and conquer (cosmography). In this context *world* was as much a concept as a concrete place; it meant not just physical creation but also the environment in which humans function. It is interesting how a shift in understanding the cosmos gave rise to a sense of *world* different from the pre-axial period. Prior to the axial period—for example, among the ancient Egyptians and Mesopotamians—the world was thought to be a flat, two-tiered structure, with the sky above and earth below. The Greeks introduced the concept of space and conceived of the cosmos as a three-dimensional sphere with height, depth, and width. One could suggest that awareness of a spatial, three-dimensional cosmos impelled the ancient Greeks to separate human from world in a way that allowed them to discover a cosmos. In other words the human was no longer part of an interdependent nature; now the human had self-consciousness and consciousness of "other" that was called world. The word *catholicity* was coined to describe a consciousness of the whole, cosmos, the whole physical order of things to which the human was connected but distinct from; cosmos was the source for guiding human action.

It was Plato who gave the word *cosmos* its meaning as *world*. His *Timaeus* provided the first description of reality as forming an ordered whole, being both good and beautiful. The cosmos, according to Plato, was created by a divine craftsman who strove to render his work as similar as possible to the perfect model.[12] The Good, the supreme principle, exercises power over physical reality and influences the conduct of the human person who, through the Good, turns his or her soul into a coherent whole (ethics) and gives the public sphere the unity it would otherwise be without. The *Timaeus* describes cosmology required by a particular anthropology. The plan for human life is an imitation of the cosmos. The wise person knows the cosmos and sees in it

---

[11] Brague, *The Wisdom of the World*, 19–20.
[12] Ibid., 22.

the mirror of his or her own wisdom. The individual soul was to imitate the regularity of the movements of the soul of the world. Nature has drawn us upright that we might be inspired by what is "cosmic." In Plato's world we stand upright to contemplate the stars.

The cosmos was a mirror for human action. The human was not simply in the world; the world was also in the human. It gave rhythm to our history, defined our aspirations, and directed our physical structure. The human (women were not allowed into Plato's academy!) was to contemplate superior things, intelligible things, whose harmonious disposition reveals profound mysteries to us.[13] Plato's cosmology influenced thinkers of late Antiquity and the Middle Ages; the cosmos influenced what one ought to be and what one was to do. Justice was the result of the agreement between cosmos and humanity, each with its own nature, instilled by God. Brague writes: "Cosmology had an ethical dimension. In turn, the task of transporting such good into the here below where we live enriched ethics with a cosmological dimension."[14]

The celestial influence on terrestrial life led Greek thinkers to posit a cosmologization of history.[15] The Greek word *catholicity* finds its root meaning in the link between *cosmos* and *anthropos* (human). Catholicity is not a physical order or a spiritual one; it does not connote geographical extension. *Kath' holou* (according to the whole) is not the same as *kata pantos* (according to all things); catholicity belongs not to the phenomenal and empirical but to the noumenal and ontological plane; it describes the essential nature of reality, not the external manifestations. Catholicity is what contemporary Jesuit philosopher Bernard Lonergan called "notional being," an orientation of being toward wholeness or leavening the stuff of life to create a greater whole.[16] For

---

[13] Ibid., 101.

[14] Ibid., 121.

[15] Brague, *The Wisdom of the World*, 98. By using this term, Brague suggests that, for the Greeks, the celestial bodies influence the earth and their circular movement governs the linear temporality of human history. Christian polemics against astrology will change this relationship and speak of a historization of cosmology.

[16] Bernard Lonergan, *A Second Collection*, ed. William Ryan and Bernard Tyrrell (Toronto: University of Toronto Press, 1996), 80.

the Greeks, catholicity was how the human stood in relation to the stars and listened to the wind, aware that the movements of nature guided the movements of human life.

Christian Catholicity

If catholicity is a consciousness of the whole, how did it find its way into the Christian sphere? In the New Testament the Church is simply called *church*. Jesus used the word *church* twice in the Gospels, both in Matthew. He said, "I will build my church" (Mt 16:18), not *churches* but one visible, recognizable church, *ecclesia*, a new family united as community in God. After the death and resurrection of Jesus, Christian identity was formed in tension with the Jerusalem community. As early as the first century we find the author of the *Didache*, one of the earliest Christian writings, offering a caveat concerning false prophets (11:2). The early Christians were very concerned that the new band of Jesus's disciples would stay together and hold fast to the teachings they received from the apostles. This desire for coherent unity prompted the earliest use of the word *catholic* by the bishop-martyr Ignatius of Antioch. It is interesting that a bishop would be the first to use the word *catholic* for the newly formed Christian church. It would take someone familiar with Greek philosophy to find an appropriate word that could describe the meaning of the Christian church as the gathering of disciples together into a new whole, a new creation, centered in Jesus Christ. If the Greeks understood catholicity as human consciousness of the wider cosmos, Christians appropriated catholicity as a consciousness of the whole centered in Christ.

Ignatius was immersed in the living tradition of the local church in Antioch, where the believers in Christ were first called Christian (Acts 11:26). On his way to Rome, under military escort to the Coliseum, where he was martyred for his confession of faith, he wrote, "You must all follow the bishop as Jesus Christ follows the Father, and the presbytery as you would the Apostles. Wherever the bishop appears, let the people be there; just as wherever Jesus Christ is, there is the Catholic Church."[17]

---

[17] Ignatius of Antioch, "Epistle to the Smyrnaeans," 8.

Similarly, Polycarp, the bishop of Smyrna, is associated with the word *catholic* by those who witnessed his martyrdom (CE 155). In "The Martyrdom of Polycarp," written at the time of Polycarp's death, begins, "The Church of God which sojourns at Smyrna, to the Church of God sojourning in Philomelium, and to all the congregations of the Holy and Catholic Church in every place." In the early second century Christians used the word *catholic* as a consciousness of gathering together around the bishop as successor to the apostles, and in the name of Jesus Christ, to create a new whole, a new creation.

Between the second and fourth centuries the Church encountered opposition and various splinter groups such as the Gnostics and Montanists who either rejected the incarnation of God (Gnosticism) or focused on the Spirit and prophecy (Montanism). The constant threat of turning Jesus's message into a political agenda impelled theologians to define what *catholic* meant in both doctrine and practice. Irenaeus of Lyons provides an important link between the apostolic Church and its later institutional forms by illuminating the meaning of catholicity in history. If the Greeks were about the cosmologization of history, that is, human events such as ethics and political action governed by the physical order of the cosmos, Christians were about eschatology, or the final destiny of all things. For Christians, catholicity was not about human action alone; rather, the whole order of things, including the stars, was directed toward a final end, the fullness of Christ.

The gathering of the Church both was and is to share in the first fruits of the new creation in Christ. For Irenaeus this meant an emphasis on the Church not as institution but as active presence of the Spirit: "For where the Church is, there is the Spirit of God; and where the Spirit of God is, there is the Church, and every kind of grace."[18] Irenaeus was a genuinely catholic thinker for whom nothing is left out of the economy of salvation and for whom truth is always found in history. The most distinctive mark of Irenaeus's theology is its inclusive concern for the whole of creation. He challenged the Gnostics (those who denied the

---

[18] Irenaeus of Lyons, *Against Heresies* 3.24.1, Eng. trans. *The Ante-Nicene Fathers*, vol. 1, ed. A. Roberts and J. Donaldson (Grand Rapids, MI: Eerdmans, 1987), 458.

incarnation of God) by saying that God entered history to heal and make whole and thus reconcile humanity to God. We know God not according to his greatness, he indicated, but according to his love. Salvation is not a flight to God *from* what is human (Gnostics), but the realizing of God's likeness and the sharing of his life *in* what is human. Catholicity, for Irenaeus, is attentiveness to the Spirit of God, that is, the Spirit of healing and wholeness. When we are inwardly whole, we can attend to the cosmos in all its beauty.

From Cosmology to Orthodoxy

Within some three hundred years after the death of Jesus and with the conversion of the Emperor Constantine, Christianity became legal and recognized as the official religion of the empire. The Nicene Creed was composed in the fourth century as a creedal confession of faith that would consolidate the Christian faith in the empire: "I believe in one God, the Father Almighty, Creator of Heaven and Earth. . . . I believe in one, holy, catholic, and apostolic church." Surprisingly, the word *catholic* became equated with *universalis* (universal). The word *universal* means "to turn as one" (from the Latin *vetere* and the prefix *uni*); however, in light of its Greek origin, catholicity is *not* universality, although one can see how universality became equated with catholicity, or wholeness with oneness. Rather, catholicity is awareness of the whole that moves one to act toward wholeness or unity. The rise of Constantine the Great in the fourth century created a turning point for catholicity. Christianity became a state religion, and the consequences were enormous. The relationship among catholicity, universality (oneness), and cosmology (wholeness) was blurred by politicizing Christian faith; politics trumped cosmology, and universality trumped catholicity.

The development of doctrine in a politicized religion became a hot topic among Christians. The core of the arguments centered on the meaning of *incarnation*. What did it mean to say that God became flesh? How could this be understood within a single human life, that is, in Jesus of Nazareth? Could God truly be united to physical matter, which changes and decays? Religion was "in the air," and no matter what a person's position in society, everyone had a vested interest in the debates: "If in this city you ask a shopkeeper for change, he will argue with you about whether the Son is begotten or unbegotten. If you inquire about the quality of bread, the baker will answer, 'The Father is greater, the Son is less.' And if you ask the bath attendant to draw your bath, he will tell you that the Son was created ex nihilo [out of nothing]."[19] The core of the controversy was the question of Jesus himself—was Jesus truly God or not? The source of the debate was a priest named Arius, who preached that Jesus was the firstborn son of the Father but not equal to the Father. His supporters, the Arians, defended this position vehemently.

Richard Rubenstein provides a scathing account of the rise of orthodoxy at the Council of Nicea in 325 CE. Arians argued that Jesus was a perfect representative of God—just as a painting or statue represents its subject—but not the subject itself. Jesus was the exact image of God, but Jesus himself was not God. Rubenstein tells us that what was at stake between the two camps (Arians and Orthodox) was a passionate monotheism fundamentally at odds with the premises of pagan thought. He claims that disputes as serious as the Arian controversy virtually compelled the ordinary churchgoer to choose between rival theologies. He writes: "These clashes between Christians were traumatic, raising questions that would haunt the Church for generations to come. Did Jesus' life provide a realistic model for human behavior or was it an ideal reachable only by a handful of saints and martyrs?"[20]

The Arian controversy sparked intense conflict as the Church sought its identity in the empire. The main question was, When did Jesus became God? The answer, according to Rubenstein, was at the Council of Nicea. Constantine detested Judaism and desired a "New Rome"; he thought that Christianity could be used to unite his people. The council itself was like a gripping novel: crime, coverup, motive, dangerous ambition, power

---

[19] Richard E. Rubenstein, *When Jesus Became God: The Epic Fight over Christ's Divinity in the Last Days of Rome* (New York: Harcourt Brace, 1999), 6.

[20] Ibid., 40.

mongering, fear, intimidation, intrigue, back stabbing, conniving, bludgeoning, and terrorizing. The cause for the tumultuous event was the word *homoousios* (what we have come to translate as "consubstantial"), which meant that the Son is one in essence (or substance) with the Father. Most of the bishops did not like the term, because it was a Greek philosophical term not found anywhere in scripture. But this word came to define Jesus as truly God and forms the linchpin of orthodoxy. Rubenstein writes:

> A look into the future, then, shows us Nicea as a watershed. While it looks forward to the ultimate resolution of the Arian controversy from the Catholic point of view—the identification of Jesus Christ as God—it also represents the last point at which Christians with strongly opposed theological views acted civilly towards each other. When the controversy began, Arius and his opponents were inclined to treat each other as fellow Christians with mistaken ideas. Constantine hoped that his Great and Holy Council would bring the opposing sides together on the basis of a mutual recognition and correction of erroneous ideas. When these hopes were shattered and the conflict continued to spread, the adversaries were drawn to attack each other not as colleagues in error but as unrepentant sinners: corrupt, malicious, even satanic individuals.[21]

The Arian controversy is of importance not only with regard to the divinity of Jesus, but even more so because it distorted the essential meaning of catholicity. Christians forgot how to read the stars or see God amid the stars as attention was focused away from the cosmos toward defending the doctrine of truths. The Arian controversy created such an embattled church at Nicea that consciousness of the whole—catholicity—was broken. After Nicea the Church became defined as *Catholic* not with a sense of the whole but with a sense of the true. Catholicity was no longer a function of cosmology but orthodoxy. The embroiled Christian religion became ensnared by political factions to the extent that catholicity lost its noumenal dimension and was

---

[21] Ibid., 87–88.

reduced to the constraints of orthodoxy. Nicea disconnected cosmos from anthropos.

The Whole Becomes Divided

With the decline and fall of Rome in the fifth century, the Roman Church assumed both temporal and spiritual authority in the West and had enormous influence on the development of art and culture of the Western world. In the fourth century the renowned Bishop Augustine asserted the widespread use of the word *catholic*. He writes, "We must hold to the Christian religion and to communication in her Church which is Catholic, and which is called Catholic not only by her own members but even by all her enemies."[22] And again, "The very name of Catholic, which, not without reason, belongs to this Church alone, in the face of so many heretics, so much so that, although all heretics want to be called Catholic, when a stranger inquires where the Catholic Church meets, none of the heretics would dare to point out his own basilica or house."[23] Augustine, following Nicea, identified the Catholic Church as the locus of orthodoxy and true faith. The Church was not so much a gathering into a new creation as the mirror of truth in a hostile world. When the Western Roman Empire began to disintegrate, Augustine developed the concept of the Catholic Church as a spiritual City of God, distinct from the material Earthly City. His thoughts profoundly influenced the medieval worldview.

In 1054, a formal split occurred between the Roman Catholic and Eastern Orthodox churches. As the Church grappled with the person of Jesus as fully divine and fully human, debates and discussions raged not only over whether Jesus was truly "consubstantial" with the Father, but also whether the Holy Spirit was a divine Person. The doctrine of the Trinity formulated by Augustine in the West and the Cappadocian Fathers in the East maintained no radical distinctions among the three divine Persons; however, disagreement as to the procession of the Holy

---

[22] Augustine, *The True Religion*, 7.12.
[23] Augustine, *Against the Letter of Mani Called "The Foundation"* 4.5.

Spirit lingered into the Middle Ages. The *Filioque* (with the Son) question was fiercely debated in the Middle Ages because it was the central question of the Trinity and at the heart of the Church's creedal confession. The Western church used a version of the Nicene Creed that included the *Filioque* ("We believe in the Holy Spirit, the Lord, the giver of life, who proceeds from the Father *and the Son*, who with the Father and the Son is adored and glorified"), while the Eastern church emphasized that the Holy Spirit proceeds only *from the Father* ("and in the Holy Spirit, the Lord, the giver of life, who *proceeds from the Father*. With the Father and the Son he is worshiped and glorified.") The two churches resolved the Filioque question in the fifteenth century but the union did not last. The debate was not only about orthodoxy but also about the authority of the pope to define what was and was not orthodox. The Eastern and Western churches have since worked toward unity, but the distinctions and ecclesial divisions remain.

What we find in the first five centuries of the Church is a mutation of catholicity from a sense of cosmos as order and harmony to a fixation on orthodoxy. Even pre-axial people had an implicit catholicity that was lost in the post-Constantinian church, as bishops fought over the formulation of doctrine. We see something of a renewal of catholicity in the Middle Ages, as the Church moved beyond the Arian controversy, but the scars of Nicea remain with us even today.

Chapter 2

The Humpty Dumpty Earth

Macrocosm-Microcosm

For the Greeks, the concept of world belonged to the realm of nature; with the Judeo-Christian tradition the world entered the realm of history. Christian writers reversed the correspondence between the larger, physical world (macrocosm) and the smaller, human world (microcosm) in favor of the human, who was created on the sixth day in the image of God (Gn 1:26). The nobility of the human person made the human the center of the stable, fixed cosmos described by Ptolemy. The entire world became a theology for the human, a book that enabled a person to know the mind of its Author.[1] While catholicity was trumped by political factions in the early Church, it found a new breath of life in the Middle Ages, a time when the harmony of heaven and earth seemed so synchronous that the whole universe resounded "like an immense zither."[2] Ancient and medieval ethics took the regularity of the world as a model. To know God was to contemplate the Book of Nature, and contemplation of nature was the model for moral practice. The entire world became a source of theology. As Bernard of Clairvaux writes: "The trees and the rocks

---

[1] Rémi Brague, *The Wisdom of the World: The Human Experience of the Universe in Western Thought*, trans. Teresa Lavendar Fagan (Chicago: The University of Chicago Press, 2003), 172.

[2] Marie Dominique Chenu, *Nature, Man, and Society in the Twelfth Century*, trans. Jerome Taylor and Lester K. Little (Chicago: University of Chicago Press, 1973), 8.

will teach you more than you could ever learn from professors."[3] The world was inhabited rightly by those who could freely orient themselves there, without being held on a leash by the stars.

At the School of Chartres (twelfth century), correspondence between microcosm and macrocosm formed the core of the curriculum. Scholars such as William of Conches and Thierry of Chartres promoted study of the natural cosmos, along with grammar and scripture, so that knowledge of the cosmos would lead to knowledge of God.[4] All that is, they believed, exists as a harmonious whole. Because the cosmos is ordered and rational, it can be investigated, studied, and known.[5] Peter Ellard describes this deep, integral relationship among the human person (microcosm), the cosmos (macrocosm), and the role of learning (study) in the School of Chartres:

> Rather than seeing the sense world as lacking value or goodness and as being distant from God, William and Thierry presented it in most positive terms as a way to God. They recognized its sacred character not in and of itself simply because it does not and cannot exist in and of itself. Its existence is tied to—and cannot be understood apart from—God. The cosmos, for William and Thierry, is a sacred image of God and it contains the Spirit of God in its very being. Humanity's primary task is to experience the world, to contemplate and understand it, and thereby to proceed to knowledge of God and, ultimately, to union and consummation with God.[6]

We find this same integration of cosmos, God, and human in the theology of Bonaventure and Thomas Aquinas. Bonaventure's doctrine of exemplarism, in particular, speaks to the deep relationship between God and cosmos. He describes creation as a limited expression of the infinite and dynamic love among the

---

[3] Bernard of Clairvaux, *Letters* 106.2.

[4] Peter Ellard, *The Sacred Cosmos: Theological, Philosophical, and Scientific Conversations in the Twelfth-Century School of Chartres* (Scranton, PA: University of Scranton Press, 2007), 16.

[5] Ellard, *The Sacred Cosmos*, xxiv–xxv,n.1.

[6] Ibid., 204.

Father, Son, and Spirit, exploding into "a thousand of forms" in the universe. He uses the term *emanation* to describe the birth of creation from the womb of the triune God of love. Creation, he writes, is like a beautiful *song* that flows in the most excellent of harmonies. It is a song that God *freely* desires to sing into the vast spaces of the universe. Creation is the finite loving outflow of an infinitely loving God; its beauty is in the order and harmony of the things. It is not a mere external act of God, an object on the fringe of divine power; rather, it is rooted in the self-diffusive goodness of God's inner life and emerges out of the innermost depths of divine life.

Bonaventure compared the rich variety of creation to the stained-glass windows of a great cathedral. Just as light strikes the various panes of glass and diffracts into an array of colors, so the divine light emanates through the divine Word of God and diffracts in the universe, producing a myriad of things; everything reflects the divine light. The world is a mirror of the Divine. It is also a book in which the Trinity shines forth.[7] Every grain of sand, every star, every earthworm, and every flower reflects the power, wisdom, and goodness of God. The world, therefore, is sacramental; it is a symbolic world full of signs of God's presence. Catholicity is a consciousness of divine presence, an awareness of divine love throughout the whole of life. Bonaventure saw this catholicity in the life of Francis of Assisi:

> In beautiful things he contuited Beauty itself and through the footprints impressed in things he followed his Beloved everywhere, out of them making for himself a ladder through which he could climb up and lay hold of him who is utterly desirable. . . . He savored in each and every creature that fontal goodness and . . . sweetly encouraged them to praise the Lord.[8]

---

[7] Ilia Delio, *A Franciscan View of Creation: Learning to Live in a Sacramental World*, ed. Elise Saggau, vol. 2, The Heritage Series, ed. Joseph P. Chinnici (New York: Franciscan Institute, 2002), 40.

[8] Bonaventure, "The Major Legend of Saint Francis," in *Francis of Assisi: Early Documents*, vol. 2, *The Founder*, ed. Regis J. Armstrong, J. A. Wayne Hellmann, and William J. Short (New York: New City Press, 2000), 596–97.

Francis contemplated the footprints of God impressed on the things of creation, and he found God wherever he went in the world. As he experienced divine love within himself, so too he saw that same love throughout creation—in birds, trees, clouds, rabbits, even wolves. The world was the self-revealed gift of God, created to lead humans to what it signified, a deep, personal unity in love. Contemplation of the world was indistinguishable from the contemplation of God.

Catholicity and the Divided Brain

There is no doubt that the medieval mind was truly catholic in the sense that there was a consciousness of cosmic wholeness in God. Knowledge of God was based on experience of the cosmos, and reflection on that experience is how one made sense of the whole. Scholars note that in the twelfth century there was a new emphasis on the individual through the influence of Cistercian spirituality and, in particular, the writings of Bernard of Clairvaux.[9] Bernard's emphasis on the concrete reality of the incarnation meant that a personal relationship with Jesus was the starting point for union with God.[10] This emphasis on individual relationship with God placed the cosmos in the background of human salvation. But it was the rise of Scholasticism that severed the relationship between cosmos and anthropos in a way that ultimately would unravel the whole and throw catholicity back into the arms of orthodoxy.

Scholasticism arose in the twelfth century as the university emerged out of the cathedral school and the need to consolidate theological writings became important for education of the

---

[9] Colin Morris, *The Discovery of the Individual 1050–1200* (New York: Harper and Row, 1973), 139–40; Caroline Walker Bynum, *Jesus as Mother: Studies in the Spirituality of the High Middle Ages* (Berkeley and Los Angeles: University of California Press, 1982), 17.

[10] See Bernard of Clairvaux, Sermon 20.6: "I think this is the principal reason why the invisible God willed to be seen in the flesh and to converse with men as a man. He wanted to recapture the affections of carnal men who were unable to love in any other way, by first drawing them to the salutary love of his own humanity, and then gradually to raise them to a spiritual love."

clergy. Scholasticism was an objective way of reasoning to truth that departed from the experiential method of monastic theology, which began with the prayerful reading of scripture *(lectio divina)* and reflection on that experience. Scholasticism was a new scientific method of theological reasoning based on the *sic et non* (yes and no) of Peter Abelard (d. 1142) and, because of its scientific approach to theological questions, was readily incorporated into the university curriculum. Peter Lombard (d. 1164) was a Scholastic theologian and Bishop of Paris who gathered all the writings of the fathers of the Church and organized them into four main books known as the *Sentences*. The *Sentences* covered the four main areas of theology: God, creation, incarnation, and church (including the sacraments). The theology of Lombard's *Sentences* was in the Scholastic form of the *questio*, a dialectical form of reasoning by which one reads the established positions on a question (yes), the counter positions (no), and then offers one's own reasoned opinion. Everyone who studied theology at the university became familiar with the *Sentences* of Peter Lombard. Brague argues that Western philosophical eccentricity was not the result of medieval thinkers picking and choosing ancient Greek ideas to fit their needs, but rather of the dialectical demise of ancient cosmology-cosmography. From ancient times cosmology had an anthropological and ethical relevance; the order of the cosmos was the framework to which it was necessary to adapt oneself and an example to be followed. With Scholasticism the cosmos became an area of abstract reasoning, as students sought to understand the truths of God based on logic and analytical reasoning. If catholicity was sublated into orthodoxy with the Arian controversy, it became absorbed into logical thinking by Scholasticism.

In an interesting study on the human brain, British psychiatrist Iain McGilchrist argues that a predominance of left-brain function emerged for the first time in Western civilization just as Greek culture was beginning to pass its peak. From the sixth to the fourth centuries BC, there was an almost unparalleled flowering of science and the arts based on the best of what both right and left hemispheres in conjunction could offer. To appreciate his thesis, it is helpful to understand how the right and left hemispheres pay attention to the world, reaching out a hand toward it (the meaning of the word *attention*) in different ways or with different sets of priorities and values. The right hemisphere begins with relationship to the world at large, not seeing it as a separate object, ripe for manipulation. The right brain is our connection to the natural world as well as a sense of the uniqueness of the individual, whose interests need to be harmonized with those of the community. It is involved with new experiences, new events, things, ideas, words, skills, music or what is present to the mind. The right hemisphere is present or "presences" us. Its attention is not in the service of manipulation but in the service of connection, exploration, and relation.[11]

The left hemisphere narrows things to a certainty while the right hemisphere opens them up to possibility. The predominance of the left brain is shown in either/or thinking (either science or religion, for example). It is adept at procedures, but it sees them as ends in themselves. It is not in touch with the world. It is not good at understanding the world. Its attention is narrow; its vision is myopic; and it cannot see how the parts fit together. It is good for only one thing: manipulating the world and controlling the parts. It neglects the incarnate nature of human beings and reduces the living to the mechanical. It prioritizes procedure without having a grasp of meaning or purpose. It requires certainty where none can be found.[12]

In Western Christianity dominant left-brain thinking emerged with the rise of Scholasticism in the Middle Ages and consolidated with the Galileo affair and the rise of modern science. The shift to linear, analytical thinking among Scholastic theologians not only produced the great *summas* of theology, such as we find with Thomas Aquinas, but laid the foundation for modern science and the scientific method. According to McGilchrist, this left-brain dominance left the world stripped of meaning because the left hemisphere takes over whatever it is presented with and breaks the data into small bits of information by which the brain abstracts and generalizes. With left-brain dominance very little returns to the right brain of passion and

---

[11] Iain McGilchrist, *The Master and His Emissary: The Divided Brain and the Making of the Western World* (New Haven, CT: Yale University Press, 2009), 32–53.

[12] Ibid., 42–44.

connectivity and thus creativity. The rise of the left brain made a way to the systematization of knowledge but stripped the world of wholeness as things were reduced to parts. Science rose to prominence, as the Church retreated from the world. Catholicity was sacrificed on the high altar of Scholastic theology and modern science.

The Rise of Modern Science

The strain in relationship between religion and science, brain and world, cosmology and catholicity became paralyzed with the collapse of the Ptolemaic cosmos and the rise of heliocentrism (a "sun-centered" cosmos). Cosmology was part of theology as long as the cosmos was believed to be God's creation.[13] The rise of heliocentrism changed this God-world relationship. When astronomers discovered that the earth was not stationary and center of the cosmos, but rather circling around the sun, the Church was not ready for the major upheaval of a moving earth. The older cosmology set the eternal celestial realm in opposition to the terrestrial scene of change and decay; the gradual "hierarchy of being" approached perfection as it approached the Divine. But the new cosmology erased the distinction between corruptible and incorruptible and applied uniform natural categories to the whole universe. Heliocentrism snuffed out cosmological wisdom by relegating the human person to the margins of a spinning planet. The displacement of the human person from the centered earth disconnected the human from creation; the human person was no longer connected to the whole. God was no longer the One who gave the whole creation its meaning and purpose and shared with creation a deep relationship of expression. Rather, God was the efficient cause who set the world machine in motion and otherwise was aloof and dispassionate. Catholicity shrank to the level of law and order in the same way that earth shrank from heaven; love from electromagnetism; and the right brain from the left brain of details and logic.

---

[13] Raimon Panikkar, *The Rhythm of Being: The Gifford Lectures* (Maryknoll, NY: Orbis Books, 2010), 186.

With the rise of modern science cosmology lost its relevance in two ways. On the one hand, its ethical value was simply neutralized as cosmology was considered amoral; on the other hand, it became disconnected from anthropology and thus from shaping ethical action.[14] The image of the world that emerged from physics after Copernicus, Galileo, and Newton was a confluence of blind forces where there was no place for consideration of the Good. "For the first time in the history of cosmologies, there was no longer a place where the physical became the spiritual. It was physical all the way out, possibly to infinity."[15] The modern cosmos was ethically indifferent. The very concept of world was repositioned by the modern, post-Galilean physics of Kepler and Descartes, whereby the idea of order became determining, and world became contrasted with chaos.[16] The West ceased to have a viable religious cosmology with the rise of modern science.

If catholicity is consciousness of the whole, such wholeness was disrupted as the earth was seen to move around the sun. The center of the stable cosmos, the earth, as well as the center of the earth, the human person, became ec-centric. The "disenchantment of the world" meant that humans could possess nature. The human person no longer discovered the world; now the human person mastered the world. The right brain lost its connectivity to the outer world, making it possible for the left brain to rise to control: "The objective became swallowed up into the immanence of subjectivity."[17] René Descartes sought to rescue God from the clutches of a changing world by searching for true and certain knowledge in the human person. His famous "I think, therefore I am" drew a strong line of separation between matter and spirit and shifted the certainty of knowledge from God to the individual. This "turn to the subject" imposed a burden on each person to make sense of the world individually and to unify

---

[14] Brague, *The Wisdom of the World*, 194.

[15] Nancy Ellen Abrams and Joel R. Primack, *The New Universe and the Human Future: How a Shared Cosmology Could Transform the World* (New Haven, CT: Yale University Press, 2011), 12.

[16] Brague, *The Wisdom of the World*, 189.

[17] Mark Taylor, *After God* (Chicago: University of Chicago Press, 2007), 44n.3.

it by rational thought alone; objectivity came to be "constituted by and to exist *for the sake of* subjectivity."[18] The rise of the self-thinking subject became a substitute for the transcendent self of the ultimate whole. Modern science stripped the cosmos of its sacred character. The world of nature became brute matter organized by internal laws and mechanisms. The wholeness of catholicity found itself in a culture of modern philosophy and science marked by brute matter and the self-thinking subject, the autonomous individual who alone bore the weight of truth. Rational thought supplanted an ethics of love. The world became a confluence of blind forces where there was no place to ponder a God whose love moves the sun and the other stars.

Lawful Catholicity

In the modern period catholicity was conflated into official church theology and reduced to a set of rules and instructions found in the *Denzinger*,[19] which favored the juridical approach rather than a theology rooted in the real. Knowledge of God and the things of God were found in reason and law, carefully analyzed and systematized, not in the experience of body, self, and world. Consonant with left-brain dominance, theology was abstract and speculative, not experiential and creative. Truth was seen as internal coherence to divine law and order. Like Newton's world, the Church was governed by law and order; a mechanistic church in a mechanistic world.[20] The task of theology was to prepare concise and clear definitions for the revealed truth. Catholicity was reduced to a set of rules and instructions, leaving the world of nature defenseless and meaningless other than as the stage for human salvation. Seminary education became what Karl

---

[18] Ibid., 318.

[19] The *Denzinger* is a compendium of brief doctrinal definitions and statements that was published in Germany in 1845 by the German priest Heinrich Denzinger; it was revised several times afterward.

[20] For a discussion on Newton and the mechanistic universe see Ilia Delio, *The Unbearable Wholeness of Being: God, Evolution, and the Power of Love* (Maryknoll, NY: Orbis Books, 2013), 10–13.

Rahner called "Denzingertheologie." An updated publication of the *Denzinger* states:

> In this age of doctrinal latitude and speculative innovation there is a pressing need for a comprehensive source book on authentic Catholic dogma that is magisterially anchored while at the same time both practical and non-voluminous. You have such a book in this English translation of Father Heinrich Denzinger's *Enchiridion Symbolorum et Definitionum*. Since it was first published a century and a half ago, this handbook or collection (enchiridion) of articles (symbols) of faith and morals has enjoyed universal appeal and approbation since the pontificate of Blessed Pope Pius IX. The *Enchiridion* has been updated periodically; the edition being offered here by Loreto is that issued in 1957. The collection includes all articles and creeds of the Catholic Faith beginning with that of the twelve apostles, all dogmatic definitions stamped with the Petrine authority of the apostolic See (ex cathedra), decrees of the solemn magisterium, papal bulls, encyclicals and letters, as well as some of the more weighty decisions of the Holy Office prior to 1957. Although not every entry in this 653 page compendium of Church teaching is definitional (i.e. ex cathedra) it still should be considered the "locutus est" for every wayfaring Catholic whose patria, this side of heaven, is Roma.[21]

Although renowned theologians such as Rahner and Yves Congar eventually contributed to this manual, Congar criticized the way the manual was used in theological education of the clergy, mainly for the Roman rite. Essentially, the manual favored modern Catholicism's inclination to the juridical approach rather than a theology attached to life. Denzinger theology became linked with an understanding of the Church governed solely by laws and instructions; faith is a process that ends in definitions, and the task of theology is to prepare concise and clear definitions. Hence, the teaching church, the magisterium, became a

---

[21] *The Sources of Catholic Dogma* (Fitzwilliam, NH: Loreto Publications, 2009), product description on Amazon.com.

detailed set of juridical statements detached from the life of faith. Clergy were educated in Denzinger theology, and they, in turn, were to instruct the faithful. Catholic was infused with the "-ism" of institutional control, cultic priesthood, and an uneducated laity indoctrinated with manual theology.

Worldly Alienation

If catholicity is consciousness of the whole, it was reduced in the modern period to law, grace, and personal salvation, leaving the natural world bereft of any sacred meaning other than its usefulness in serving humanity. The human person was burdened by the depravity of a sinful world and a narrow individualism that fed on rational order, fixed truths, and canon law. The Catholic Church did not hesitate to bank on this new way of the individual in its pursuit of moral order and objective truth. To be Catholic at the dawn of the twentieth century was to be obedient to the institutional Church, the primacy of the pope, and the teachings of the magisterium. Since most Catholics knew little of either scripture or church history, a catechism of essential truths was instilled universally. Thinking was not essential to salvation.

At the turn of the twentieth century the world was considered a spiritually dangerous place. God created humans not for this "vale of tears," but for his kingdom in the next world. The existential choice was between a blissful heaven and a sinful world.[22] The salvation of souls and the world hereafter trumped all other concerns. Aspirations for human (or spiritual) fulfillment in this world were vain, misguided, and fleeting. The brevity and fallen nature of humanity was emphasized, including the vanity of

---

[22] This composite summary of pre–Vatican II Catholic spirituality draws on Joseph P. Chinnici, OFM, "Organization of the Spiritual Life: American Catholic Devotional Works, 1791–1866," *Theological Studies* 40 (June 1979): 229–55; idem, *Living Stones: The History and Structure of Catholic Spiritual Life in the United States* (Maryknoll, NY: Orbis Books, 1996); Joseph P. Chinnici, Christopher J. Kauffman, and Angelyn Dries, eds., *Prayer and Practice in the American Catholic Community* (Maryknoll, NY: Orbis Books, 2000), 246; and Jay P. Dolan, *Catholic Revivalism: The American Experience: 1830–1900* (Notre Dame, IN: University of Notre Dame Press, 1979).

earthly things, the harshness of God's punishment, the precariousness of eternal life, the importance of sacrifice, the necessity of choosing between heaven and a sinful world, and the imperative for order, regularity, control, penance, self-discipline, self-denial, and self-mortification. Personal moral weaknesses, the necessity of moral rigor, and reparation for sin were dominant motifs. The impetus to mortify the flesh and "control the passions," notably sexual ones, was paramount. Through ubiquitous reminders of death, divine retribution, punishment, and themes of calamity, pre–Vatican II Catholic culture reinforced this otherworldly sensibility that pitted an empire of grace against an empire of nature.[23]

The sources of Catholicism's tendency to downplay human fulfillment in the secular world and to accentuate a negative conception of the spiritual life reflected a longstanding historical ambivalence within the Christian tradition regarding the world and humanity's place in it. This ambivalence derived in part from an undercurrent of neo-Platonic influences promoting liberation from embodiment and an emphasis on ascending into the transcendent and universal/eternal.[24] But even more so it resulted from the rejection of modern science. It was reflected in the role of religious life and the monastic contemplative ideal as models of a higher order, striving for spiritual perfection, and a holier calling than available to laity in "the world." Christ's kingdom was not of this world; suffering and death were ever-present realities; the greatest glories lay in the world to come. Although various apostolic orders enshrined active service (charity,

---

[23] As Chinnici points out, the incarnation, and with it the world and the individual, lost its positive dimension as an act of creative love in the context of this emphasis on the "corruption" and "nothingness" of the human person and on the subsequent "debasement" and "humility" of Christ becoming a person like us ("Organization of the Spiritual Life," 240).

[24] The lingering influences of Gnosticism, Manichaeism, and, in the more modern European/American context, Jansenism, along with other tendencies exaggerating the division between body and spirit accentuated the negative side of this world-nature ambiguity. An excellent summary and discussion of these influences can be found in Anna Peterson, "In and Of the World," *Journal of Agricultural and Environmental Ethics* 12, no. 3 (2000): 237–61.

almsgiving) on a somewhat equal plane with "interior" spiritual exercises, the purely contemplative life was seen as the superior one.[25] A spiritually threatening world fed the impetus to withdraw in both literal and symbolic ways.[26] The religious/monastic ideal represented the more perfect response to this imperative.

Aside from the theological presuppositions animating Catholicism's negative spirituality of the nineteenth and early twentieth centuries, the view was also a reaction to a world characterized by Protestant apostasy, dramatic political upheavals, the corrosive influence of materialistic science, the social disruptions of urbanization and industrialization, a worldwide Great Depression, two catastrophic World Wars, the global spread of "atheistic communism," and the emergence of historical consciousness. These collective traumas psychologically reinforced a deep sense of sin, alienation, and estrangement, along with an apocalyptic sense of living in a sinful world facing the last days. Little wonder that so many of the Church's pronouncements and theological reflections at the time, especially on the errors of modernism, accentuated the rhetoric of calamity, unbelief, avarice, ungodliness, libidinous passions, and so forth. A corrupt and unwieldy world of sin, pride, materialism, and incredulity necessarily faced an imminent eternal judgment by God.[27]

An Unfortunate History

Whereas the Protestant Reformation artificially separated God from the cosmos, positing God as a supernatural, omnipotent Being who governed from above, Neo-Scholastic Catholicism separated the human from the cosmos by instilling fear, guilt, and self-doubt. By the beginning of the twentieth century both Protestantism and Catholicism had become anti-catholic

---

[25] Patricia Wittberg, *From Piety to Professionalism—and Back? Transformations of Organized Religious Virtuosity* (New York: Rowman and Littlefield Publishers, 2006), 6–7.

[26] Chinnici, "Organization of the Spiritual Life," 246.

[27] William D. Dinges and Ilia Delio, OSF, "Teilhard de Chardin and the New Spirituality," in *From Teilhard to Omega: Co-creating an Unfinished Universe* (Maryknoll, NY: Orbis Books, 2014), 170–71.

(separate, divided, isolated) in the most literal sense. In this respect historian Lynn White lamented the impact of Christianity
(both Protestant and Catholic) on the ecological crisis. A sense
of sin and guilt made Christians self-focused, not focused on the
earth. White argued that no religion had been more anthropocen-
tric than Christianity and none more rigid in excluding all but
humans from divine grace and in denying any moral obligation
to lower species. Christianity made it possible to exploit nature
in a mood of indifference to the feelings of natural objects.[28]
A piety of self-righteousness and otherworldly consciousness,
garnished with the promise of heaven, caused many Christians,
both Catholic and Protestant, to neglect the natural world and/
or to exploit it for purposes of human consumption. We will
continue to have an ecological crisis, White said, until we reject
Christian axiom that nature has no reason for existence except
to serve us.[29]

Wholeness Unraveled

Descartes's division of the world into thinking stuff and material stuff created havoc in the modern period as technology and
industrialization began to show their effects on a wounded earth.
Whereas the ancient and medieval models aimed for harmony
between the heavens and earth, in the modern period there was
no longer any connection between cosmology and ethics or any
relationship between the physical universe and the way humans
thought about themselves.[30] The idea of a moral or religious
imitation of nature became impossible because our concept of
nature changed. The world could no longer help us to become
human persons. On the religious level God was more to be feared
than loved, utterly transcendent rather than intimately near. It
was left up to the self-thinking subject to make sense of the
whole, even in its shrunken parts, and to make way to heaven.
Catholicity came undone after the Middle Ages and maybe even

---

[28] Lynn White Jr., "The Historical Roots of Our Ecological Crisis,"
Science 155 (March 10, 1967): 1205.

[29] Ibid., 1207.

[30] Brague, *The Wisdom of the World*, 216.

before then. Once heliocentrism became the accepted cosmological model, catholicity was reduced from a consciousness of the whole to a level of individual concern and personal salvation. The left brain became detached from the right brain.

Despite the power of the Catholic Church and its universal presence, the worldly lure of scientific achievement created a new culture of the individual. The rise of science and technology, the growth of industrialization, and the pursuit of capitalism all took place at the expense of the cosmos, even though some of the best scientists and inventors of the modern period were Christian, such as Michael Faraday, who discovered electromagnetism, and Lord Kelvin, who contributed to the area of thermodynamics. To work hard, to use one's intellectual gifts, and to glorify God were part of the Protestant ethic. However, technology developed to master nature and to wrench from nature that which it could not produce by itself, the spread of good and the containment of evil. Knowledge was power and should be pursued at all costs.[31]

The Vatican II Council, which opened in 1962, was a revolutionary moment for the Catholic Church. The shrinkage of catholicity into the stale, abstract lawfulness of Catholic life coupled with a manual theology led Pope John XXIII to declare that something was deeply amiss in the pastoral presence of the Church in the world. The council sought to open up the Church "windows" to a world of change and historical complexity, to recognize the people of God as a people in history. As the marvelous opening paragraph of *Gaudium et spes* states: "The joys and the hopes, the griefs and the anxieties of the men of this age, especially those who are poor or in any way afflicted, these are the joys and hopes, the griefs and anxieties of the followers of Christ" (no. 1). The Church called for new vision, a new Pentecost, a new people of God who would help make the gospel alive in a world where religion would be less institutional and more personal. The conciliar Bishops of Rome, John XXIII and Paul VI, realized that if radical action was not taken, the Church would become an artifact of history.

The cautious growth of the Church in the contemporary world has created an anxious restlessness that can no longer be satisfied by the institution alone. For some, the longing for a new

---

[31] "Francis Bacon: The Natural Philosopher," kepler.edu website.

Church in which laity and clergy, men and women, can participate in mutual relatedness is a pipedream supplemented by other
religious practices such as Buddhist meditation or belonging to
multiple religious groups; others take a more apologetic stance,
adhering strictly to the doctrines and teachings of the Church.
While a plurality of viewpoints and ideologies is characteristic
of the postmodern era, a polarization of positions within the
Church has enervated its ability to do new things. What we find
today is domesticated insularity, the inability to move beyond
one's ideological comfort zone while barely tolerating the differences of others.

The Modern Challenge

The artificial separation between humans and cosmos, Teilhard de Chardin said, lies at the core of our contemporary moral
confusion. Similarly, Nancy Abrams and Joel Primack, who have
devoted their work to reconnecting cosmology and anthropology, state: "There is a profound connection between our lack
of a shared cosmology and our increasing global problems. We
have no sense how we and our fellow humans fit into the big
picture. . . . Without a big picture we are very small people."[32]
Small, fragmented, lost in space, the human person has become
radically disconnected from the whole.

We humans have forgotten how to read the stars. We have
become the most unnatural of species, disconnected from nature
and from one another. Abrams states that "the human race needs
a coherent, believable picture of the universe that applies to all of
us and gives our lives and our species a meaningful place in that
universe."[33] The future of the earth depends on a shared vision
and shared life. The new science awakens us to our connectedness to the stars and the swirling galaxies. Biology has discovered
the miniature world of the cell, and through it we see a dynamic
energy that weaves together all of life in a cosmic communion
of wonder and awe. Science discloses a fantastic world that is

---

[32] Abrams and Primack, *The New Universe and the Human Future*,
xi–xii.

[33] Ibid., xiv.

in search of meaning and purpose—a new narrative. According to Abrams and Primack, the new science story is our hope for a new future and a sustainable earth:

> The new scientific picture differs from all earlier creation stories not only because it's based on evidence but also because it's the first ever created by collaboration among people from different religions, races, and cultures all around the world. . . . The new universe picture excludes no one and sees all humans as equal. It belongs to all of us, not only because we're all part of it but also because around the world the work to discover it has been largely funded by the public. The fruit of this transitional collaboration could become a unifying, believable picture of the larger reality in which Earth, our lives, and the ideas of all our religions are embedded.[34]

A new age has dawned with a new universe story. It is an invitation to a new consciousness, a new catholicity in which wholemaking can be renewed: the whole of life imbued with the wholeness of God. The world is not an objective "other" outside the human person or an obstacle to God. Rather, it is the outflow of human creativity, freedom, and imagination. What this means for Christian life and the Church in *our* cosmos is the challenge and the journey ahead.

---

[34] Ibid., 6.

Chapter 3

Big Bang Catholicity

Catholicity and New Cosmology

The Greeks knew that the human person belongs to the cosmos, and the cosmos makes sense only in light of the human person. To separate human from cosmos is not only unnatural but creates confusion. Catholicity lives between cosmos and anthropos. It is an orientation toward the whole by one who has a sense of the whole. Catholicity begins, therefore, not with religion but with the whole; catholicity begins with the cosmos. Twentieth-century science has given new meaning to the word *cosmos* in a way anticipated by the Greeks but much more expansive. Whereas the Greeks understood cosmos as that which is brought together by a sense of the whole order of things, modern science understands the deep interrelatedness between consciousness and matter. Modern cosmology is the study of the space-time continuum that is our universe. If twentieth-century science has returned to us the word *cosmos*, we now know this word to be charged with new meaning. Science tells us today that we are part of the whole from the beginning and to sever ourselves from the whole, in any way, is to disrupt the flow of life. In light of science, catholicity finds fresh new meaning in contemporary science.

The modern cosmos story, which began with Copernicus and the rise of heliocentrism, found its most significant description in the work of Sir Isaac Newton. Exploring an understanding of how material things are held together in an orderly way, Newton discovered the laws of motion and the law of gravity. The material universe comprised myriad particles interacting against a backdrop of absolute space and absolute time. These interactions were assumed to be causal, deterministic (predictable), and independent of a detached observer. Nature was permeated by a stark dualism; subject and object, mind and matter, and the cosmos was pictured as a giant machine that functioned mechanistically.[1] This nice, neat universe of perfect order, running according to the Newtonian laws of motion, was destroyed, however, in 1905, when Albert Einstein published a paper that upset the world of physics. Einstein was captivated by the mystery of matter. His deep religious sense and his quest for spiritual truth motivated his scientific mind. But what attracted Einstein to plumb the mystery of nature? Part of the answer is found in the nature of matter itself. In *Einstein and Religion*, Max Jammer gives Elsa's account of the day her husband discovered relativity:

> The Doctor came down in his dressing gown as usual for breakfast but he hardly touched a thing. I thought something was wrong, so I asked what was troubling him. "Darling," he said, "I have a wonderful idea." And after drinking his coffee, he went to the piano and started playing. Now and again he would stop, making a few notes then repeat: "I've got a wonderful idea, a marvelous idea!" I said: "Then for goodness' sake tell me what it is, don't keep me in suspense." He said: "It's difficult; I still have to work it out."
>
> She told me he continued playing the piano and making notes for about half an hour, then went upstairs to his study, telling her that he did not wish to be disturbed, and remained there for two weeks. "Each day I sent him up his meals," she said, "and in the evening he would walk a little for exercise, then return to his work again. Eventually, he came down from his study looking very pale. 'That's it,' he told me, wearily putting two sheets of paper on the table. And that was his theory of relativity."[2]

---

[1] David Pruett, *Reason and Wonder: A Copernican Revolution in Science and Spirit* (Santa Barbara, CA: Praeger, 2011), 222.

[2] Max Jammer, *Einstein and Religion: Physics and Theology* (Princeton, NJ: Princeton University Press, 1999), 56.

For three hundred years Newton's vision of absolute space and time was the sacred dogma of scientific cosmology. Space, for Newton, was an empty stage on which the drama of physics played out, a constant emptiness everywhere and at all times. Time, too, was constant. No matter where one stood in the universe, time flowed at the same rate. Einstein's short, revolutionary paper swept away in a single stroke absolute space and time. Space is not an empty stage, nor does time flow at a fixed rate. Rather, space and time form a single continuum, each relative to the other. "Space and time could shrink or expand depending on the relative motion of the observers who measured them."[3] According to Adam Frank, "The new universe was a *hyperspace*, a world with an extra dimension. . . . in relativity every object becomes four-dimensional as it extends through time."[4] Scientists today believe that the universe is at least four dimensions or multidimensional.

Einstein's creative insight eventually yielded to a new understanding of gravity that, for Newton, was "the force between massive objects that pulled them toward each other."[5] The elastic nature of space-time impelled Einstein to think of gravity not as a substance but as a curvature of space-time by matter. The heaviness of matter not only stretches or shrinks distances (depending on their direction with respect to the gravitational field) but also appears to slow down or "dilate" the flow of time. In other words gravity acts to structure space, which is the basic ingredient of the universe containing fields or spatial structures in the fabric of space itself. Einstein's discovery of relativity changed our understanding of the universe dramatically. He

---

[3] Adam Frank, *The Constant Fire: Beyond the Science vs. Religion Debate* (Berkeley and Los Angeles: University of California Press, 2009), 146; Simon Singh, *Big Bang: The Origin of the Universe* (New York: HarperCollins, 2004), 120–28. For a succinct description of the new cosmology see Brian Swimme and Thomas Berry, *The Universe Story: From the Primordial Flaring Forth to the Ecozoic Era—A Celebration of the Unfolding of the Cosmos* (New York: HarperOne, 1994); Judy Cannato, *Radical Amazement: Contemplative Lessons from Black Holes, Supernovas, and Other Wonders of the Universe* (Notre Dame, IN: Sorin Books, 2006).

[4] Frank, *The Constant Fire*, 147.

[5] Ibid.

wondered about the relationship between energy and matter, especially because Newton thought matter was substance that had mass and occupied space, distinct from energy. In Newton's time particles were visualized as discrete entities forming molecules, and electromagnetic radiation was conceived as wave motion involving changing electric and magnetic fields. Michael Faraday (d. 1867) showed that electricity and magnetism are not two separate phenomena but a single field phenomenon. It was Einstein's theory of special relativity, however, that changed our conventional visualization of the physical world by disclosing matter as a form of energy. In physical terms the mass of a body is a measure of its energy content. Mass and energy are not identical but equivalent. Einstein's famous equation $E = mc^2$ showed that the energy E of a physical system is numerically equal to the product of its mass m and the speed of light c squared; matter can be converted into energy and energy into matter. In nuclear physics, for example, this exchange occurs when a positively charged proton bonds with a charged neutral neutron. Any time that matter interacts and binds with other matter, matter disappears; any time that matter "falls" apart (like in alpha and beta decay) matter is created. The invisible world of energy has a direct and solid connection to the concrete world of matter. Whereas Newton thought the material universe was made of inert matter, we now know that the material universe is fundamentally energy. Scientists identify different forms of energy such as kinetic energy, potential energy, or thermal energy. Energy is all around us. We can hear energy as sound; we can feel energy as wind; we can see energy as light. We use energy when we sing or read a book. It is energy that enables birds to fly, rain to fall, students to learn, and leaves to fall. Energy is work, and work is the force that moves things from one place to another. There is potential energy, mechanical energy, heat energy, and kinetic energy. Every aspect of life is charged with energy.

Relativity theory states that matter and energy are really different forms of the same thing—but what is the *thing* they are forms of? Einstein himself was perplexed by the mysterious nature of matter as a form of energy and had problems with quantum physics. A particle split in two, for example, can communicate over vast distances between the two halves, almost instantaneously, what Einstein and his colleagues called *entanglement*.

How could this be? Only if the vast seemingly empty spaces of the universe are really not so empty after all, but rather complex layers of energy fields. Einstein's equations led to a most startling insight—that the elastic nature of the universe implies change—an insight Einstein himself was not comfortable with.

In 1916 Dutch physicist Willem de Sitter constructed a universe that could stretch in different directions "like taffy," a theoretical insight that received experimental support in 1928 when astronomer Edwin Hubble, "using the most powerful telescope of his day, found that every galaxy in the sky was moving away from us."[6] He saw that ours was not the only galaxy; rather, there were many other galaxies with large empty spaces between them. "The more distant a galaxy was from our own, the faster it appeared to be rushing outward."[7] If the universe was contracting instead of expanding, we would see distant galaxies radiate a blue light intensity (measured by the Doppler effect) proportional to their distance. However, Hubble noticed a redshift, indicating that the distance between galaxies is expanding. "This is exactly what observers riding on debris from an explosion would see. In an explosive release of matter all the bits of shrapnel appear to move away from all the others."[8]

The idea that the universe is dynamic and changing was confirmed in 1964 when two scientists working at Bell Laboratories in New Jersey discovered *cosmic microwave background* that was left over from the beginning of the universe more than 13 billion years ago. Adam Frank writes:

> New Jersey seems an unlikely place for the origin of the universe to reveal itself, but that is exactly where the story of the Big Bang starts. . . . At the time the two astronomers were working on the new technology of microwave communications. . . . The problem was an annoying, low level of "noise" that persisted regardless of which direction the antenna pointed. It was a microwave hiss that refused to go away. . . . The microwave signal . . . wasn't noise but the ultimate prehistoric relic. . . . It was a pervasive electro-

---

[6] Ibid., 149: Singh, *Big Bang*, 214–29.
[7] Frank, *The Constant Fire*, 149.
[8] Ibid.

magnetic memory of the universe's origin and a direct link to the time of the Big Bang.[9]

Up to the time of the discovery by Wilson and Penzias, scientists believed that the cosmos had an eternal, steady state. British scientist Fred Hoyle suggested that even as galaxies moved away and the universe expanded, matter was slowly added to the universe. Hoyle did not accept the Big Bang theory of the universe proposed by Belgium priest George LeMaitre because it smacked of a Creator God. Hoyle's steady-state model, however, was not convincing against the discovery of cosmic microwave background. Rather, the elastic space-time universe glowing with the relics of a primeval explosion supported the idea that the universe had a beginning, a Big Bang; the universe developed from an extremely dense and hot state.

Einstein's revolutionary ideas sparked a new vision of the cosmos, a new genesis story. As Frank writes:

> *In the beginning* [emphasis added] there was a single geometrical point containing all space, time, matter and energy. This point did not sit in space. It was space. There was no inside and no outside. Then "it" happened. The point "exploded" and the Universe began to expand. . . . The universe had a temperature of 100 billion degrees at this point and was so dense that a single teaspoon of cosmic matter would weigh more than a thousand tons. . . . At one one-hundredth of a second after the Big Bang the entire universe was about the size of our solar system. It was a universe pervaded by dense, primordial gas: an ultra-smooth, ultra-hot sea of protons, neutrons, and other subatomic particles. . . . In this dense soup photons, which are quantum particles of light, mixed easily with matter. . . . As the cosmic clock ticked off the instants expansion continued to stretch space, and with it the particle-photon sea thinned and cooled. . . . Protons and neutrons collided and combined to form nuclei of light elements such as helium and lithium. . . . This cosmic nuclear furnace stopped just three minutes after the Big Bang when the universe dropped

---

[9] Ibid., 150; see also Singh, *Big Bang*, 422–37.

below the temperatures and densities at which nuclear reactions can be sustained. At this point all creation was a mix of photons, protons, electrons, and light nuclei. . . . After 300,000 years of expansion and cooling, negatively charged electrons were moving slowly enough to get caught by positively charged protons. Each capture created a new atom of hydrogen. Once the process started, the universe rapidly made the transition from a mix of free photons and electrons to a vast gas of electronically neutral atomic hydrogen. . . . As the eons passed a vast cosmic network of form emerged from these humble beginnings. One by one a hierarchy of cosmic shapes was born. Galaxies appeared first. Then clusters of galaxies were swept together by their mutual gravitational pull. . . . Gravity alone constructed a cosmic architecture that is filamentary and beautiful. . . . [But] the universe is also composed of tremendous quantities of something else, something that emits no light. . . . This 'dark matter' constitutes the majority of mass in the universe. . . . It is dark matter . . . that sculpts the large-scale structure. . . . The visible galaxies we see strewn across space are nothing more than strings of luminous flotsam drifting on an invisible sea of dark matter.[10]

Today we know our universe to be ancient, large, dynamic, and interconnected. The universe is about 13.8 billion years old, with a future of billions of years before it. Some scientists estimate that the future age of the universe will be 100 trillion years, although the sun will die out long before then, perhaps six to nine billion years from now. It is a large universe stretching light years in diameter, one of many universes that occupy space. Our own galaxy, the Milky Way, is a mid-size galaxy consisting of billions of stars and stretching about 100,000 light years in diameter. The galaxies are often grouped into clusters—some having as many as two thousand galaxies. We are one of billions or maybe even a trillion galaxies. What is entirely amazing about this story is that we are here to tell it. Although the new universe story is complex, there are certain features to be noted. First, the "what" of the universe appears like a quantum leap

---

[10] Frank, *Constant Fire*, 152–55.

into existence. The beginning of the universe is unknown, except in the beginning there was energy. Second, after the Big Bang, the universe was a hot, dense soup of particles, including Higgs bosons, quarks, and what we now refer to as dark matter. It began to expand and cool. As this happened, the Higgs field as we know it went into effect and gave elementary particles mass. Quarks and gluons began clumping together to form protons and neutrons, which then began to form nuclei.[11] The universe from the beginning has been in constant motion, a constant, "workaholic" bundle of energy in which vast fields of energy connecting across cosmic spaces continuously form, a hyper-energetic mass of bursting mind-like stuff, spewing molecules into the atmosphere with the creativity of an artist.

The Quantum World

Quantum physics is the study of the behavior of matter and energy at the molecular, atomic, nuclear, and microscopic levels. The birth of quantum physics began with Einstein's theory of relativity. French physicist Louis De Broglie was excited by this theory and proposed that light waves could behave as particles, for instance, electrons, and particles could behave like waves. In the famous double-slit experiment an electron seems to pass through two separate openings simultaneously. However, only one of those two behaviors, wave or particle, can be observed at any moment. This wave-particle duality, also known as comple-mentarity, is the basis of quantum physics. Quantum objects manifest both wave-like and particle-like behaviors. Danish physicist Niels Bohr remarked, "Anyone who is not shocked by quantum theory has not understood it."[12]

Quantum physics has taught us that what we think of as matter is actually the manifestation of energy, what physicists call quanta or little packets or lumps of energy manifesting themselves out

---

[11] Kathyrn Jepsen, "The Early Universe," *Symmetry* (November 26, 2013).

[12] Quoted in John Gribbin, *In Search of Schrödinger's Cat* (Toronto: Bantam Books, 1984), 5.

of an infinite field. The realization that light, which had been primarily understood to be waves, actually exhibited properties we call photons, little quanta of energy, led physicists to ask: if light can behave like particles, can particles behave like waves? This question led scientists to do the famous double-slit experiment with electrons.[13] In this experiment a background board is set up with two slits. As a particle goes through one slit or another, its wave-function goes through both slits and suffers interference. Since the wave-function guides the particle's motion, it is impossible to measure the wave-function without affecting the particle's position. Since "there is no separate stage of wave-function collapse, if you measure a particle's position and find it *here* that is truly where it was a moment before the measurement took place."[14] Scientists found that light has a dual nature; in some cases it behaves as a wave, and in other cases it behaves as a photon. So which is it? When it looks like a particle, it *is* a particle. When it looks like a wave, it *is* a wave. *It is meaningless to ascribe any properties or even existence to anything that has not been measured.* What quantum physics tells us is that *nothing is real unless it is observed*; it is a participatory universe. The only reality that exists is that which is observed. John Gribbin writes, "When we try to look at the spread-out electron wave, it collapses into a definite particle, but when we are not looking it keeps its options open. . . . unless someone looks, nature herself does not know which hole the electron is going through."[15] Niels Bohr called this wave/particle aspect of reality complementarity, which means "neither description is complete in itself, but there are circumstances when it is more appropriate to use the particle concept and circumstances where it is better to use the wave concept."[16]

---

[13] For a discussion on the double-slit experiment see Jack Geis, *Physics, Metaphysics, and God* (Bloomington, IN: AuthorHouse, 2003); Shan Gao, *God Does Play Dice with the Universe* (Suffolk: Abramis, 2008).

[14] Brian Greene, *The Fabric of the Cosmos: Space, Time, and the Texture of Reality* (New York: Vintage Books, 2004), 206.

[15] Gribbin, *In Search of Schrödinger's Cat*, 171.

[16] Ibid., 184.

German physicist Werner Heisenberg proposed that uncertainty is part and parcel of nature itself; that is, nature is fundamentally indeterminate. Heisenberg showed that the more precisely the position of a particle is determined, the less precisely its momentum is known. The consequences of the uncertainty principle significantly changed our fundamental understanding of nature. We do not live in a deterministic universe; in Heisenberg's view what cannot be measured cannot take place exactly. It is a participatory universe with no distinction between the process of observation and what is observed; that is, there is no line between subject and object. Reality is what we observe. At the most fundamental level of existence there are no discrete pieces of inert matter. Rather, there are clusters of interrelated probabilistic events that change their nature when observed. In this sense there is no true objective reality; only what can be observed can be known. We are actors, therefore, rather than spectators in the universe.

Evolution

While the discovery of Big Bang cosmology radically altered our understanding of the large-scale universe, and quantum physics transformed our understanding of the fundamental stuff of life, evolution has affected our understanding of how life develops. Evolution describes the process of unfolding life, including, but not limited to, biological life. It involves an interplay of forces and can be thought of as "a broad set of principles and patterns that generate novelty, change, and development over time."[17] The idea of evolution emerged among the nineteenth-century biologists such as Alfred Wallace but was made famous by Charles Darwin in his *Origin of the Species*. What Darwin sought to show was that natural life unfolds primarily through the process of natural selection, "a process that promotes or maintains adaptation and, thus, gives the appearance of purpose or design."[18] The idea that life unfolds from simple to complex

---

[17] Carter Phipps, *Evolutionaries: Unlocking the Spiritual and Cultural Potential of Science's Greatest Idea* (New York: Harper, 2012), 18.

[18] Francisco J. Ayala, "Biological Evolution: An Introduction," in *An Evolving Dialogue: Theological and Scientific Perspectives on Evolution*, ed. James Miller (Harrisburg, PA: Trinity Press International, 2001), 13.

structures or that nature is marked by a twofold movement of convergence and divergence now holds true not only on the level of biology but on just about every level of life in the universe. In the area of physics, for example, we know that the universe is much different than that which Newton described in the late seventeenth century. The mechanistic view of the world associated with Newtonian physics has been replaced with a dynamic, open-ended view of the universe that is described as ancient, dynamic, and expanding. John Polkinghorne states that "the story [of the cosmos] moves from an initial cosmos that was just a ball of expanding energy to a universe of stars and galaxies; then, on at least one planet, to replicating molecules, to cellular organisms, to multicellular life, to conscious life and to humankind." [19]

The whole history of the universe, particularly the history of biological life on earth, has been characterized by the steady emergence of complexity. Teilhard de Chardin described evolution as a "biological ascent," a movement toward more complexified life forms in which, at critical points in the evolutionary process, qualitative differences emerge. This progressive evolutionary movement, according to Teilhard, is one in which the consistence of the elements and their stability of balance lie in the direction not of matter but of spirit. [20] This movement from matter to spirit marks "the fundamental property of the cosmic mass to concentrate upon itself . . . as a result of attraction of synthesis." Thus, "there is only one real evolution, the evolution of convergence, because it alone is positive and creative." [21] In 1940 Teilhard completed his most important work, *The Phenomenon of Man,* in which he described the fourfold sequence of the evolution of galaxies, earth, life, and consciousness. The human person is not a ready-made fact but the outflow of billions of years of evolution, beginning with cosmogenesis and the billions of years that

---

[19] John Polkinghorne, *Science and Theology* (Minneapolis: Fortress Press, 1998), 44.

[20] Pierre Teilhard de Chardin, *Activation of Energy,* trans. René Hague (New York: Harcourt Brace Jovanovich, 1970), 387–403; idem, *The Phenomenon of Man,* trans. Bernard Wall (New York: Harper and Row, 1959), 46–66.

[21] Pierre Teilhard de Chardin, *Christianity and Evolution,* trans. René Hague (New York: Harcourt Brace Jovanovich, 1971), 87.

led to biogenesis. Thomas King states: "Throughout the ages life has constructed organisms of ever greater complexity, and with this increased complexity the organism has also shown an increase in consciousness, that is, an increase of intention, of acting with a goal."[22] Teilhard saw evolution of the human person as part of the whole natural process of creativity and generativity.

Scientists today realize that human evolution is much more complex and fascinating than previously thought. For one thing, climate change has had a significant effect on evolution, an idea proposed by Charles Darwin, who claimed, according to Peter N. deMenocal, that "large-scale shifts in climate can shake up the kinds of food, shelter and other resources available in a given region, eventually leading to adaptation, extinction or evolution into different species."[23]

> Each of the "big five" mass extinctions over the fossil record of life on earth during the past 540 million years was accompanied by an environmental disruption. During each of these events, between 50 and 90 percent of all species perished, but this was followed by bursts of new, very different species. These episodes define the major chapters in the history book of life, when new biotic worlds emerged and flourished. We mammals owe a debt of gratitude to the Manhattan-size meteorite that struck the Yucatán Peninsula in what is now Mexico about 66 million years ago. It killed off the dinosaurs . . . ushering in the rapid radiation and diversification of mammals.[24]

Homo sapiens is a rather late arrival in the evolutionary story. More than four million years ago our ancestors began to move from trees to ground, becoming upright and two-legged

---

[22] Thomas M. King, *Teilhard's Mysticism of Knowing* (New York: The Seabury Press, 1981), 33.

[23] Peter N. deMenocal, "Climate Shocks," *Scientific American* 311 (September 2014): 50.

[24] Ibid.

(Hominins).[25] Recent studies show that the genus, Homo, developed with larger brains than those of the early bipeds and seemed to develop different independent lineages: *Homo neanderthalensis* in Europe, *Homo erectus* in Asia, and *Homo sapiens* in Africa. It is likely that these various lineages existed simultaneously. The modern human physique probably first appeared in Africa about 150,000 years ago and then spread into the rest of the Old World, replacing existing populations of archaic human forms.[26]

The two main influences on evolution (hence, the development of different lineages) are culture and climate change. Genetic and fossil evidence shows closely related Hominin species shared the planet many times in the past few million years, making it more challenging for scientists to identify direct ancestors of modern humans.[27] The development of tools and environmental changes

---

[25] The word *hominin* is a recent one that reflects a development in the understanding of what it means to be human. Until the 1980s paleoanthropologists, when they spoke of the various species of humans, generally followed the taxonomic system followed by eighteenth-century scientist Carl Linnaeus. The family of Hominoids included the subfamily of Hominids (humans and their ancestors) and Anthropoids (chimps, gorillas, and orangutans). The problem is, recent molecular studies show that humans, chimps, and gorillas are closer to one another than orangutans. Scientists, therefore, have split the Hominoids into two subfamilies: Ponginae (orangutans) and Homininae (humans and their ancestors, chimps, and gorillas). We still need a way to discuss humans and their ancestors as a separate group, however, so researchers have proposed a further breakdown of the Homininae subfamily to include Hominini (humans and their ancestors), Panini (chimps), and Gorillini (gorillas). So, roughly speaking, a Hominin is what we used to call a Hominid, a creature that paleoanthropologists have agreed is human or a human ancestor. These include all of the Homo species (*Homo sapiens, H. ergaster, H. rudolfensis*), all of the Australopithecines (*Australopithecus africanus, A. boisei*, etc.) and other ancient forms like *Paranthropus* and *Ardipithecus*. See archaeology.about.com website.

[26] Denis Edwards, *Ecology at the Heart of Faith: The Change of the Heart That Leads to a New Way of Living on Earth* (Maryknoll, NY: Orbis Books, 2008), 12–13.

[27] Bernard Wood, "Welcome to the Family," *Scientific American* 311 (September 2014): 45–46.

favored evolution of the *Homo sapiens* who eventually adapted and flourished.[28]

When we look at the vast sweep of evolution and the complexities of emergent biological life, we see that the human person is not a chance arrival but an integral element of the physical world. The human species has existed on earth for a relatively short time, only about 0.04 percent of the 4.5 billion years of the earth's existence. Teilhard described the human person as distinct in three ways: (1) The extreme physical complexity (apparent in the brain) marks the human person as the most highly synthesized form of matter known to us in the universe; (2) in light of this complexity, the human is the most perfectly and deeply centered of all cosmic particles within the field of our experience; and (3) the high degree of mental development (reflection, thought) places the human person above all other conscious beings known to us.[29] The human person is integrally part of evolution in that we rise from the process but in reflecting on the process we stand apart from it. Teilhard defines reflection as "the power acquired by a consciousness to turn in upon itself, to take possession of itself *as an object* . . . no longer merely to know, but to know that one knows."[30] He quotes a phrase of Julian Huxley's, "Man is nothing else than evolution become conscious of itself." To this idea he adds, "The consciousness of each of us is evolution looking at itself and reflecting upon itself."[31] Thus, the human person emerges from the evolutionary process and is integral to evolution. The human person is "the point of emergence in nature, at which this deep cosmic evolution culminates and declares itself."[32]

To realize that humans are part of a larger process that involves long spans of developmental time brings a massive change to all of our knowledge and beliefs. Evolution is the

---

[28] Ian Tattersall, "If I Had a Hammer," *Scientific American* 311 (September 2014): 57–58.

[29] Pierre Teilhard de Chardin, *The Future of Man*, trans. Norman Denny (New York: Harper, 1964), 90.

[30] Teilhard de Chardin, *The Phenomenon of Man*, 165.

[31] Ibid., 221.

[32] Pierre Teilhard de Chardin, *Human Energy*, trans. J. M. Cohen (New York: Harcourt Brace Jovanovich, 1969), 23.

process that describes cosmological as well biological movement toward greater complexity. Complexity refers to the quality of a thing based on the number of elements and their organization. For example, the atom is more complex than the electron, and a living cell is more complex than the highest chemical nuclei of which it is composed, the difference depending not only on the number and diversity of the elements but on the correlation of the links formed among these elements. "It is not therefore a matter of simple multiplicity but of organized multiplicity: not simple complication but centered complication."[33] At some point evolution reaches a reflexive state that generates the idea of evolution, namely, the human person.

Emergence

The new science of emergence holds particular interest in this dynamic worldview marked by evolution and complexity. "In ordinary language emergence refers to processes of coming forth from latency, or to states of things arising unexpectedly."[34] Emergence is produced by a combination of causes or events but cannot be regarded as the sum of their individual effects. Webster's Third New International Dictionary stresses the factor of newness in one of its definitions: "appearing as or involving the appearance of something novel in a process of evolution." Philip Clayton defines emergence as "genuinely new properties which are not reducible to what came before, although they are continuous with it."[35] He writes: "Emergent properties are those that arise out of some subsystem but are not reducible to that system. Emergence is about *more than but not altogether other than*. . . . Emergence means that the world exhibits a recurrent

[33] Teilhard de Chardin, *The Future of Man*, 105.

[34] Niels Henrik Gregersen, "Emergence and Complexity," in The Oxford Handbook of Religion and Science, ed. Philip Clayton and Zachary Simpson (New York: Oxford University Press, 2006), 767.

[35] Philip Clayton, "Neuroscience, the Person, and God: An Emergentist Account," in *Neuroscience and the Person: Scientific Perspectives on Divine Action*, ed. Robert John Russell, Nancey Murphy, Theo C. Meyering, and Michael A. Arbib (Vatican City: Vatican Observatory; Berkeley, CA: Center for Theology and the Natural Sciences, 1999), 211.

pattern of novelty and irreducibility."[36] Something is constituted from components in such a way that it has new properties which are not reducible to the properties of the components.[37]

Niels Henrik Gregersen notes that emergence theory was formed as a meta-scientific interpretation of evolution in all its forms—cosmic, biological, mental, and cultural—by British scientists in the 1920s. Although emergentists differ in metaphysical orientation, he writes, they usually share three tenets: (1) Emergents are qualitative novelties, which should be distinguished from mere resultants that come about by a quantitative addition of parts (weight, for example, is an aggregate of matter, whereas water emerges from the combination of compounds, hydrogen and oxygen, and is thus composed of but different from them). (2) Nature is a nested hierarchy of ontological levels, so that the higher emergent levels include the lower levels on which they are based. (3) Higher levels are not predictable from our knowledge of their constituent parts, and their operations are often in principle irreducible to the lower levels.[38] The mark of emergence is *irreducible novelty,* which pertains not only to the properties of the new emerging entity but to the entity itself as new.

According to Gregersen, the notion of a nested hierarchy in nature has its precursors in classic tradition. The concept of emergence can be found in rudimentary form in Aristotle's principle of entelechy,[39] Plotinus's doctrine of emanation, Henri Bergson's idea of creative evolution, Hegel's philosophy of emerging Spirit, and Marx's dialectical economics.[40] Plotinus's doctrine of emanation is of particular interest precisely because much of Christian thought is influenced by Neoplatonism. Following Plotinus's philosophy, Arthur Lovejoy's *Great Chain of Being* (1936) argued that higher forms include lower forms. Thus,

---

[36] Philip Clayton, *Mind and Emergence: From Quantum to Consciousness* (New York: Oxford University Press, 2004), 39.

[37] Denis Edwards, *Breath of Life: A Theology of the Creator Spirit* (Maryknoll, NY: Orbis Books, 2004), 136.

[38] Gregersen, "Emergence and Complexity," 767.

[39] Entelechy refers to the internal principle of growth and perfection that directs the organism to actualize the qualities that it contains in a merely potential state (see Clayton, *Mind and Emergence,* 7).

[40] Ibid., 7–9.

human beings include the features of animal and plant life, just as biological processes include the physical processes. According to the principle of plenitude we live in a "filled world" in which all potentialities are presented. While the great chain of being contains both hierarchy and holism, what is absent is evolutionary novelty. Something more does not come out of something less. Rather, in Plotinus's philosophy of emanation, in which all things flow from the One, the occurrence of new things takes place as *devolution*, as a thinning out of the power of being that resides in the divine Principle prior to the process of creation.[41] Emanation from the One is a sharing of being in such a way that created being derives being from Being and hence participates in Being without becoming something new. This is the classical metaphysical scheme that underlies Christian theology today.

By contrast, emergentists subscribe to a robust scientific naturalism, according to which mental processes supervene on biological processes and biological processes on physical processes. There are two broad categories of emergence. Strong emergentists maintain that evolution in the cosmos produces new, ontologically distinct levels, which are characterized by their own distinct laws or regularities and causal forces. By contrast, weak emergentists insist that, as new patterns emerge, the fundamental causal processes remain those of physical interactions; that is, different sorts of causal interactions seem to dominate "higher" levels of reality. Both views maintain that cosmic evolution repeatedly includes unpredictable, irreducible, and novel appearances.[42] Clayton states that emergence is everywhere, beginning with the Big Bang. He writes: "Once there was no universe and then, after the Big Bang, there was an exploding world of stars and galaxies. Once the earth was unpopulated and later it was teeming with primitive life forms. Once there were apes living in trees and then there were Mozart, Einstein and Gandhi."[43] Emergence is a combination of holism with novelty in a way that contrasts with both physical reductionism and dualism. It is irreducible novelty of increasing complexity in nature

---

[41] Gregersen, "Emergence and Complexity," 769.
[42] Clayton, *Mind and Emergence*, 9–10, 39.
[43] Philip Clayton, "Emerging God," religion-online.org website.

and underscores the fact that time is irreversible; in nature, there is no turning back.

Wholeness and Community

Looking at evolution through the lens of emergence helps us realize that cosmic and biological life are marked by the development of increasing wholeness in nature, from the beginning of the Big Bang universe. Wholeness is not a static concept but a dynamic one.[44] It emerges in evolution with biological complexity and is marked by corresponding degrees of consciousness. As elements converge and complexity rises, so too does consciousness. What is interesting from the point of nature is that, no matter where one looks in nature, there is an "unbearable wholeness"; nature works as cooperative local systems with various degrees of communication and, we might add, compassion—at least on the higher levels of biological life. "Our ability to cooperate in large societies," Frans de Waal writes, "has deep evolutionary roots in the animal kingdom."[45] In the past scientists thought that competition and the struggle for survival accounted for the predominance of our species. Now we realize that cooperation is essential to survival. Recent studies show that cooperation is not based on family ties but on reciprocity, empathy, and mutualistic cooperation, which is the most ubiquitous form of cooperation in the animal kingdom. Mutual cooperation is marked by working together toward an obvious goal that is advantageous to all and depends on well-coordinated action and shared payoffs. De Waal writes:

---

[44] It is interesting to note that the Vatican document *Jesus Christ: The Bearer of New Life*, composed under the auspices of the Pontifical Council of Culture, dismisses the contemporary emphasis on "wholeness" as "new age" and indicates that belief in the radical immanence of God and the indwelling Spirit reflect pantheism and a distortion of the doctrine of Jesus Christ. What is missing here is a cogent understanding of the sciences and the import of the new science for an understanding of nature as science now discloses it, including concepts of space, time and consciousness.

[45] Frans de Waal, "One for All," *Scientific American* 311 (September 2014): 69.

This kind of cooperation can spawn more subtle cooperative behaviors such as sharing. If one hyena or pelican were to monopolize all rewards, the system would collapse. Survival depends on sharing, which explains why both humans and animals are exquisitely sensitive to fair divisions. Experiments show that monkeys, dogs and some social birds reject rewards inferior to those of a companion performing the same task; chimpanzees and humans go even further by moderating their share of joint rewards to prevent frustration in others. We owe our sense of fairness to a long history of mutualistic cooperation.[46]

We are relational beings through and through, and our primal relation is to the whole, including family, community, nation, globe, and planet earth. In other words, the evolution of wholeness is intrinsic to being human; catholicity is wired into our DNA. If evolution is the rise of wholeness and consciousness, it is also the rise of catholicity. We emerge from the whole; we belong to the whole; and we are endowed with the capacity to evolve to higher levels of complexity and consciousness. Nature reveals intrinsic wholeness, but the whole is not constrained by biological life; rather, on the level of the human person the whole is open to becoming more whole, oriented to transcend itself, as life stretches toward absolute unity.

---

[46] Ibid., 71.

Chapter 4

Quantum Consciousness

Matter and Mind

The question of evolution is not simply one of existence, of why we are here; rather, it is the startling fact that, after 13.8 billion years, we *are* here—and we know we are here! Amazingly, a Gallup poll on June 2, 2014, showed that 42 percent of the American population still believe that God created humans in their present form at one time within the last ten thousand years.[1] This inability to modify core religious beliefs according to what we now know about ourselves, such as the doctrine of creation, goes hand in hand with the power of religious myth to form a coherent picture of the world and one's own place within it.[2] Studies have shown that rejection of modern science by religious people is not due to a lack of the knowledge of science; rather, the power of religious myth runs deeper than science, even though the beliefs are based on outmoded notions of the physical cosmos.

The Christian story is still based on an ancient cosmology described by the Greek astronomer Ptolemy (d. 168 CE). Early Christian writers adopted Greek science and philosophy, including Ptolemy's earth-centered cosmology, Plato's division between

---

[1] "Evolution, Creationism, Intelligent Design," gallup.com/poll website.

[2] Danah Zohar, *The Quantum Self: Human Nature and Consciousness Defined by the New Physics* (New York: Quill/William Morrow, 1990), 217.

matter and spirit, and Aristotle's notion of matter and form. In the modern period Newtonian physics took the older Platonic and Christian notion that matter was something base, inert, and shapeless and sharpened it considerably. Matter was something that had weight and extension; it was atomistic, consisting of tiny corpuscles that behaved like billiard balls. It was solid, influenced other matter mechanically by touching it, and was wholly mindless. Matter had no purpose or intention; it held no room for spirit or consciousness. The physical world was set against the mental, and, in turn, the mental came to be seen in terms that were not physical. These two radically different realms of existence still remain with us today.[3] We are bodies with minds that reflect atomic or neural processes.

The discoveries of modern science and the traditional doctrines of the Church with their Greek philosophical foundations are no longer consonant. The Christian confession of faith—"I believe in one God, Creator of heaven and earth, of all things visible and invisible"—still leads many people to believe that heaven and earth are two distinct places, that matter is distinct from spirit, and that the soul is separate from the body. There is a profound dualism that still runs through much of Christian thinking, and this dualism has been unhelpful to catholicity. In the previous chapter we discussed the main features of the new science, including Big Bang cosmology, evolution, and quantum physics. Teilhard de Chardin described evolution as the rise of consciousness. We once thought that mind was a peculiar feature of the human person, as Descartes described. We shaped our world accordingly, stripping it of any sacred meaning, making it a left brain, analytical, logical mechanistic world, running on the engines of law and order. Now we see that mind is a property of matter. With quantum physics the separation of matter and mind has come to an end.

The Rise of Consciousness

Consciousness is integral to all aspects of cosmic life. The universe is brimming with consciousness all the way from the

---

[3] Ibid., 93–94.

most elementary particles to vast galaxies, from the Big Bang to Einstein. We can trace our consciousness back to something we share in a basic sense with every living thing, what physicists call *quantum coherence*. Perhaps we can say it this way: In the beginning was the quantum, and the quantum was with God, and the quantum was God. All things were in the quantum, and apart from the quantum nothing could exist or come to be. The quantum vacuum (QV) is the basic, fundamental, and underlying reality of everything in this universe, including ourselves. Although we think of a vacuum as empty space, the quantum vacuum is just the opposite; it is bursting with energy. Shortly after the Big Bang there was space, time, and the vacuum, a "field of fields" or a "foam-like" sea of potential. This vacuum contains no particles and yet all particles come about as energy fluctuations within it. "The vacuum," Danah Zohar writes, "is the substrate of all that exists."[4] The universe emerged from this plenum of quantum foam at the time of the Big Bang and has been evolving ever since—for some 13.8 billion years.[5]

There is no doubt that quantum physics has altered our understanding of the universe in radical ways. Solid matter is now understood as invisible waves existing in a field of mathematical probabilities. Time and space form a background in which relativistic quantum fields float, completely different from the reliable time ticked off by clocks and the space enclosed inside rooms where solid objects find a place. Everything we consider real, either to our senses or to scientific investigation, first passed through the so-called Planck era (a state so minuscule, brief, and turbulent that it cannot be penetrated; a mathematical formulation that describes the limit of what we can know) and entered the phase of general expansion that created matter, energy, stars, galaxies, and biological life. I think the quantum vacuum can be seen as a modern scientific understanding of what Saint Au-

---

[4] Ibid., 225.

[5] Scientists now speculate that the universe began when a star in a four-dimensional universe collapsed to form a black hole; that is, our universe may have emerged from a parent universe that collapsed into a black hole. See Niayesh Afshhordi, Robert B. Mann, and Razieh Pourhasen, "The Black Hole at the Beginning of Time," *Scientific American* (August 2014): 38–43.

gustine called the *rationes seminales,* a doctrine whereby all the seeds of creation (the potential powers of everything that could be) were given in the first instance of creation.[6] Similarly, the quantum vacuum means that everything, including consciousness, is present in the Big Bang.

Consciousness is not a human phenomenon; nor does it pertain to the human brain alone. Up to the twentieth century and the rise of quantum mechanics, consciousness was identified with the human mind, especially since our notion of consciousness was based on human experience. It was believed that as long as the brain functioned, there was consciousness; when the brain shut down, consciousness vanished. We know now that this is not true, and that the operations of the human brain mirror in some way the underlying operations of the universe. In fact, by understanding brain activity in light of quantum physics, we have come to understand consciousness as a cosmic phenomenon. But to make sense of this phenomenon, we need to revisit the relationship between matter and energy.

Quantum Wholeness

The Newtonian-Cartesian paradigm held two radically different realms of existence that still remain fixed with us today in our everyday lives: the realm of matter and the realm of mind (or spirit/energy). Recall that Newton's idea of matter (like Descartes') was inert substance. The Newtonian world of individual particles could be likened to a world of billiard balls; each separate and individual ball could bounce against another ball or strike another ball in a way that the balls would be externally related. The bouncing or striking of the balls against one another did not alter their inner qualities. Rather, each ball retained its own mass, position, and momentum. The energy of the balls resided in the force of attraction between them as well as the force of resistance.

---

[6] On Augustine's doctrine of *rationes seminales* see Michael John McKeough, *The Meaning of Rationes Seminales in St. Augustine* (Washington, DC: Catholic University Press, 1926).

Einstein's special theory of relativity changed our understanding of matter and energy: mass is a property of energy, and energy is a property of mass. Since mass and energy are two forms of the same thing, matter can be converted to energy and energy to matter, while conserving mass. Einstein's theory provided the basis for the double-slit experiments of the early twentieth century, which opened up a whole new meaning of matter. We previously thought that matter is composed of atoms. Now we know that atoms are composed of electrons, and electrons are simultaneously waves and particles.

> As a consequence of the wave-like aspects of reality, atoms do not have any shape, that is, a solid outline in space, but the things they form do have shape; the constituents of matter, the elementary particles, are not in the same sense real as the real things that they constitute. Rather, left to themselves they exist in a world of possibilities, "between the idea of a thing and a real thing," as Heisenberg wrote.[7]

Instead of imagining a set of billiard balls in a box, imagine a group of electrons bouncing around in a box. Because electrons are waves and particles, their wave aspects will interfere with one another; they will overlap and merge, drawing the electrons into an existential relationship whereby their actual inner qualities such as mass, charge, and spin, as well as their position and momentum, become indistinguishable from the relationship among them. All properties of the electrons are affected by the relationship; in fact, they cease to be separate things and become parts of a whole. The whole will, as a whole, possess definite properties of mass, charge, and spin, but it is completely indeterminate as to which constituent electrons are contributing to this whole. Indeed, it is no longer meaningful to talk of the constituent electrons' individual properties, as these continually change to meet the requirements of the whole. This kind of internal relationship exists only in quantum systems and has been called *relational holism*.[8]

---

[7] Lothar Schäfer, *In Search of Divine Reality: Science as a Source of Inspiration* (Fayetteville: University of Arkansas Press, 2014), 111.

[8] Zohar, *The Quantum Self*, 99.

Imagine that the original quantum vacuum or foam was bubbly, energy-charged stuff and that this foam was a system of electrically charged molecules (dipoles with a positive charge at one end and a negative charge at the other end) vibrating rapidly and emitting electromagnetic vibrations (photons). Imagine then that a rapid level of vibration caused the molecules to vibrate in unison. By vibrating together, they pulled one another into the most ordered form of condensed phase possible, an ordered whole or what is known in physics as a *Bose-Einstein condensate*.[9] This foamy wholeness is the basis of all cosmic life and the basis of consciousness.

Quantum mechanics means that quantum-level "matter" is not very "material." In place of billiard balls we have patterns of active relationships, electrons and photons, mesons and nucleons, that tease us with their elusive double lives as their position, momentum, particle, wave, mass, and energy all change in response to one another and to the environment. The paradigm of quantum physics is wave-particle duality, but this description of matter as wave-particle duality is metaphorical or, better, analogical for mathematical formulas in science. The formulas do not describe the behavior of a single particle-wave in isolation, but rather the way the system operates as a whole; the parts cannot be separated from the whole. The terms *particle* and *wave* are expressions of different types of measurement and are not properties that the underlying quantum reality possesses independent of the measurements. A particle is understood as the location in a specific position, and thus the actualization of one of the possible positions given by the wave function. The wave is a wave of probability of places (energy states) in which the electron might be found.

---

[9] The Bose-Einstein condensate is a state of matter in which separate atoms or subatomic particles, cooled to near absolute zero kelvin, coalesce into a single quantum mechanical entity—that is, one that can be described by a wave function—on a near-macroscopic scale (britannica.com website). Zohar writes that "the many parts that go to make up an ordered system not only *behave* as a whole, they *become* whole; their identities merge or overlap in such a way that they lose their individuality entirely" (*The Quantum Self*, 83).

The wave-particle duality of matter can be described as *relationship-existence*. Quantum relationships create something new by drawing together things that were initially separate and individual. Consciousness is the pattern of active relationship, the "wave side" of the wave-particle duality. Consciousness is relationality that includes communication and the flow of information. The flow of information is the creative relationship made possible by overlapping waves or perhaps, we can say, overlapping energy states. The relationality of these energy states would account for a flow of information or information processing.[10] As more electron waves overlap, consciousness increases. Two electrons whose wave functions are overlapping cannot be reduced to the individual characteristics of the two electrons; the two have become one new whole so that the relationship between the waves cannot be reduced to the activity of the vibrating molecules. An analogy that might be helpful here is the experience of love. The bond between two persons is so deeply personal, like a third person, that it cannot be reduced to the two uniting persons. Similarly, the bond between two electron waves is a third that cannot be reduced to the electrons. What we need to keep in mind is that overlapping waves are not exactly neighbor electrons, as if two electrons live next door to each other and share space. Rather, in the quantum world, elementary particles can act without delay on each other, no matter how far apart they are.

The quantum world is a continuous dance of energy in which relationships form reality. At the foundation of physical reality, the nature of material things reveals itself as nonmaterial, that is, quantum virtual states. At the level of elementary particles, idea-like states become matter-like. Non-locality refers to the non-separability of reality. Two quantum particles that at one time interact and then move away from each other are forever bonded and act as though they were one thing regardless of the distance between them.[11] The material world is non-local.

---

[10] David Chalmers, *The Conscious Mind: In Search of a Fundamental Theory* (New York: Oxford University Press, 1996); idem, "Consciousness," plato.stanford.edu website.

[11] Lothar Schäfer, "Quantum Reality, the Emergence of Complex Order from Virtual States, and the Consciousness in the Universe," *Zygon* 41, no. 3 (2006): 508.

If reality is non-local, that is, if things can affect one another despite distance or space-time coordinates, then nature is not composed of material substances but deeply entangled fields of energy; the nature of the universe is undivided wholeness. Because our consciousness has emerged from this wholeness and continues to be part of it, then what accounts for the human mind is active in the universe.

Quantum relationships create something new by drawing together things that were initially separate and individual. Such relationship is both the origin and meaning of the mental side of life.[12] Whereas consciousness is the wave side, physicality originates in the particle side of that duality. The information that flows from wave-overlapping organizes particles into matter and, in turn, into form, resulting in physical structure. If we had to speculate on which type of particles are responsible for consciousness, we might vote for bosons. Bosons, which include photons, virtual photons, w particles (+/-), gluons, and gravitons, are particles of relationship. They carry the forces that bind together the universe. Their wave functions can overlap to the degree that they merge totally, thus causing them to share their identities and surrender all claims to individuality.[13] Fermions are the particles that give us the solid stuff of matter. Fermions include electrons, protons, and neutrons. Their wave functions can overlap somewhat but never entirely. Fermions tend to be antisocial and individual. Because bosons and fermions are present throughout nature, scientists are beginning to see that consciousness is also present throughout nature. By seeing consciousness as a quantum-wave phenomenon, we are able to trace the origin of our mental life back to our cosmic beginning.

Mind *in* Matter

Catholicity, as the Greeks first conceived it, may be the best word to describe our universe today, since from the beginning it is a web of consciousness and undivided wholeness. The Big

---

[12] Zohar, *The Quantum Self*, 100.
[13] Ibid., 105–6.

Bang universe emerged out of quantum wholeness. Life began with consciousness and wholeness. In the beginning was quantum foam, and the foam was overlapping waves, and the whole thing—from the beginning—was (and still is) brimming with consciousness. Zohar writes: "What is interesting is that the many parts that go to make up an ordered system not only *behave* as a whole, they *become* whole; their identities merge or overlap in such a way that they lose their individuality entirely."[14] One body, one whole, one unified field of energy. Doesn't this sound like the "body of Christ"?

If wholeness is intrinsic to cosmos from the beginning, then it is worth noting that mind is intrinsic to wholeness. In the 1930s astrophysicist James Jeans wrote:

> The universe looks more like a great thought than a great machine. Mind no longer appears as an accident intruder into the realm of matter. . . . Mind may be the creator and governor of the realm of matter—not of course our individual minds, but the mind in which the atoms out of which our individual minds have grown and exist as thoughts. The quantum phenomena make it possible to propose that the background of the universe is mindlike.[15]

Emerging out of a sea of energy means that what we call real is made of stuff that cannot be considered real; in other words, the basis of the material world is nonmaterial. This is difficult for our minds to grasp, since we live in the everyday world of materiality. But this macro world of things is, in a sense, an optical illusion, blurring the entangled wholeness of reality.

Teilhard de Chardin gave primacy to consciousness as the stuff of the universe. For Teilhard, life is "a specific effect of matter turned complex; a property that is present in the entire cosmic stuff."[16] Teilhard considered matter and consciousness not as "two substances" or "two different modes of existence,

---

[14] Ibid., 83.

[15] James Jeans, *The Mysterious Universe* (New York: Macmillan, 1931), 158.

[16] Pierre Teilhard de Chardin, *Man's Place in Nature*, trans. Noel Lindsay (New York: Collins, 1966), 34.

but as two aspects of the same cosmic stuff." From the Big Bang onward there is a "withinness" and "withoutness," or what he called radial energy and tangential energy.[17] The universe orients itself toward intelligent, conscious, self-reflective life. Teilhard indicated that life cannot be considered in the universe any longer as a superficial accident but, rather, must be considered to be under pressure everywhere—ready to burst from the smallest crack no matter where in the universe—and, once actualized, is incapable of not using every opportunity and means to arrive at the extreme of its potentiality, externally of complexity, and internally of consciousness.[18]

Ken Wilbur states that every level of interior consciousness is accompanied by a level of exterior physical complexity; as physical complexity rises, so too does consciousness. For example, the reptilian brain stem is accompanied by a rudimentary interior consciousness of basic drives such as food and hunger; the more complex mammalian limbic system includes complex feelings, desires, emotional-sexual impulses, and needs. As evolution proceeds to even more complex structures such as the human brain with its neocortex, consciousness expands to a world-centric awareness of "all of us" and a transcendent awareness of a divine Other.[19] Thus, the greater the exterior levels of physical complexity, the greater the interior levels of consciousness. More recently, Thomas Nagel has said that the mind has eluded physical explanation because "the great advances in the physical and biological sciences excluded the mind from the physical world."[20] What we are saying is that the whole of life, from the Big Bang onward, is the emergence of mind or consciousness. A system is conscious if it can communicate or process information that, in turn, serves as its organizational function. Anything capable of self-organizing possesses a level of consciousness. But, of course,

---

[17] Pierre Teilhard de Chardin, *The Phenomenon of Man*, trans. Bernard Wall (New York: Harper and Row, 1959), 56–64.

[18] Pierre Teilhard de Chardin, *The Future of Man*, trans. Norman Denny (New York: Harper, 1964), 211–17.

[19] Ken Wilbur, *The Integral Vision: A Very Short Introduction to the Revolutionary Integral Approach to Life, God, the Universe, and Everything* (Boston: Shambala, 2007), 57.

[20] Thomas Nagel, "The Core of 'Mind and Cosmos,'" online.

this raises a question of whether there is a distinction between the consciousness of living and nonliving things? Can we speak of a stone as being conscious? Ilya Prigogine, whose work on complex, dynamical systems won him the Nobel Prize, said that communication or consciousness exists even in chemical reactions where molecules know, in some way, what the other molecules will do even over macroscopic distances. Throughout all of life there is creative dialogue between matter and consciousness; neither is reducible to the other and, yet, neither can function without the other. Teilhard writes:

> There is no doubt: the so-called brute matter is certainly animated in its own way. . . . Atoms, electrons, elementary particles, whatever they may be if they be anything at all outside of us, must have a rudiment of immanence; i.e., a spark of consciousness. Before on this planet the physic-chemical conditions allowed the birth of organic life, the universe was either not yet anything in itself, or it had already formed a nebula of consciousness.[21]

Ultimately, we can trace our consciousness back to a special kind of relationship that exists wherever two bosons meet, to their propensity to bind together, to overlap, to bunch together, and to share an identity; to super-socialize. According to scientist Fritz Popp, the difference between a living and nonliving system is the radical increase in the occupation number of the electronic levels.[22] In living systems photons are exponentially more bunched together or squashed into a coherent Bose-Einstein condensate; in nonliving systems they are less tightly packed. The difference of consciousness between living and nonliving is one of degree not principle.[23] Nature seems to have a built-in awareness of its own integral wholeness.

---

[21] Pierre Teilhard de Chardin, *Science and Christ*, trans. René Hague (New York: Collins, 1965), 75.

[22] Fritz-Albert Popp, "On the Coherence of Ultraweak Photoemission from Living Tissues," in *Disequilibrium and Self-Organization,* ed. C. W. Kilmister (Dordrecht and Boston: D. Reidel, 1961).

[23] Zohar, *The Quantum Self,* 223.

The Matter of Mind

Quantum cosmology has given us a new story of the universe, from the quantum vacuum to human life. The universe is tied to conscious acts of observation all the way from the most elementary particles to vast galaxies. If consciousness is related to complexity, then mind is an emergent process of complexification and consciousness. Joseph Bracken suggests that mind is the place where synthesizing activity occurs. Mind is itself an instance of an activity that is going on everywhere in the universe at the same time. To reflect upon the mind as an instance of pure activity is to gain an insight into the nature or deeper reality of the universe as a whole. In Bracken's view, "Creativity is at work in atoms and molecules unconsciously, even as it is at work both consciously and unconsciously in the workings of the human mind."[24] Life evolves in the biosphere, not from nothing but from the actualization of virtual states whose order exists long before it is actualized. We emerge by way of biological evolution in a way that involves quantum mechanics at the levels of natural selection and adaption. Evolution, we might say, is the emergence of complex order from virtual states. Lothar Schäfer writes:

> The quantum perspective of biological evolution—emergence of complex order from virtual states—enables a path to complexity that the classical perspective of evolution—emergence of complex order from nothing—does not afford. . . . Virtual states contain states for all possible life forms, including complex ones. Thus, if all states are actualized with equal probability, virtual state actualization must lead to increased complexity in some cases, which natural selection will then preserve. The complex order that evolves in the biosphere evolves not out of nothing but out of the quantum structure of molecular systems. The emerging structures are not created by chance but result from the quantum properties and conditions of a system.[25]

---

[24] Joseph Bracken, *Does God Play Dice?* (Collegeville, MN: Liturgical Press, 2012), 26.

[25] Schäfer, "Quantum Reality," 519–20.

In our everyday existence it is difficult to see how we can be part of a reality that is an indivisible wholeness, without parts and divisions; the only way we can understand this is to acknowledge the presence of Mind in the universe as an intrinsic aspect of all things in space and time. The Mind or consciousness that permeates nature is the same flow of activity that each of us inherits in a unique way. In and through our minds we are part of an undivided whole that is our home, the cosmos.

Nobel Prize–winning scientist Roger Sperry says that the human mind is an emergent property of the brain as a whole. Only when the brain is understood as a single integrated system, according to Sperry, can we understand the nature of mind.[26] Gerald Edelman and Giulio Tononi propose that there is a "dynamic core" responsible for human consciousness.[27] Human consciousness depends not only on a particular region in the brain, however, but also on its complexity. Brain complexity is a function of the degree of interconnectedness, which is increased exponentially through feedback and feed-forward loops. Of the brain's 10^{14} neurons, some 10^7 are sensitive enough to register quantum-level phenomena at any one time.[28] The human brain is a collection of nerve cells that operates like a multilayered frequency receptor. Due to initial conditionings early in life, each receptor becomes wired to perceive a particular wave frequency. As the brain's receptors tune in to a particular pattern of frequency waves, a pattern-recognition response is received by the brain and interpreted according to the perceptions allotted to the frequency. In other words, the act of *tuning in* involves picking up familiar frequency patterns out of the ocean of frequencies that surround us constantly.

---

[26] Roger Sperry, "A Modified Concept of Consciousness," *Psychological Review* 76 (1969): 532–36; idem, "New Mindset on Consciousness," theosophy-nw.org website.

[27] Gerald M. Edelman and Giulio Tononi, "Reentry and the Dynamic Core: Neural Correlates of Conscious Experience," in *Neural Correlates of Consciousness: Empirical and Conceptual Questions*, ed. Thomas Metzinger (Cambridge, MA: MIT Press, 2000), 139–53; Gerald M. Edelman, *A Universe of Consciousness: How Matter Becomes Imagination* (New York: Basic Books, 2001); cf. Jean Askenasy and Joseph Lehmann, "Consciousness, Brain, Neuroplasticity," ncbi.nlm.nih.gov website.

[28] Zohar, *The Quantum Self*, 79.

By tuning in to the same patterns again and again, we rein-
force a particular reality set. We are thus tuning in to a consensus
reality pattern unconsciously and forming our perceptions continually from this. Unfamiliar patterns often get ignored, because
they do not fall within our receptor limit. Perceptions are thus
formed moment by moment as the brain constantly scans the
bands of frequencies that surround us; yet, we are often unaware
that we are filtering from a limited set of perceptual patterns.
However, if this pattern-recognition behavior does not evolve
over time, our perceptual development is in danger of becoming
stalled. The result is that we become fixed—or trapped—within
a particular reality.

Integral Wholeness

The quantum worldview transcends the dichotomy between
mind and body, inner and outer, by showing us that the basic
building blocks of mind (bosons) and the basic building blocks
of matter (fermions) arise out of a common quantum substrate
(the vacuum) and are engaged in a mutually creative dialogue
beginning with the Big Bang. Mind is relationship and matter is
that which it relates. Neither on its own could evolve or express
anything; together they give us ourselves and our world.[29] Once
we have seen that the physics of human consciousness emerge
from quantum processes within the brain and that, in consequence, human consciousness and the whole world of its creation
shares a physics with everything else in this universe—with the
human body, with all other living things and creatures, with the
basic physics of matter and relationship, and with the coherent
ground state of the quantum vacuum itself—it becomes impossible to imagine a single aspect of our lives that is not drawn into
a coherent whole.[30] Relationship is the basis of all that is. Our
world comes about through a mutually creative dialogue between
mind and body, between the individual and the individual's personal and material context, and between human culture and the
natural world. The quantum world gives us a view of the human
self that is free and responsible, responsive to others and to its

---

[29] Ibid., 236.
[30] Ibid.

environment, essentially related and naturally committed, and at every moment creative.[31]

Understanding the emergence of mind and consciousness in terms of quantum reality provides a basis to understand the role of the human with regard to the whole of cosmic life. It is certainly not the entire story, but it provides the starting point for a new story of our place in the universe. David Bohm, the great contemporary of Einstein, spoke of the undivided wholeness of life in which everything (and everyone) shares in the same cosmic process.[32] Quantum consciousness undergirds the complex evolution of biological life. To be human is to know that we know.[33] We are evolution become conscious of itself, which means we are part of something much more interconnected and conscious than our immediate selves. Biologist Lynn Margulis writes, "Independence is a political, not a scientific fact."[34] Yet, we have become conditioned by a mechanistic way of thinking about ourselves and our world as separate parts. Lothar Schäfer writes:

> The barbaric view of reality is mechanistic. It is the easy view of classical science and of common sense. In epistemology, mechanism is naive realism, the view that all knowledge is based on unquestionable facts, on apodictically verified truths. In physics, mechanism is the view that the universe is clockwork, closed, and entirely predictable on the basis of unchanging laws. In biology, mechanism is the view that all aspects of life, its evolution, our feelings

---

[31] Ibid., 237.

[32] David Bohm, *Wholeness and the Implicate Order* (New York: Routledge, 2002; originally published in 1980); David Bohm and Basil Hiley, *The Undivided Universe: An Ontological Interpretation of Quantum Theory* (New York: Routledge, 1995; originally published in 1993).

[33] Recent studies show that humans may not be the only animals capable of introspection. Scientists have found that western scrub jays can plan for the future. They are able to remember past events and are known to store their food in anticipation of hunger. What is surprising, however, is that experiments show a level of reasoned planning. See Jason G. Goldman, "The Thinker," *Scientific American* 311 (September 2014): 30.

[34] Lynn Margulis and Dorian Sagan, *What Is Life?* (New York: Simon and Schuster, 1995), 26.

and values, are ultimately explicable in terms of the laws of physics and chemistry. In our legal system, mechanism is the view that the assumption of precise procedural technicalities constitutes perfect justice. In our political system, mechanism is the view that the assertion of finely formulated personal rights constitutes the ideal democracy. In our public administration, it is the view that responsible service manifests itself by the enforcement of finely split bureaucratic regulations. All of these attitudes are the attitudes of barbarians.[35]

To overcome our Cartesian anxiety of dualistic thinking, we need to shift our focus from objects to relationships. Only then can we realize that identity, individuality, and autonomy do not imply separateness and independence but rather *interdependence*. The discovery of the quantum phenomena has established a new covenant between the human mind and the mindlike background of the universe. It is now possible to see that the human mind recapitulates Mind or consciousness in the universe. We are part of a creative whole of unlimited potential whereby our self and our world are constantly drawn into new existence together. In the words of Albert Einstein:

> A human being is part of the whole, called by us 'Universe'; a part limited in time and space. One experiences oneself . . . as something separated from the rest—a kind of *optical delusion of one's consciousness* [emphasis added]. . . . Our task must be to free ourselves from this prison by widening our circle of compassion to embrace all living creatures and the whole of nature in its beauty.[36]

If we are part of a whole, then religion tells us about the whole; it gives meaning and direction to the whole. It is on the level of mind or consciousness that religion is awakened in us. We reach a level of consciousness where we are not alone; divinity is at the heart of life itself. How we respond to this divine lure is how we live in the dynamic energy of catholicity.

---

[35] Schäfer, *In Search of Divine Reality*, 115.
[36] Albert Einstein, "Letter of 1950," *New York Times* (March 29, 1972) and *New York Post* (November 28, 1972).

Chapter 5

Jesus and Creative Wholeness

Jesus, the Strange Attractor

Jesus emerged by way of evolution, just as you and I did. The carbon in his body came from the stars, and the elements in his blood were first in the explosion of the Big Bang 13.8 billion years ago. His distant ancestors, like ours, were the ancient primitive cyanobacteria that blanketed earthly life about 3.8 billion years ago. Jesus was born as a particular baby and given a particular name. He learned to walk and talk and "grew in wisdom" (Lk 2:40). Gerhard Lohrfink describes Jesus as a faithful Jew who strove to restore the Tribe of Israel—not to start a new religion.[1] Jesus was a "strange attractor," a new pattern of religious life amid an established pattern of Jewish customs and laws. The term *strange attractor* comes from chaos theory. It describes a basin of attraction that is both within a system and yet different from the system. Jesus was a Jewish prophet and teacher whose radical teaching on the immanent presence of God gave rise to a new, strange pattern of life that was shocking to the Jews and puzzling to those who knew his family: "Isn't this the carpenter's son?" (Mt 13:55), they asked. Something about Jesus was outrageous and unique, a new way of living the Torah unlike anything ever seen before. The strange attraction of Jesus's

---

[1] Gerhard Lohfink, *Jesus of Nazareth: What He Wanted, Who He Was*, trans. Linda M. Maloney (Collegeville, MN: Liturgical Press, 2012), 342–47.

life lured those around him into new patterns of relationship centered in the in-dwelling presence of God.

A Jewish carpenter hardly seems likely to be the prophet of the messianic kingdom, but indeed, the life of Jesus is the paradox of God's wisdom. He emerged on the scene from the small town of Nazareth, boldly walked in the Temple on the Sabbath, and took the elder rabbis by surprise, announcing that the prophecy of Isaiah was being fulfilled in their midst (Lk 4:21). Jesus embodied a radical spirit of newness and creativity, a new direction of religious energy centered in God. He was radically caught up in an all-embracing relationship with the living God and addressed God as "Abba," a title expressing intimacy, boundless trust, and commitment. As a practicing Jew, he likely recited the Shema twice a day: "Hear, O Israel, the Lord our God is One. . . . You shall love the Lord your God with all your heart, with all your soul and with all your strength." His deep, God-centeredness was the source and secret of his being, message and manner of life. He had "an immediate awareness of God as a power cherishing people and making them free," a God of personal love and liberation.[2]

Jesus expressed the liberating engagement of God with the world using the ancient Hebrew idea of the kingdom of God or the reign of God, which, in the time of Jesus, could mean liberation from Roman occupation or, for the Pharisee, faithfulness to the law of God. However, Jesus took religion out of the abstract and dogmatic and placed it in the concrete flesh and blood of human persons. His message was one of vision, reflected in his frequent use of words such as *behold, look, see*—"the kingdom of heaven is among you" (Lk 17:21). To see is an act of consciousness; it brings what is seen into conscious reality. Jesus's desire to see required an open heart. It was not simply to "take a look"; rather, he called his disciples to gaze, to have an inner spaciousness of the heart to receive another into it. Denis Edwards writes that "the kingdom is God's future, but it is a future anticipated in the healing, liberating ministry of Jesus . . . a future already present in all the good that ordinary women and men do, in every act of genuine love and in every work of peace and

---

[2] Edward Schillebeeckx, *Jesus: An Experiment in Christology* (New York: Seabury Press, 1979), 268.

justice."[3] To see with new eyes and to realize a new wholeness emerging through God's in-breaking love is to be part of God's creative Spirit through prayer, community, and prophetic action.

Jesus's Catholicity

At the beginning of his public ministry Jesus underwent baptism by John the Baptist, placing him in the charismatic and prophetic stream of Judaism. His baptism symbolized his mission and was a sign of his deep God-centeredness. Shortly afterward he was led into the wilderness where he was tempted to forgo his mission. His temptations in the desert showed his deep humanity, as he struggled between fear and trust, reliance on self and reliance on God. The themes of trust and surrender weave throughout the stories of Jesus, interspersed with the social and political crises of his day. The Torah gave meaning and direction to Jewish life, but to be faithful to the Torah was difficult because of the Roman occupation, with its pagan practices, political corruption, and exploitative taxation. Many people were displaced from their land and unemployed because of Roman taxation; further, the Roman officials were often insensitive to Jewish religious duties, including tithing, and could be extraordinarily brutal in punishment. Edwards writes:

> In response to the Roman occupation it seemed important to close ranks and resist assimilation. A high value was placed upon keeping oneself separate from all that was unclean. In first century Palestine it seemed the way of survival as well as the way of fidelity. Each of the major renewal groups in Palestine, the Essenes, the Pharisees and the revolutionary movement, intensified, in its own way, the idea of separation from all that was unclean. The main sanction against those who did not conform to the code of separation from all that was unclean was to ostracize the offenders, and deny them table fellowship.[4]

---

[3] Denis Edwards, *Jesus and the Cosmos* (Mahwah, NJ: Paulist Press, 1991), 45.

[4] Ibid., 47.

Jesus began his mission by announcing the dawn of a new age, a new humanity unified in the love of God and committed to the reign of God. He challenged the social pattern of exclusivity and sought to replace it with the values of compassion and mercy. His inner oneness with God became manifest on the level of community, where he sought to overcome divisions by giving priority to men and women as coequal in God's reign and by empowering the poor, lowly, and marginalized. The reign of God is not an abstract ideal, he indicated, but a concrete reality. It begins with a consciousness of God and a desire to live in accord with God's law of love. Jesus's deep oneness with God empowered his sense of catholicity, a non-dual consciousness of belonging to the whole and the whole belonging to God. He lived from this wholeness by going "all over Galilee, teaching in their synagogues, preaching the good news of the kingdom, and healing people from every kind of disease and sickness" (Mt 4:23). He constantly challenged others to *see,* to awaken to the presence of God, and to be part of an undivided whole, the kingdom (or "kin-dom") of God, where Jew and Gentile, rich and poor, male and female are invited as equals to the divine banquet.

Jesus internalized the Torah so that obedience to God was not dutifully following the law but the human heart centered in God. He challenged those who claimed to see but were blinded by their own ambitions and addiction to power, leading them to "bind up heavy loads and put them on the shoulders of men and women" (Mt 23:4). He chastised those who substituted legalism for charity, looked down on others, or separated themselves from others as if they were superior (see Lk 18:9–11). Instead, he ate with outcasts and sinners (Mk 2:15) and accepted those declared untouchable as friends, revealing God's merciful love. The Gospels consistently show Jesus's outreach to the economically poor and oppressed; to those who were diseased, disabled, or possessed; and to society's outcasts, including prostitutes, tax collectors, and other public sinners. Over and over again in the Gospels we see Jesus criticized by those who burdened the poor and defenseless and who wielded power over others: "Truly, I say to you, the tax collectors and the prostitutes are entering the kingdom of God ahead of you" (Mt 21:31). He reached out to everyone and invited each person into a new relatedness with God and neighbor, challenging the powerful and raising up the poor. Jim Marion claims that "Jesus saw there was no separation between himself and any other person. . . . He saw all human beings (and indeed the whole created universe) as part of himself."[5] For Jesus, money, power, violence, greed, and self-righteousness are divisive and oppose God's desire for unity in love. The self-righteous Jews, in particular, were confronted by Jesus because, in the name of religion, they opposed God's desire for all people to share in the banquet of life. Jesus confronted the legalism of the Pharisees. When he and his disciples picked corn on the Sabbath because they were hungry, for example, some of the Pharisees complained: "Look, why are they doing what is unlawful on the Sabbath?" (Mk 2:23–24). Jesus replied: "The Sabbath was made for humans not humans for the Sabbath" (Mk 2:27). Jesus transposed the Greek ideal of "know thyself" into the higher ideal of "love thyself," for when one really loves oneself as "self-loved-by-God," one is free to love another with a oneness of heart. His words are enduring, "You are to love God with all your heart and all your soul, and to love your neighbor as yourself" (Mk 12:31).

Jesus's mission of renewal called for an inner spirituality of surrender, prayer, mercy, and compassion. Living in Omega begins with letting go and allowing the truth of things to enter one's field of vision: "Blessed are the poor in Spirit," Jesus said, "theirs is the kingdom of heaven" (Mt 5:3). Jesus was not a literalist nor was he superficial. His gospel "be-attitude" of poverty is a way of being inwardly free, liberated from the enslavement of possessions, and therefore alive to the beauty of the goodness of things throughout all reality. Happy are those who are inwardly free, unencumbered by preoccupations, anxieties, and material things. Blessed are those who have inner space to see and receive what they see into their lives, for those who can see the truth of reality already know heaven. Heaven unfolds when we see things for what they are, not what we think they should be, and when we love others for who they are, and not what we expect them to be. The catholicity of Jesus's message is this: we are to realize the whole we are part of and to love the whole; to find a conscious voice of praise and glory to God in the whole;

---

[5] Jim Marion, *Putting on the Mind of Christ: The Inner Work of Christian Spirituality* (Charlottesville, VA: Hampton Roads, 2000), 8.

and to participate creatively in this unfolding reign of God. His message of "good news" was also a reality check, a wake-up call to the fact that humans can be unnaturally violent to one another, divisive, arrogant, and brutal. Jesus called his disciples to a new future, to create a new, transformed earth, a "kin-dom" of equality and inclusivity, where tax collectors, sinners, women, children, lawyers, housewives, and rabbis are one in justice, mercy, and peace. His Jewish renewal program transcended the Greek cosmos and ushered in a new cosmos, a new order of life centered in the wellspring of divine love; a new cosmic family, a new household of relationships where the members are mothers, sisters, and brothers. Interestingly, Edwards notes, "Fathers are not mentioned and the disciples are instructed: 'Call no one on earth your father' (Mt 23:8–12). With a God who was Abba, there was apparently no place in the new community for the role of the patriarchal father."[6] This radically new community under God is like a new Big Bang, a new whole that requires a new level of consciousness and participation. In Jesus we see not only a new direction but a new catholicity.

The Book of Nature

The problem of wholeness, in Jesus's view, is a human one. Nonhuman nature shows us what it means to belong to God's creation, and Jesus asks us to contemplate nature in its holiness: "Consider how the wild flowers grow. They do not labor or spin. Yet I tell you, not even Solomon in all his splendor was dressed like one of these" (Lk 12:27). Nature lives according to the law of wholeness; everything participates in the whole. Shared life is natural life. Thomas Merton writes: "The little yellow flowers that nobody notices on the edge of the road are saints looking up into the face of God."[7] We humans are caught up in the drive for mastery and success, addicted to power and control. We are blind and full of ourselves, running after false idols. We treat the world as an object for our use and dispense with everything that is in

---

[6] Edwards, *Jesus and the Cosmos*, 51.
[7] Thomas Merton, *New Seeds of Contemplation* (New York: New Directions Books, 1961), 30.

the way of our agendas. We are good at unraveling relationships by brute force and power. We are a most uncatholic species; we prefer self-interest over the interest of others, the law over the spirit, sowing where we do not reap and condemning without mercy. If nature is an evolving whole, the human person is constantly threatening to destroy the whole. This is sin: consciously to disrupt or sever what is otherwise part of the whole.

Jesus saw that all life is shared life. He went out of his way to emphasize the all-inclusiveness of God's merciful love, and he tried, at every opportunity, to raise the level of consciousness to a higher level, in order to attract a new wholeness. Jim Marion writes:

> He deliberately praised the faith of the pagan Roman centurion as superior to many in his religion (Luke 7:9). He did the same in the case of the pagan Canaanite woman (Matt 15:21–28). Jesus deliberately spoke at length with the Samaritan woman even though, in his culture, men almost never discussed serious matters with women, and even though Samaritans were considered heretics and therefore shunned by orthodox Jews (Jn 4:7–26). He deliberately told the story of the good Samaritan who, unlike the priest and the other Jewish religious officials, showed himself the true neighbor to the man robbed and beaten along the road (Lk 10:30–37). And to the constant scandal of the morally separatist and righteous, Jesus made a habit of associating with people, such as tax-collectors and even prostitutes, whom his society considered sinners (Matt 9:10).[8]

His law of love is the law of the whole. His acts of healing expressed God's compassionate love for the wounded of this world, showing that God desires to liberate us from suffering, if we desire to be made whole. "What do you want me to do for you?" Jesus asked the blind man, Bartimeus. "Rabbi, I want to see," he said. "Go, your faith has healed you" (Mk 10:49–51). God's desire for healing must be our desire for healing, just as God's desire for unity must be our desire for unity. Salvation is not a spiritual grace alone; it is a physical and bodily healing

---

[8] Marion, *Putting on the Mind of Christ*, 8–9.

that "embraces health, sanity, relationships, community and wholeness."[9] God's healing love embraces the whole of reality, but one must be receptive to God's love for wholeness to be realized.

To follow Jesus is to be a wholemaker, essentially to love the world into new being and life. But the message of Jesus was grossly misunderstood, distorted, and turned against him in an effort to destroy him. His radical message of love and forgiveness was conflictual in the Jewish community and ushered in his untimely and brutal death at the hands of Roman torturers. Jesus wept over those who were hard of heart (see Lk 19:41–44); he wept for those who were blind, self-righteous, full of themselves, judgmental, critical, and addicted to power. He publicly chastised the blindness of the Pharisees: "If you were blind you would have no sin but because you say you see your sin remains" (Jn 9:40). That is, if you lived with a consciousness of Omega and saw the presence of God in others, you would not judge so harshly or condemn others, but since you are unconscious of the humility of God and insist that God judges from above, then you bring judgment upon yourself because you destroy the whole and, by destroying the whole, you destroy yourself. Blindness divides the whole into thousands of little pieces that God cannot repair without our consent and cooperation.

Death and Dying into Love

Jesus's catholicity was a new consciousness and a new cosmos, a living banquet of life empowered by God. His program of life was not only to be attentive to the whole, of which each of us is a part, but to create a new whole by receiving the Spirit, the life-giving energy of God, and participate in the emerging "kin-dom" of mutuality and shared life. We might call the way of Jesus not only the gospel life but *creative catholicity.*

For too long we have interpreted the life, death, and resurrection of Jesus as the reparation for sin. Medieval theology focused attention on original sin and the fall of Adam and Eve. The need

---

[9] Edwards, *Jesus and the Cosmos,* 54.

to repair fallen creation and restore humanity to God became the reason for the incarnation.[10] The story of Adam and Eve, however, was constructed against the background of the static, fixed Ptolemaic cosmos. It was a way of explaining evil and death in the patristic era. We simply do not live in a static, fixed cosmos. We live in an evolutionary and self-organizing cosmos where each person is co-extensive with the entire universe.[11] Ours is not a "fallen" humanity but a "deep" humanity, embedded in nature from the Big Bang onward. While original sin no longer makes sense as an act of disobedience in an otherwise perfect creation, we might interpret the "Adamic" disconnect (the entire *Homo sapiens* species) as the power to say "no" (I will not obey). The human person is distinguished by self-reflective consciousness and symbolic language; hence, the human is the first in cosmic history consciously to reject God and thus participation in the undivided wholeness of being. The human "no" is the act of symbolic self-assertion and independence that disrupts nature's catholicity. Fifth-century theologian Maximus the Confessor said that Adam's "no" was the peak of human freedom.[12] Adam thought that only a person who can say "no" is truly free, that if one is to achieve one's freedom, the human must be able to say "no" to God. Adam's "no" was the first real "no" to integral wholeness in the history in the universe; the conscious "no" uttered as an act of freedom over and against God; the "no" that splintered the undivided whole of cosmotheandric love into a thousand little pieces. The "no" is the language of rejection that defies catholicity.

That is why the death of Jesus is significant. His "yes" to the immanent love of God was a result of a life lived in fidelity to the demands of love. Edwards writes: "He so identified himself with God and God's concern for humanity, that he accepted the consequences, the experience of profound failure, desertion by most of his community, and even seeming abandonment by the God

---

[10] Saint Anselm of Canterbury, *Cur Deus Homo: "Why God Became Man,"* Amazon digital services (January 1, 2012).

[11] Pierre Teilhard de Chardin, *Activation of Energy*, trans. René Hague (New York: Harcourt Brace Jovanovich, 1970), 218.

[12] Pope Benedict XVI, "St. Maximus the Confessor."

in whom he had trusted."[13] Jesus's suffering and death was the final expression of his life lived for others. His mission of creative wholeness restores humanity to its integral nature within the whole of evolutionary nature. Through the life of Jesus we can see ourselves as part of an ongoing process of creative and emergent life (evolution) and are called to realize our participation in this unfolding of life, as creation seeks its ultimate fulfillment in God. The radical nature of death can frighten us—and Jesus feared for his life at the end—but we also see in his surrender to God that death is part of the fullness of life. Death is not due to sin and evil; it is not the opposite of life. Rather, death is integral to life. Without death, there can be no new life. Jesus realized he had to risk death if his mission was to be authentically of God and not of human design. He knew that he had to go because the disciples would have turned him into an idol and made him king: "Unless I go," Jesus said, "the Spirit cannot come to you" (Jn 16:7). He had to die, just as everyone (and everything) must die, because the limits of human life oppose the fullness of God's love. Every limit must be transcended in the longing for eternal life. The death of Jesus is the resolution of opposites; it is the first full act of human freedom not constrained by ego and self-doubt. His death on the cross was a culmination of his living out of a deep oneness with the Father. It symbolized his "yes" to his consciousness of unity with God, and, from the side of divinity, we see God's yes of unconditional love. Jesus is the "thisness" (haecceity) of God. God is like "this," and "this" is what God is like. God is not greater than the humanity of Jesus; God is not more glorious or more powerful than the humanity of Jesus. All that can be said of God is expressed in the person of Jesus Christ. This is difficult for us to grasp if we think of God as a "Super Being" governing us from up above. But the haecceity of the incarnation means that God is in the particulars and, explicitly, in the particularity of Jesus. All that God is, is revealed in the death of Jesus:

> When the Crucified Jesus is called the image of the invisible God, the meaning is that *this* is God, and God is *like this*. God is not greater than he is in his humiliation. God is not

---

[13] Edwards, *Jesus and the Cosmos*, 57.

more glorious than he is in this self-surrender. God is not more powerful than he is in this helplessness. God is not more divine than he is in this humanity.[14]

Our minds are often baffled by this infinite mystery of love. We want God to lord it over us, to be superior to, to judge, and to condemn so that we may be vindicated in our judgments and condemnations of others. This God of condemnation was constructed by the medieval church and later by the Reformers—the wrathful God, the harsh judge. But this is not the God of Jesus Christ—and this is where Christian ethics has become distorted by condemning, judging, separating out, and dividing what does not fit our beliefs. The God of Jesus Christ, the omnipotent God, is revealed in the powerlessness of the cross: "The Father and I are One," Jesus said (Jn 10:30). The stretching of the crucified body of Jesus on the cross *is* the humility of God—God is not greater, more powerful, or more glorious that what appears on the cross. The opposites of God and world are so fixed in our dualistic mentality that we cannot fathom that the power of God is shown in the powerlessness of the cross. But this *is* the incarnational mystery and the power of evolution. Cardinal Walter Kasper writes:

The cross is not a de-divinization of God but the revelation of the divine God. . . . God need not strip himself of his omnipotence in order to reveal his love. On the contrary, it requires omnipotence to be able to surrender oneself and give oneself away; and it requires omnipotence to be able to take oneself back in the give and to preserve the independence and freedom of the recipient. Only an almighty love can give itself wholly to the other and be a helpless love. . . . God on the cross shows himself as the one who is free in love and as freedom in love.[15]

---

[14] Jürgen Moltmann, *The Crucified God: The Cross of Christ as the Foundation and Criticism of Christian Theology*, trans. R. A. Wilson and John Bowden (New York: HarperCollins, 1991), 205.
[15] Walter Kasper, *The God of Jesus Christ*, trans. Matthew J. O'Connell (New York: Crossroad, 1999), 194–95.

God is radically involved with the world, empowering the world toward fullness in love, but God is unable to bring about this fullness without the cooperation of humans. Human and divine cannot co-create unto the fullness of life without death as an integral part of life. Isolated, independent existence must be given up in order to enter into broader and potentially deeper levels of existence. Bonaventure speaks of life in God as a "mystical death," a dying into love: "Let us, then, die and enter into the darkness; let us impose silence upon our cares, our desires and our imaginings. With Christ Crucified let us pass out of this world to the Father."[16] The wisdom of the cross reveals the wisdom of God; it shatters all other forms of knowledge and opens one up to a depth of life that is lasting and true.

Jesus's self-gift, born into freedom on the cross, symbolizes the type of life that contributes to the fullness of life up ahead: "Unless a grain of wheat falls to the ground and dies, it remains a single grain of wheat but if dies it produces an abundant harvest" (Jn 12:24). The paradox of Jesus's message still eludes us. In the Christian view death is not the end but beginning of the absolute wholeness of life. To refuse death—even the "little deaths" of personal differences, career disappointments, or loss of loved ones—is to die. Every time we grab and grip, holding tightly so as to control completely, we kill the whole by snuffing out the Spirit. The refusal of the many deaths along the way is rejection of the Spirit. We suffocate the life of the Spirit within us by controlling the space around us. To say "I will not die" is to die. To be willing to die by surrendering to the freedom of the Spirit is to live forever.

Jesus knew that every choice is a thousand renunciations. Through his own conscious "yes" to the ultimate costliness of life, he shows us that it takes all that we have and all that we are for a new creative wholeness of life to emerge. God suffers the sufferings of this age out of an abundance of love, and only a consciousness of one's freedom in love can help transform the sufferings of this world into the peace of God's "kin-dom." Only by dying into God can we become one with God, letting go of

---

[16] Bonaventure, *Itinerarium mentis in Deum* 7.6. Engl. trans. Ewert H. Cousins, *Bonaventure: The Soul's Journey into God, The Tree of Life, The Life of St. Francis* (New York: Paulist Press, 1978), 16.

everything that hinders us from God. Clare of Assisi spoke of the "mirror of the cross" in which she saw in the tragic death of Jesus our own human capacity for violence and, yet, our great capacity for love.[17] Empty in itself, the mirror simply absorbs an image and returns it to the one who gives it. Discovering ourselves in the mirror of the cross can empower us to love beyond the needs of the ego or the need for self-gratification. We love despite our fragile flaws when we see ourselves loved by One greater than ourselves. In the mirror of the cross we see what it means to share in divine power. To find oneself in the mirror of the cross is to see the world not from the foot of the cross but from the cross itself. How we see is how we love, and what we love is what we become.

Quantum Resurrection

The core of Christian salvation rests on the resurrection of Jesus from the dead: "If Christ has not been raised, our preaching is useless and so is your faith" (1 Cor 15:14). This core belief, however, is still linked with Adam's sin: O *felix culpa*, the Easter Exsultet proclaims, for had Adam not sinned, Christ would not have come. For a brief moment Christians rejoice—and then daily life goes on, as if God is not really involved in what we do. Belief in the resurrection does not empower us to create new wholes, to live with a higher consciousness of wholemaking, or to surrender ourselves into the arms of love. Can we understand the resurrection in light of the new science? Can new insights on matter and energy create within us a new consciousness of catholicity? A quantum understanding of immortality may shed new light on the death and resurrection of Jesus Christ.

In the quantum view a person is a constellation of relationships, inner and outer: the degree of one's relationships extends throughout space-time and endures in those who live on. Belief in the resurrection of Jesus undergirds the fact that life creates the universe, not the other way around. Space and time are not absolute; rather, they are "tools" of our mind to help organize

---

[17] Ilia Delio, *Clare of Assisi: A Heart Full of Life* (Cincinnati: Franciscan Press, 2007), 26–41.

our world. Death and immortality exist in a world without spatial or linear boundaries. Every act of physical death is an act of new life in the universe. The resurrection of Jesus reveals to us new cosmic life. Death is not the end; our bodies do not become dust, while the soul goes to heaven. Rather, through the lens of quantum physics, we now realize that death is the collapse of our "particle" aspect of life into the "wave" dimension of our relatedness. While I am alive, I am changing and growing from one moment to the next. This is true of both my body and my character, indeed of the whole pattern that is "me." The "I" that exists now, though woven in part from the cloth that was "me" yesterday, is an evolved person in whom yesterday's "I" is sublated into the new "I" of the present moment. My childhood self no longer exists exactly as the child that I was, and yet it lives on in me, partly to make me what I am and partly to experience its own growth through me. Thus I am always investing my future in another. While I am alive that other is "me"—my many selves that I am becoming; after I am dead, that other is "you" because my own self is woven into yours. "I" am not just my atoms or my genes; rather, the pattern that is me will be part and parcel of all that is to come because my growing does not cease. The process of my becoming continues. We live on in our relationships, and, in and through our relationships, we are continuously created.[18]

This living on in and through relationships undergirds the resurrection of Jesus, an event without eyewitnesses but recounted by those who experienced Jesus in a new way after his death: on the road to Emmaus; in the breaking of the bread; on the shore of Like Tiberias; and behind locked doors, where the human finger of Thomas touched the wounds of Christ. Jesus lives on in heart of the universe in a new relatedness; his death was not the end but the beginning of new life in God. Resurrection means that we too will live on to the extent that we live now; that is, to the extent that we focus our passion, loyalty, and care to family, friends, community, nation, to transcend ourselves in love. The magnitude of our relatedness is the breadth of our lives, and the degree to which we live on in the evolution of life. To live eternal life is to live in the *now* unconditionally and wholeheartedly, to lose ourselves for the sake of love. The resurrection of

---

[18] Zohar, *The Quantum Self,* 150–51.

Jesus Christ anticipates the destiny of the cosmos—a new field of theandric energy embracing the cosmos.[19] If the resurrection anticipates our future in God, then the one who is raised from the dead shows the kind of future God intends. The resurrection happens in the present moment, but it is a present moment bathed in future, a new relationship with God, a new union, a new wholeness—a new catholicity—by which life is wholly unified.

Baptism and Eucharist as Entanglement

A quantum understanding of the resurrection of Jesus Christ helps us renew a sacramental sense of participating in creative wholemaking underlying the emerging "kin-dom" of God. We might consider the sacraments of baptism and Eucharist as quantum entanglement with the life of Jesus. The term *entanglement* comes from quantum physics; it is based on the interaction of particles and the enduring bond between them after their separation. Entanglement is known as non-local action at a distance. It means that once two parties interact, they are bound together forever and can affect each other. Each particle can affect the other directly and reciprocally despite spatial distance.

Baptism is initiation into entanglement whereby human life enters into the theandric (divine-human energies) complex so that a person becomes part of the cosmotheandric whole. We are, in a sense, "grafted" onto God in a way that our life is now part of God's life and God's life is part of our life; we "put on" Christ. Melito of Sardis (c. 165) spoke of all creation participating in a "cosmic baptism" as part of the sacramental life:

> If you wish to observe the heavenly bodies being baptized, make haste now to the Ocean, and there I will show you a strange sight. If you look there you will see the heavenly

---

[19] The term *theandric* was coined by Maximus the Confessor and refers to the union of divine and created energies. See Lars Thunberg, *Man and His Cosmos: The Vision of Saint Maximus the Confessor* (Crestwood, NY: St. Vladimir's Press, 1985); Andrew Louth, *Maximus the Confessor* (New York: Routledge, 1996).

bodies being baptized. At the end of the day, they make haste to the Ocean, there to go down into the waters, into the outspread sea, and boundless main, and infinite deep, and immeasurable Ocean, and pure water. The sun sinks into the sea, and when it has been bathed in symbolic baptism, it comes up exultantly from the waters, rising as a new sun, purified from the bath. What the sun does, so do the stars and moon. They bathe in the sun's swimming pool like good disciples. By this baptism, sun, moon and stars are soaking up pure brilliance.[20]

This "cosmocentric baptism," as Linda Gibler calls it, becomes, on the human level, a conscious "yes" to Omega-love, bearing witness to this love, rendering love for love, and thus participating in the evolution of Christ.[21] In this respect, baptism is not something done *to* us; it is done *by* us, a willing consent to be affected by God, as God seeks to evolve life toward greater unity in love. Through baptism we are to be more consciously aware of a new power at the heart of our lives and at the heart of the universe, the power of the risen Christ, the invasion of the present by what is yet to come. To be baptized is to give oneself wholeheartedly to this unfolding reality.

The eyes of the baptized are called to see Christ as the innermost center of the universe and to sacramentalize this reality through the celebration of the Eucharist. Jesus left us a memorial of his life by sharing his body and blood in a way that we would "re-member" or be "membered to" his life, creating and widening the fields of love, mercy, and compassion: "Do this in memory of me" (Lk 22:19). Jesus's "Do this in memory of me" are words of entanglement, saying that my life affects your life, and your life affects my life—we are mutually and reciprocally related. By celebrating the sacrament of the Eucharist we are not simply saying thank you to God, as if saying, "how nice of you

---

[20] Cited in Kilian McDonnell, *The Baptism of Jesus in the Jordan: The Trinitarian and Cosmic Order of Salvation* (Collegeville, MN: Liturgical Press, 1996), 50–51.

[21] See Linda Gibler, *From the Beginning to Baptism: Scientific and Sacred Stories of Water, Oil, and Fire* (Collegeville, MN: Liturgical Press, 2010), 111–22.

to remember me." Eucharist means being an active participant in the cosmic body of Christ, a body evolving unto fullness, the cosmic Person, through the rise of consciousness and unity in love.

Jesus's memorial is an invitation to be "membered to" the life of God in and through the concrete realities of this world, to suffer through the "no's" and rejections of human relationships into the "yes" of God's love. It calls us to a new level of consciousness and to new levels of relatedness by which energy fields of mercy, compassion, peacemaking, forgiveness, and charity are formed in and through us. The concept of morphogenetic fields is helpful to appreciate the eucharistic life as a field of energized patterns drenched with divinity. Biologist Rupert Sheldrake postulated that repetitive behavior creates informational fields that can influence similar behavior in an unrelated area. These morphogenetic fields are formative fields that carry information and are available throughout time and space without any loss of intensity after they have been created. According to Sheldrake, these fields of habitual patterns link all people. The more people have a habit or pattern—whether of knowledge, perception, or behavior—the stronger it is in the field and the more easily it replicates in a new person (or entity).[22] As more and more people learn or do something, it becomes easier for others to learn or do it.[23] A eucharistic community is a morphogenetic field of gospel values; that is, the community itself has a pattern of relatedness that reflects the life of Jesus. As new members engage in the community, the pattern widens and the bonds deepen so that a field of resonance strengthens, making it possible for others outside the community to tap into these gospel values. When the sacramental life of baptism and Eucharist is reduced to duties and obligations, we are in the Newtonian world of lifeless,

---

[22] Rupert Sheldrake, *The Presence of the Past: Habits of Nature* (Rochester, VT: Park Street Press, 1995), 177–81; idem, *A New Science of Life: The Hypothesis of Formative Causation* (Los Angeles: J. P. Tarcher, 1981), 99–115.

[23] Judy Cannato, *Radical Amazement* (Notre Dame, IN: Sorin Books, 2006), 84, 90; idem, *Fields of Compassion: How the New Cosmology Is Transforming Spiritual Life* (Notre Dame, IN: Sorin Books, 2010), 25–32.

inert matter in which the sacramental life is nothing more than dutiful obligations.

Theologian John Dourley speaks of recovering a wider sense of the holy by which humanity births a new myth of the co-redemption of the divine and human in one single and histori-cally prolonged process.[24] Divinity and humanity have, from the birth of consciousness, been opposites united in an ongoing process of mutual redemption. Both divinity and humanity are related to each other from the outset and attain the completion of their respective consciousness in the reciprocity of their re-lationship. For both, a new moral imperative is implicit in this dialectic. Morality is no longer an arbitrary imposition by a God foreign to the fabric of humanity. For both, the basis of morality lies in the human task of making God real and conscious in his-torical processes through ushering into human consciousness that divinity which appears to become more fully real and responsible to it. Because divine and human are always opposites in tension, the Spirit reconciles the coincidence of opposites constitutive of divine and human life. The symbolic relation of the Father to the Son corresponds to the relation of unconscious to consciousness. The incarnation is the consciousness of God entering into un-conscious matter and raising it to consciousness. In the Spirit the opposites of God and world are beyond the threat of dissolution; hence, divine life, intensely alive in the interplay of its polarities, rests always in Spirit-filled resolution beyond disintegration.[25] German mystic Jacob Boehme (d. 1624) said that the opposites in the divine life are not united in eternity, as traditional trinitar-ian theology would have it. Divinity necessarily creates to unite in finite consciousness the opposites it could neither perceive nor unite in itself.[26] Hence, the life of Jesus *is* the revelation of God, and we are called into this mystery, through the life of Spirit, to share in the consciousness of Jesus by sharing in his oneness of cosmotheandric love. However, at the same time, it is

---

[24] John P. Dourley, *Jung and the Religious Alternative: The Reroot-ing*, Studies in the Psychology of Religion (Lewiston, NY: Edwin Mellen Press, 1995), chap. 4.

[25] John P. Dourley, *Paul Tillich, Carl Jung, and the Recovery of Re-ligion* (New York: Routledge, 2008), 65.

[26] Ibid., 66.

to realize the transcendent nature of this love. God's revelation continues to transcend itself in and through us until the warring absolutes of divinity and humanity are resolved in higher forms of consciousness and compassion. This is the work of the Spirit, by which the opposites of God are beyond the threat of dissolution. The Spirit raises the unconscious christic life to the consciousness of being part of a whole, oriening one's life to the whole, so that "holiness" is consciousness of belonging to God-Omega. To be entangled with Jesus Christ is to live in the fields of love and compassion, contributing to the mutual completion of God and humanity in the future pleroma. We are drawn to surrender our separate selves and to be part of a greater whole in the evolution of love.

Chapter 6

Evolution and the Four Last Things

The Conflict of Heaven and Hell

When the spirit of catholicity emerged in the life of Jesus, it did so in tension with the world around him: "My kingdom is not of this world" (Jn 18:36). There seems to be constant tension between Jesus and his surrounding community because his radical message of love, justice, and inclusivity placed the spirit of love over the duty of law. Jesus, the strange attractor, was within the Jewish community and yet different from it. The gospel writers interpreted the words of Jesus in view of their prevailing cosmology. The words "my kingdom is not of this world" were read against the static, fixed Ptolemaic universe where the immobile earth was center of the cosmos, and the sun and planets circled around the earth; heaven was above the firmament of stars and the underworld was below. In later Jewish literature Gehenna came to be associated with a place of torment and unquenchable fire and punishment for sinners. It was thought that lesser sinners might eventually be delivered from the fires of Gehenna, but by the age of the New Testament punishment for sinners was deemed to be eternal.[1] In the Middle Ages the Italian poet Dante

---

[1] "All authorities admit this word is derived from the name of the narrow, rocky valley of Hinnom just south of Jerusalem where trash, filth, and the bodies of dead animals were burned in Bible days. Here is a quote from *Bible Facts* by Jenny Roberts, 'Gehenna meant "the valley of Hinnom," and was originally a particular valley outside Jerusalem, where children were sacrificed to the god Moloch (2 Kings 23:10;

Alighieri composed the *Divine Comedy*, which carved heaven and hell into the Catholic imagination. By the end of the Middle Ages the four last things—death, judgment, hell, and heaven—along with the seven deadly sins were foremost in the minds of Catholics. The chapters of a seventeenth-century document on the four last things still resonates with us today: "the terror of death," "the assaults of Satan at the hour of death," "the spirits of darkness," and "the fear of hell."[2]

While modern theology and scriptural interpretation have moved beyond the dreaded anticipations of death, judgment, and hell, the image of a place above (heaven) or a place below (hell) still governs the lives of many believers and, more so, motivates religious action. The maxim "do good and avoid evil" carries an implicit sense of reward. The person who does good deeds and follows God's law will receive favorable judgment and the reward of heaven. The person who does bad things and does not follow the law of God will be condemned. The motivation for action is eternal reward, and the failure to act is eternal damnation. Despite our sophisticated knowledge about quantum physics, lasers, and the Big Bang, catholicity is still framed by an ancient cosmology of heaven and hell.

Is there a way to understand the four last things—death, judgment, heaven, and hell—in light of the Big Bang cosmos in which we live? Can we understand the finality of life in view of evolution, where matter is converted into energy, and energy is taken up into new life? Exploring these questions in detail would require another book; however, it is important that we recognize the limits these categories impose, not only on religious thinking but on religiously motivated action. The greatest obstacle to a more unified, just, and peaceful world is a religious belief that

---

2 Chron. 28:3; Jer. 32:35). In later Jewish literature Gehenna came to be associated with a place of torment and unquenchable fire that was to be the punishment for sinners. It was thought by many that lesser sinners might eventually be delivered from the fires of Gehenna, but by New Testament times punishment for sinners was deemed to be eternal'" (Hobie, "The Bible on Hell (as Tartarus and Gehenna and Hades)," Christian-faith.com, August 15, 2009).

[2] See Father Martin VonCochem, OSFC, "The Four Last Things—Death, Judgment, Hell and Heaven," catholictradition.org website.

God and world are in conflict and that doing good in earthly life will reap a reward in eternal life. Catholicity is stifled by the polar opposites of heaven and hell and many people live fearfully in between.

Teilhard's Contribution

Teilhard de Chardin believed that "we can be saved only by becoming one with the universe."[3] The problem, as he saw it, is the inability to resolve the conflict between the traditional God of revelation and the "new" God of evolution or to see salvation as becoming one with the universe. N. Max Wildiers writes, "The conflict we are suffering today does indeed consist in the conflict between a religion of transcendence and a secularized world, between the 'God of the Above' and the 'God of the Ahead,' between a 'religion of heaven' and a 'religion of the earth.'"[4] Teilhard's solution to the problem of the God-world conflict is to rid ourselves of the old God of the starry heavens and embrace the God of evolution. Only in this way, he indicates, is God truly revealed in the world, which is a "divine milieu." To reject evolution is, in a sense, to reject God because God is the power of evolution, Omega, who is within and ahead.

Teilhard used the term *Christogenesis* to describe evolution as the genesis of the total Christ, "the triumph of the personal at the summit of the mind."[5] He envisioned the evolutionary process as one moving toward evolution of consciousness and ultimately toward evolution of spirit, from the birth of mind to the birth of the whole Christ.[6] He urged Christians to participate in the process of Christogenesis, to risk, get involved, aim toward union with others, for the entire creation is waiting to give birth to God. He opposed a static Christianity that isolates its followers instead

---

[3] Pierre Teilhard de Chardin, *Christianity and Evolution*, trans. René Hague (New York: Harcourt Brace Jovanovich, 1971), 128.

[4] N. Max Wildiers, "Foreword," in ibid., 10.

[5] Pierre Teilhard de Chardin, *The Phenomenon of Man*, trans. Bernard Wall (New York: Harper and Row, 1959), 297.

[6] Pierre Teilhard de Chardin, *The Future of Man*, trans. Norman Denny (New York: Harper and Row, 1964), 309.

of merging them with the masses, imposing on them a burden of observances and obligations, and causing them to lose interest in the common task. "Do we realize that if we are to influence the world it is essential that we share in its drive, in its anxieties and its hopes?"[7] We are not only to recognize evolution but to make it continue in ourselves.[8] We are to "christify" the world by immersing ourselves in it, plunging our hands into the soil of the earth and touching the roots of life. Union with God is not withdrawal or separation from the activity of the world but a dedicated, integrated, and sublimated absorption into it.[9] Before, he said, the Christian thought that he or she could attain God only by abandoning everything. Now he writes, "We must make our way to heaven *through* earth.[10]

By bringing together evolution and Incarnation in a single vision, Teilhard reshaped the meaning of gospel life. The gospel call to "leave all and follow me" does not mean leaving the world but rather returning to the world with new vision and a deeper conviction to take hold of Christ in the heart of matter and to further Christ in the universality of his incarnation.[11] We humans are evolution made conscious; hence, our choices for and in the world shape the future of the world. What we have to do, Teilhard says, "is not simply to forward a human task but to bring Christ to completion . . . to cultivate the world. The world is still being created, and it is Christ who is reaching his fulfillment through it."[12] The Christian of today must gather from the body all the spiritual power it contains, and not only from the personal body but from the whole immense cosmic body that is the world stuff in evolution. We are to harness the energies of love for the forward movement of evolution toward the fullness of Christ. This means to live from the center of the heart where

---

[7] De Lubac, *Teilhard de Chardin*, 124.

[8] Ursula King, *Christ in All Things* (Maryknoll, NY: Orbis Books, 1997), 80.

[9] Pierre Teilhard de Chardin, *The Divine Milieu: An Essay on the Interior Life*, trans. Bernard Wall (New York: Harper and Row, 1960), 62–73.

[10] Teilhard de Chardin, *Christianity and Evolution*, 93.

[11] Ibid., 170.

[12] Ibid., 49.

love grows and to reach out to the world with faith, hope, and trust in God's incarnate presence. The Christian is one who sees the world in its divine depth, which is shown precisely in the worldliness of human activities and earthly affairs. This means to be conscious of the larger dimension of our efforts, laboring in the midst of the world, so that our activities become part of the unfolding of the earth process itself. Human activity is to benefit all of life, human and nonhuman, seeing in nonhuman creation the inherent dignity of all creatures and our mutual relatedness to all created things.

Teilhard's mysticism of action calls for oneness of heart with God. Heaven is the place of God, and earth is the place of heaven: heaven and earth are two sides of the same conjugate. We are called to make our way to heaven through earth. Heaven is not an otherworldly world but this world clearly seen. Paul Tillich writes: "In the midst of the old creation there is a New Creation, and this New Creation is manifest in Jesus who is called the Christ."[13] To enter the new creation, we must be grasped by it and surrender to it. Sacrifice is part of the costliness of life and of life in evolution. Mary Evelyn Tucker describes a backward movement or entropy phase and a forward movement or energy phase in evolution. The presence of evil in the cosmic order is part of the fragmentation or multiplicity that must be overcome in the movement toward greater unity. She writes: "Events such as natural disasters, sickness, and tragedies are part of the groping of nature including the human to fulfill its deepest purposes." Struggle provides a stimulating value for self-transcendence. Tucker continues: "Without the limits of struggle there can be no heroic potential of the human to overcome his or her particularity."[14] In an essay entitled "The Significance and Positive Value of Suffering," Teilhard ingeniously turns suffering inside out, from the dark, sinful curse of God to the power of human energy to unite what is fragmented and incomplete, transforming the scattered pieces of life into a greater unity. He sees suffering as a higher

---

[13] Paul Tillich, *The New Being* (New York: Charles Scribner's Sons, 1955), 18.

[14] Mary Evelyn Tucker, "The Ecological Spirituality of Teilhard," *Teilhard Studies* 51 (Fall 2005): 14.

form of creativity, releasing tremendous energy that enkindles creative union.

> Human suffering, the sum total of suffering poured out at each moment over the whole earth, is like an immeasurable ocean. But what makes up this immensity? Is it blackness, emptiness, barren wastes? No, indeed: it is potential *energy*. Suffering holds hidden within it, in extreme intensity, the ascensional force of the world. The whole point is to set this force free by making it conscious of what it is capable. . . . If all those who suffer in the world were to unite their sufferings so that the pain of the world should become one single grand act of consciousness, of sublimation, of unification, would not this be one of the most exalted forms in which the mysterious work of creation could be manifested to our eyes?[15]

If the whole evolutionary process, of which we are part, is a *via dolorosa* waiting to give birth to its fullness—a "yes" to the crushing "no" of evil forces within it—then it is because God is within this process; the whole evolution is Christ coming to be. Here, says Teilhard, we have the truth that makes us free. There is a single "mysterious divinity" moving in the world, liberating unsuspected powers, promising and delivering more being, more unity, and more freedom. It is God active in creation, embodied in the universe. The object of evolution is that God should become manifest in the world and the world should attain its final unification in God. However, this can only take place if the world is united according to that which is its peak, a self-reflected consciousness, which we find in the human person. We are the synthesizers of the new creation. Heaven unfolds when we see this world for what it truly is, "pregnant with God."[16] Heaven is earth transformed by love when earthly life is lived in love; the suffering of earth is transformed into a foretaste of heaven when one sees and hears from the inner center of love. Even in

---

[15] Pierre Teilhard de Chardin, *Hymn of the Universe*, trans. Simon Bartholomew (New York: Harper and Row, 1965), 93–94.

[16] Paul Lachance, OFM, trans., *Angela of Foligno: Selected Writings* (New York: Paulist Press, 1993), 242.

heaven the wounds of suffering will not be removed but will be transformed by divine love into new and eternal life. Heaven is not a place of eternal rest or a long sleep-in, but a life of creativity and newness in love; one with God in the transformation of all things. The young Carmelite mystic Elizabeth of the Trinity (d. 1906) said that when one dwells in God on earth, one already dwells in heaven—even in the midst of life's struggles.

Hell is the absence of love, a deep internal disconnectedness that leads to self-loathing and despising others. Hell is the final rejection of self and God. We humans live between heaven and hell (we know a bit of each during our lifetime), and the final outcome of our life depends on our choices. God creates the world in such a way that, ultimately, we always get what we choose. If I choose to jump from the top of a high building, I will bear the result of my decision—injury or death. Judgment is, in a sense, already encoded in the fields of our lives; we are judged by our own actions. If I refuse to learn, I will bear the cost of ignorance and all the painful things that go with ignorance. If I choose to hurt and humiliate others out of envy, I will bear an inner darkness and all that goes with darkness. The judgment is the law of the universe that operates now and in everything. Judgment appears in the consequences of our choices such as ignorance, failure, and darkness of the mind. The judgment of a life well-lived is the radiance of love; and the radiance of our love lives on in the fields of memory, those who follow us in the evolution of Christ. The future judgment is now, where every choice marks a thousand little deaths. Heaven, hell, death, and judgment are not future events; they are present realities centered on a radical decision to love.

Jazz Fests, Facebook, Baseball, and Catholicity

If catholicity is about wholemaking, religion is not the place where catholicity thrives today; indeed, the Church is an obstacle to its own desire for catholicity. It is deeply divided on theological, philosophical, and moral issues; it is otherworldly ("heaven" oriented); its main story competes with the new universe story, and thus our religious sensibilities are not in tune with the physical cosmos. While the Church supports many excellent programs on justice and peace, care for the poor, and care for creation, among others, these are not unique to the Catholic Church. One can find similar initiatives in other religions. For example, the Coalition on the Environment and Jewish Life states that it "strives to bring the moral passion of Jewish tradition and social action to environmental stewardship and protection of the earth."[17] In Islam, helping those in need is one of the central tenets. One of the main themes of the Qur'an is its emphasis on charity; in fact, it is an obligation for the Muslim to do so. Muslims are to give a portion of their income to the poor.[18]

In a world linked by mass communication, the Internet, and global travel, all world religions show deep concern for the welfare of humankind and the earth. All are concerned with moral action and ethical standards. None of them, however, has adjusted its religious code to a Big Bang cosmos and life in evolution. Hence, world religions are basically united on the level of human welfare but divided on human destiny. The four last things—death, judgment, heaven, and hell—mark the lines of division between world religions because the different religions are based on the same outmoded, ancient cosmology. That is, each religion has an individual line of escape because no religion has refitted its doctrine to an expanding universe and biological evolution. Religion does not make a whole in relation to the whole cosmos—nor does the cosmos impart wisdom to the whole. The refusal of monotheistic faiths to embrace modern science sustains competing theological, moral, and ethical claims and thus the artificial separation between humans and cosmos. This unnatural separation has left the earth abandoned and "unwholly."

Catholicity, as wholemaking, can best be found today in worldly activities and events. Making wholes and being part of larger wholes is behind three major cultural drivers: music, sports, and technology. Recently, I attended a jazz festival in Washington, DC. It was an outdoor festival that was free and

---

[17] Rabbi Jill Jacobs, "Social Justice and Climate Change," and Al Gore, "The Importance of Jewish Climate Change Advocacy," coejl.org website.

[18] Alfred Guillaume, *The Life of Muhammad: A Translation of Ibn Ishaq's Sirat Rasu Allah* (New York: Oxford University Press, 2002), 151–52; "Islam and Looking after the Poor," muslimdebate.org website.

open to the public. We arrived about thirty minutes after the music started. The park where the festival was held was blanketed with people, a large human quilt of vibrant colors, a patchwork of young and old, families and single persons, women and men, all part of a large whole drawn together by a trio of musicians. People of various ages spontaneously started dancing on the walkway, as the lively rhythm of the music shook the earth beneath their feet; they danced with one another—old to young, black to white, disabled, feeble, geriatric, and postmodern to one another. For a moment I had an experience of what a "christified" world might look like, a world of many different persons, nationalities, cultures, and religions, sharing the earth, joining together in the rhythm of life. I had a similar experience at a Nationals baseball game several years ago. People of all ages, sizes, cultures, colors, and languages all gathered under the same roof, sporting the Nationals logo on baseball caps, tee shirts, sweatshirts, and gym shorts. When the team made a home run, thirty thousand people shouted out and cheered with enough energy to launch a rocket.

Technology and the New Catholicity

We are relational beings through and through. We emerge out of a web of relationships; we exist in relationships, and we long for ultimate relationships of love, peace, and happiness. We find ourselves joined together by passion when something more whole than ourselves unites us. If we could harness the energies of love in these moments of collective passion, we could create a new world together. World religions promise something new, each in its own way, but they do not deliver because they are stifled by ancient thinking. They compete with one another on what is true and lasting and hold fast to ancient ideas and old conflicts. Religions separate rather than unite.

In the last sixty years computer technology has risen to meteoric heights. In 1976 Steve Wozniak singlehandedly invented the Apple computer in a California garage, but it was Steve Jobs who developed Wozniak's computer into a billion-dollar business. Jobs, the orphaned and adopted child, had a deep, almost insatiable, desire for ultimate belonging, to make a difference in the world. Wozniak's computer was Jobs's answer to prayer and, prophetically, he saw that the power of the computer could "make a dent" in human evolution, that it would connect people in an unprecedented way in human history. The Wozniak-Jobs initiative was the start of Apple Corporation. In 1997, Apple lauched a new ad campaign with the motto "think different." The text of the ad campaign read:

> Here's to the crazy ones. The misfits. The rebels. The trouble-makers. The round pegs in the square holes. The ones who see things differently. They're not fond of rules. And they have no respect for the status quo. You can quote them, disagree with them, glorify or vilify them. But the only thing you can't do is ignore them. Because they change things. They push the human race forward. And while some may see them as the crazy ones, we see genius. Because the people who are crazy enough to think they can change the world, are the ones who do.[19]

Another computer innovator is Mark Zuckerberg, who, as a Harvard undergraduate, developed Facebook. Zuckerberg was a computer "whiz kid" from an early age. As a teenager he built a software program he called ZuckNet that allowed all the computers between the house and his father's dental office to communicate with one another. At Harvard he was a socially awkward "geek" who struggled with personal relationships. He wrote a program, at age nineteen, called CourseMatch, which allowed users to make class selections based on the choices of other students; it also helped them form study groups. A short time later he created a program he initially called Facemash that let students select the best-looking person from a choice of photos. This program eventually morphed into the highly successful Facebook. In a 2010 interview with *Wired* magazine Zuckerberg said, "The thing I really care about is the mission, making the world open."[20]

---

[19] Walter Isaacson, *Steve Jobs* (New York: Simon and Schuster. 2011), 329–30. See Rob Siltanen, "The Real Story Behind Apple's 'Think Different' Campaign," *Forbes* (March 14, 2014).

[20] Steven Levy, "Mark Zuckerberg on Facebook's Future, From Virtual Reality to Anonymity," wired.com; David Kirkpatrick, *The Facebook Effect: The Inside Story of the Company That Is Connecting the*

It does not take a business degree to realize that technology is a principal driver of cultural evolution. Gordon Moore, the cofounder of Intel Corporation, predicted that the computer chip would evolve human culture exponentially. Moore's Law states that the number of transistors that can be placed on an integrated circuit for the same price will increase exponentially by a factor of two every eighteen to twenty-four months. In short, the processing power of computers will double every two years. Today, Moore's Law is also known as the Law of Exponential Growth or the Accelerating Change Law; change occurs exponentially not arithmetically. Yet, despite its relatively wide publicity, most people fail to comprehend the computer's immense power and profound implications. Computer power lies in the speed and quantity of processing information. Efficient computing power means the ability to solve problems and arrive at solutions in record time. Computers are now so fast that problems and calculations that used to take many years can be solved in fractions of a second. Recently introduced, the quantum computer basically doubles computing power. Quantum computing is based on quantum bits that can be in superposition states. Instead of computing power based on "0" or "1," quantum computing is based on "0" *and* "1," which means basically more information more quickly. Because of their amazing success in problem solving, computers have been integrated into practically every aspect of our lives. Ray Kurzweil and others predict that a world of intelligent silicon-based creatures will soon coexist with carbon-based creatures, both growing and evolving together.

Technology: The Fulfillment of Religious Desires?

The computer has given rise to a new digitized human being who is more at home in the presence of artificial intelligence and virtual reality than among flowers and trees. Children are now spending their formative years online, and recent studies show that excess computer usage is rewiring the brain.[21]

World (New York: Simon and Schuster, 2010); Lev Grossman, "Person of the Year 2010: Mark Zuckerberg," *Time* (December 15, 2010).

[21] Dave Mosher, "High Wired: Does Addictive Internet Use Restructure the Brain?" scientificamerican.com website.

Neuropsychologist Charlotte Tomaino describes a new type of compulsive disorder called OCD or "obsessive checking disorder"—excessively checking emails.[22] Philosopher Carl Mitcham notes, "A thousand or two thousand years ago the philosophical challenge was to think nature—and ourselves in the presence of nature. Today the great and the first philosophical challenge is to think technology . . . and to think ourselves in the presence of technology."[23] If technology has come to define us, it is also creating us by addressing the basic biological need for transcendence. Whereas in the past religion fulfilled the need for transcendence by harnessing the powers of the spirit, now technology is supplanting the role of religion to connect us in a way that is meaningful for us.

Although there are a wide range of technologies today to enhance human life, the term *transhumanism* refers to technologies that can improve mental and physical aspects of the human condition such as suffering, disease, aging, and death. Transhumanism is "the belief that humans must wrest their biological destiny from evolution's blind process of random variation . . . favoring the use of science and technology to overcome biological limitations."[24] Transhumanism is distinctive in its particular focus on the applications of technologies to improve human bodies at the individual level. F. M. Esfandiary writes that a transhumanist is a "transitional human, someone who by virtue of their [sic] technology usage, cultural values and lifestyle constitutes an evolutionary link to the coming era of posthumanity."[25] Transhumanists look to a postbiological future where super-informational beings will flourish and biological limits such as disease, aging, and death will be overcome. In other

---

[22] Charlotte A. Tomaino, PhD, *Awakening the Brain: The Neuropsychology of Grace* (New York: Atria Books, 2012), 63.

[23] Carl Mitcham, "The Philosophical Challenge of Technology," *American Catholic Philosophical Association Proceedings* 40 (1996): 45.

[24] Archimedes Carag Articulo, "Towards an Ethics of Technology: Re-Exploring Teilhard de Chardin's Theory of Technology and Evolution," scribd.com website.

[25] Nick Bostrom, "A History of Transhumanist Thought," *Journal of Evolution and Technology* 14, no. 1 (April 2005): 8.

words, transhumanists believe that technology will address at least two of the four last things—namely, death and heaven—in a way that favors more enhanced life. One of the primary aims today is to overcome the death barrier. Ray Kurzweil describes a new type of emerging "mindware," that is, software that "will archive a digital file of your thoughts, memories, feelings and opinions—creating a *mindfile*—and operating on a technology-powered twin or *mindclone*.[26]

Transhumanists feel that traditional religion stifles creativity and the evolution of humanity. Their goal is to develop technologies that will fulfill what religion promises. Christianity espouses salvation and liberation from death, but what better way to achieve these than by our own powers of invention? Computer scientist Daniel Crevier argues that AI (artificial intelligence) is consistent with the Christian belief in resurrection and immortality. Since some kind of support is required for the information and organization that constitutes our minds, Crevier states, a material, mechanical replacement for the mortal body will suffice. "Christ was resurrected in a new body," he says, "why not a machine?"[27] "Apocalyptic AI" is the term used by Robert Geraci to describe the eschatological implications of artificial intelligence. Michael Benedikt describes cyberspace as the new Paradise and entrance into the Heavenly City through cyberspace made possible for all people: "If only we could, we would wander the earth and never leave home, we would enjoy the triumphs without the risks, and eat of the Tree and not be punished, consort daily with angels, enter heaven now and not die."[28]

Oxford philosopher Nick Bostrom sees the root of transhumanist thinking in Renaissance humanism: "The otherworldliness and stale scholastic philosophy that dominated Europe during the Middle Ages gave way to a renewed intellectual vigor in the Renaissance. . . . Renaissance humanism encouraged people

---

[26] Ray Kurzweil, "Introduction," in Martine Rothblatt, PhD, *Virtually Human: The Promise and the Peril of Digital Immortality* (New York: St. Martin's Press, 2014), 3.

[27] Daniel Crevier, *AI: The Tumultuous History of the Search for Artificial Intelligence* (New York: Basic, 1994), 278–80.

[28] Michael Benedikt, "Introduction," in *Cyberspace: First Steps*, ed. Michael Benedikt (Cambridge, MA: MIT Press, 1991), 14.

to rely on their own observations and their own judgment rather than to defer in every matter to religious authorities."[29] While transhumanism aims for a type of autosalvation, we can also interpret it as radical incarnationalism: God is so radically one with us that we have the power to transcend ourselves. This is the point Teilhard de Chardin was trying to make. Christians believe in the Word made flesh, but they do not trust the power of incarnation, that is, the fullness of God's power within us to do new things. Transhumanists begin with the inner powers of creativity and intelligence and aim to create a new and better world, using technology toward this end.

Ray Kurzweil and Vernor Vinge believe that exponential growth trends described by Moore's Law will eventually lead to a technological singularity, a point of transition when a machine-human hybrid with human-like intelligence and self-awareness will emerge and transcend the human species, radically changing civilization.[30] The term *posthuman* is used to describe "persons of unprecedented physical, intellectual, and psychological capacity, self-programming, self-constituting, potentially immortal, un-limited individuals."[31] Kurzweil claims that machine-dependent humans will transcend death, possibly by "neurochips" or simply by becoming totally machine dependent. As we move beyond mortality through computational technology, our identity will be based on our evolving mindfile. By replacing living bodies with virtual bodies capable of transferral and duplication, we will become disembodied superminds. Kurzweil anticipates that brain scanning will eventually lead to re-creating the brain's organization on a digital-analogue computer by the third decade of the twenty-first century.[32] Geraci states, "Our new selves will

---

[29] Bostrom, "A History of Transhumanist Thought," 2.

[30] Ray Kurzweil defines the singularity as the point at which machines become sufficiently intelligent to start teaching themselves. When that happens, he writes, the world will irrevocably shift from the biological to the mechanical. See Ray Kurzweil, *The Age of Spiritual Machines: When Computers Exceed Human Intelligence* (New York: Viking, 1999), 3–5.

[31] Max More, *Lextropicon: Extropian Neologisms* (Extropy Institute, 2003).

[32] Ray Kurzweil, "The Coming Merging of Mind and Machine," *Scientific American Presents* 10, no. 3 (1999): 60.

be infinitely replicable, allowing them to escape the finality of death."[33] This futuristic "post-biological," computer-based immortality is also envisioned by Hans Moravec, who claims that the advent of intelligent machines *(Machina sapiens)* will provide humanity with "personal immortality by mind transplant." Moravec suggests that the mind will be able to be downloaded into a machine through the "eventual replacement of brain cells by electronic circuits and identical input-output functions." Moravec dreams of a world where it will be possible to create multiple copies of oneself, each experiencing different things, and then merging memories with other copies and other persons. "Concepts of life, death, and identity will lose their present meaning as your mental fragments and those of others are combined, shuffled, and recombined into temporary associations."[34]

Margaret Wertheim notes that artificial intelligence is spawning a philosophical shift from reality constructed of matter and energy to reality constructed on information.[35] This leads to the notion that "the essence of a person can be separated from their body and represented in digital form—an immortal digital soul waiting to be freed—an idea she [Wertheim] sees as medieval dualism reincarnated."[36] A new term, *cybergnosticism,* has been coined to describe the "belief that the physical world is impure or inefficient, and that existence in the form of pure information is better and should be pursued."[37] Wertheim's insights are noteworthy because she sees transhumanism as Cartesian dualism; that is, computer technology can cause a separation of mind and matter. But this is not the Cartesian dualism of

---

[33] Robert Geraci, "Spiritual Robots: Religion and Our Scientific View of the Natural World," *Theology and Science* 4, no. 3 (2006): 235.

[34] Hans Moravec, *Mind Children: The Future of Robot and Human Intelligence* (Cambridge, MA: Harvard University Press, 1988), 114–15.

[35] Margaret Wertheim, *The Pearly Gates of Cyberspace: A History of Space from Dante to the Internet* (New York: W. W. Norton, 1999; London: Virago Press, 2000), 264.

[36] Stephen Garner, "Praying with Machines," *Stimulus* 12, no. 3 (August 2004): 20.

[37] D. O. Berger, "Cybergnosticism: Or, Who Needs a Body Anyway?" *Concordia Journal* 25 (1999): 340–45; G. Mann, "Techno-Gnosticism: Disembodying Technology and Embodying Theology," *Dialog* 34 (1995): 206–12.

the Enlightenment. Recent developments indicate that while consciousness arises within the material world, it cannot be constrained by the material world. The emergence of mindfiles and cyberconsciousness suggests that technology is advancing the notion of mind beyond the human.[38] Future generations may have a consciousness of wholeness that involves a supercharged consciousness (mindfile) in a robo-human hybrid.

While we are using technology to enhance life and attain personal ideals of happiness and heaven, we need to discern whether or not we are losing sight of the whole (including the earth), or if we are conflating the whole to the level of the individual, or if a radically new transhuman whole is emerging with a new level of cyberconsciousness. The sheer expense of advanced technology threatens to leave out the poor, the marginalized, and the earth from the next stage of evolution's progress. Technology can enhance catholicity or simultaneously thwart it, if it has no other purpose than self-enhancement. Jaron Lanier, who coined the term *virtual reality*, contends that anything worthwhile in the future must be built upon compassion and empathy.[39]

The pros and cons of information technology cannot blur the fact that we are at a new level of shared consciousness today because of the World Wide Web. We are more aware of being a single human community than ever before in human history. José Casavova states that globalization is about a new social context and an awareness of the world as a single place that has implications for new social arrangements.[40] Roland Robertson, professor of sociology at the University of Aberdeen, defined globalization

---

[38] Martine Rothblatt, *Virtually Human: The Promise and the Peril of Digital Immortality* (New York: St. Martin's Press, 2014), 4–5.

[39] Jaron Lanier, "Comparative Illusions: Jaron Lanier on the Potential of Virtual Reality," *Tricycle: the Buddhist Review* 3, no. 4 (1994): 57; Alex Steffen, "What Keeps Jaron Lanier Awake at Night: Artificial Intelligence, Cybernetic Totalism, and the Loss of Common Sense," *Whole Earth* (Spring 2003).

[40] José Casavova, "Human Religious Evolution and Unfinished Creation," in *The Spirit in Creation and New Creation: Science and Theology in Western and Orthodox Realms*, ed. Michael Welker, 192–202 (Grand Rapids, MI: Eerdmans, 2012), 200.

in 1992 as "the compression of the world and the intensification of the consciousness of the world as a whole."[41] This emerging sense of unity carries with it an invitation to evolve together in a new way. But this is our dilemma; our emerging unity does not have a common story. Technology may afford a shared presence, but it does not necessarily support a shared future. Transhumanism claims that technology will achieve our desires, but these desires are still on the individual level, where many of us are controlled by our devices and addicted to the speed of computing power. We have become information gluttons and have a difficult time turning off our computers and devices. Ron Cole-Turner writes that technology is not out of control because it is a real power, but because "we cannot control what it is supposed to control, namely, ourselves."[42] As a result, we suffer from brain fatigue, compulsive checking disorders, increased loneliness and feelings of isolation, memory loss, impatience, irritability, computer addiction, sleep deprivation, and the list goes on. We have recognized our own capacity to invent and create ourselves, but we have no aim other than personal enhancement. Globalization promises a new wholeness, but we do not know how to harness the energies of our collective psychic and spiritual powers. We find ourselves in a compressed world of limited resources and in a world of religious conflict on ultimate realities, such as death, judgment, heaven, and hell. The saving grace of technology may be the new, emergent level of global mind, but we must learn how to live together on the level of shared consciousness. Cyberspace gives us the power not only to create new worlds but to enter into them, to become incarnate within them. Kevin Kelly argues that the human quest for truth may be found not in what we discover but in what we create.[43]

---

[41] Roland Robertson, *Globalization: Social Theory and Global Culture* (London: Sage, 1992), 8.

[42] Ronald Cole-Turner, "Biotechnology and the Religion-Science Discussion," in *The Oxford Handbook of Religion and Science*, ed. Philip Clayton and Zachary Simpson (New York: Oxford University Press, 2006), 942.

[43] Kevin Kelly, "Nerd Theology," *Technology in Society* 21, no. 4 (1999), 388–90.

Teilhard de Chardin and Ultrahumanism

Teilhard de Chardin was firmly convinced that the human person is a creative center. God evolves the universe and brings it to its completion through the cooperative co-creative "great work" of human beings. The world is not a place of evil or ungodliness to be renounced; rather, it is the place of divine presence in the midst of multiplicity and a complexity of forces. Human action is to help evolution advance in every field of enterprise—business, science, education, law, agriculture, social sciences, cultural and artistic pursuits—all of which are involved in a transforming process much greater than ourselves. We are not to relate to God without a world. To love God we must also love what God loves. We are called to love God in and through the world, giving birth to Christ: "Thou shalt love God in and through the genesis of the universe and of mankind."[44] To love God is to love the cosmos, the earth, the body, materiality—the stuff of life—which is one with God without being identical to God. Christian love, Teilhard states, is to be dynamized, universalized, and pantheized.[45] The Catholic Church has recently initiated a new evangelization program "inviting Catholics to renew their relationship with Jesus Christ and his Church," to be evangelized and then to go forth and evangelize.[46] One Catholic website states: "The goal of all evangelization is to help those living without the good news know the fullness of life Christ said he came to bring."[47] The sincerity, yet narrowness, of the Church's evangelization program leaves transhumanism and globalization begging for direction.

To live the good news of salvation (to evangelize) is to build one's soul by creative engagement with the world, embracing the earth with a new zest for life, uniting that which is separate, creating new wholes, and overcoming disunity through bonds of selfless love: "The Christian is now discovering that he cannot

---

[44] Teilhard de Chardin, *Christianity and Evolution*, 184.

[45] Ibid., 184.

[46] United States Conference of Catholic Bishops, "New Evangelization," usccb.org website.

[47] "Evangelization in the Catholic Church," evangelicalcatholic.com website.

be saved except through the universe and as a continuation of the universe."[48] Living from a deeper center within, Christians are to go about urging all reality toward the Omega, to the final synthesis that is constantly growing within them.[49] Each person who awakens to a new consciousness of Christ's universal presence discovers his or her own self-realization and full maturity in being-with-Christ. Therefore, "it *does* matter what the human person does, for only through his or her action can one encounter God."[50]

Teilhard was fascinated by computer technology, even though he lived at the dawn of the computer age. He saw that technology had initiated the next step of evolution, the noosphere, but we must take hold of this new level of consciousness and evolve.[51] The noosphere is a psycho-social process, a planetary neo-envelope *essentially linked with the biosphere* in which it has its root, yet is distinguished from it. It is the natural culmination of biological evolution and not a termination of it. Just as the earth once covered itself with a film of interdependent, living organisms that we call the biosphere, so humankind's combined achievements are forming a global network of collective mind,

---

[48] Teilhard de Chardin, *Christianity and Evolution*, 92.

[49] Martin Laird, "The Diaphanous Universe" *Studies in Spirituality* 4 (1994): 222–25.

[50] George A. Maloney, *The Cosmic Christ: From Paul to Teilhard* (Kansas City: Sheed and Ward, 1968), 189. See also N. Max Wildiers, *The Theologian and His Universe: Theology and Cosmology from the Middle Ages to the Present*, trans. Paul Dunphy (New York: Seabury Press, 1982), 207. Wildiers writes: "The completion of the world in Christ is not imposed on us as a necessity but is offered to us as a possibility that will not be realized without our cooperation. The further evolution of humankind ought to be our main concern."

[51] Teilhard de Chardin, *The Future of Man*, 204. "In the 1920s Teilhard coined the word *noosphere* in collaboration with his friend Edouard Le Roy. Derived from the Greek word *nous* or mind in the sense of integrating vision, the noosphere describes the layer of mind, thought, and spirit within the layer of life covering the earth." Ursula King, "One Planet, One Spirit: Searching for an Ecologically Balanced Spirituality," in *Pierre Teilhard de Chardin on People and Planet*, ed. Celia Deane-Drummond (London: Equinox, 2008), 82.

a new intersubjectivity.[52] The noosphere is a new stage for the renewal of life and not a radical break with biological life. If there is no connection between noogenesis and biogenesis, according to Teilhard, then the process of evolution has halted and man is an absurd and "erratic object in a disjointed world."[53] The noosphere is a level of shared consciousness that transcends boundaries of religion, culture, or ethnicity. It is a sphere of collective consciousness evident in the way culture is organizing itself around social networks. The age of nations has passed, Teilhard said, and unless we wish to perish, we must shake off our old prejudices and build the earth.

Cosmic Personalization

Teilhard's vision of evolution is communal and creative, spiritual and material. It is not something in evolution, he said, but *Someone*; that is, evolution is the rise of the cosmic Person. The World Wide Web and globalization, in a sense, undergird the rise of the cosmic Person, but such movement lacks aim and purpose; that is, it lacks a core religious dimension of transcendence. Hence, we are becoming more united and globalized but with no shared meaning or ultimate destiny. Teilhard was optimistic that evolution is a process of greater unification in and through the human person empowered by God-Omega. He writes, "We should consider inter-thinking humanity as a new type of organism whose destiny it is to realize new possibilities for evolving life on this planet."[54] He imagined psychic energy (or consciousness) in a continually more reflective state, giving rise to ultrahumanity.[55] By "ultrahumanity" he meant more consciousness and more being through convergence and globalization. Humankind does not dissipate itself but continually concentrates upon itself.[56]

---

[52] Michael H. Murray, *The Thought of Teilhard de Chardin* (New York: Seabury Press, 1966), 20–21.

[53] Robert J. O'Connell, *Teilhard's Vision of the Past: The Making of a Method* (New York: Fordham University Press, 1982), 145.

[54] Teilhard de Chardin, *The Phenomenon of Man*, 20.

[55] W. Henry Kenney, *A Path through Teilhard's Phenomenon* (Dayton, OH: Pflaum, 1970), 105.

[56] Teilhard de Chardin, *The Future of Man*, 316.

Hence the noosphere is a superconvergence of psychic (spiritual/mental) energy, a higher form of complexity in which the human person does not become obsolete but rather acquires more being through interconnectivity with others.

Teilhard's ultrahumanism requires humanity to enter into a new phase of its own evolution. The value of science, Teilhard indicated, can only be for the deepening of spirituality, since knowledge increases mind and mind deepens spirit. He states: "However far science pushes its discovery of the essential fire and however capable it becomes someday of remodeling and perfecting the human element, it will always find itself in the end facing the same problem—how to give to each and every element its final value by grouping them in the unity of an organized whole."[57] He saw the insufficiency of science to effect the transition to superconsciousness, that is, to effectively usher in the next stage of evolution as a higher, more "christified" stage of life. Neither science nor technology ultimately can fulfill the cosmic need to evolve. "It is not tête-à-tête or a corps-à-corps we need; it is a heart to heart."[58] Similarly, Lanier sees that technology must be combined with spirituality to form some type of collective practice that helps people become more compassionate and empathetic in society. A world grounded in love can only evolve by means of love. The noosphere is not about more information; rather, it is about "the rise of . . . a cosmic spiritual center . . . the rise of God."[59] Computer technology extends the outreach of human activity, but it depends on a broader use of human activity and how humans will control psychic, spiritual energy needs, and powers.[60] In Teilhard's words:

> It is not *well being* but a hunger for *more-being* which, of psychological necessity, can alone preserve the thinking earth from the *taedium vitae*. . . . It is upon its point (or

---

[57] Teilhard de Chardin, *The Phenomenon of Man*, 250.

[58] Teilhard de Chardin, *The Future of Man*, 75; Kenny, *A Path through Teilhard's Phenomenon*, 138.

[59] Teilhard de Chardin, *The Future of Man*, 120.

[60] Joseph A. Grau, *Morality and the Human Future in the Thought of Teilhard de Chardin: A Critical Study* (Plainsboro, NJ: Associated University Press, 1976), 274.

superstructure) of spiritual concentration, and not upon its basis (or infra-structure) of material arrangement, that the equilibrium of Mankind biologically depends.[61]

Teilhard said that materialism can bring about well-being, but spirituality and an increase in psychic energy or consciousness bring about more being.[62] Evolution in the noosphere will not happen with the impersonal but the *deeply personal* through *convergence* or the bringing together of diverse elements, organisms, and even the currents of human thought. Teilhard writes: "The future universal cannot be anything else but the *hyperpersonal*."[63] He coined the word *ultrahumanity* to describe a deepening of personhood through shared consciousness. In a sense we can assess whether or not we are on the right path with our technologies if love deepens in the human community as a unifying thread: "It is precisely this state of isolation that will end if we begin to discover in each other not merely the elements of one and the same thing, but of a single Spirit in search of Itself."[64]

World Religions

Teilhard's vision of ultrahumanity requires harnessing the psychic, spiritual powers of the earth and sharing these powers in a way such that we evolve toward greater unity, that is, toward the fullness of the cosmic Christ. As we advance from individual consciousness to collective consciousness, we see that reality is a single organic evolutionary flowing. The noosphere is not simply a new level of global mind; rather, the new level of global mind, in Teilhard's view, is the emergence of Christ. As we come together in a new level of consciousness, we have the capacity to unite in a new way. The new, emerging level of global consciousness, the noosphere, means that religions must leave behind their individual paths and converge. Casavova states that

---

[61] Teilhard de Chardin, *The Future of Man*, 317.

[62] Grau, *Morality and the Human Future in the Thought of Teilhard de Chardin*, 275.

[63] Teilhard de Chardin, *The Phenomenon of Man*, 260.

[64] Teilhard de Chardin, *The Future of Man*, 84.

world religions are becoming more at home in the presence of one another than at home because of dialogue and internet communication.[65] Dialogue among religions, as well as dialogue with scientists, technologists, and economists, is essential to fostering a future of shared life.

Teilhard realized that religion is essential to the future because religion alone can bring about a deeper unity of humankind, integrating all people with God and God with all of life. Human consciousness is on the threshold of a new age that requires entirely new dimensions and values. To this end world religions have a critical role to play. Teilhard emphasized that religions have the power to harness the deepest spiritual energies of humankind and could become the main driving force toward the evolution of a higher future. However, with the steadily progressing self-evolution of the human being, all religions must grow and redefine themselves. Describing Teilhard's vision of religion and the future, Ursula King writes: "The kind of religion we lack today cannot be found in the religious traditions of the past which are linked to static categories; what is needed is a new type of religion that can use all the 'free energy' of the earth to build humankind into greater unity."[66] The deepest beliefs of human beings must find new forms of expression. Teilhard felt that "the human world of today has not grown cold but is ardently searching for a God proportionate to the newly discovered immensities of a universe whose aspect exceeds the present compass of our power of worship."[67]

The rise of the "Nones," those who are religiously unaffiliated, reflects Teilhard's insight that institutional religions no longer meet the needs of our world. In a study done by the Center for Religion in Public Life (Trinity College), Nones comprise about 22 percent of the eighteen- to twenty-nine-year-old population. If the trend continues, Nones may well be 25 percent of the American population in two more decades. Interestingly, 61 percent of

---

[65] Casavova, "Human Religious Evolution and Unfinished Creation," 15.

[66] Ursula King, *The Spirit of One Earth: Reflections on Teilhard de Chardin and Global Spirituality* (New York: Paragon House, 1989), 105.

[67] Teilhard de Chardin, *The Future of Man,* 268.

Nones believe in evolution, while only 38 percent of Americans in general do; 51 percent of Nones believe in God or a Higher Power, and slightly more than half of these believers understand God in a non-personal way, like the Force or the Tao. Less than 10 percent of Nones are atheists, but most tend to believe that whatever God is, God does not fit into the neat packages of religion. Nones tend to be freethinkers, open-minded, and in favor of religious freedom.[68] One Jewish writer sums up the Nones by saying:

> Rather than write off Jewish Nones, I'd create a Jewish Nonery, a school for Jewish Nones that focuses on culture, language, progressive/prophetic politics, and the genius of the biblical wisdom tradition that embraces doubt, argument, and ambiguity. Will anyone do this? I doubt it. Jewish funders are still looking to revive the past and haven't a clue how to invent the future.[69]

World religions share similar challenges.

Teilhard saw a particular role for Christianity in evolution. Christians believe that God is actively involved in the history and development of the world; therefore, Christianity is essentially a religion of progress. To be a vital religion of evolution, however, Christianity needs a new consciousness, an "option for the whole," a new catholicity that integrates humankind's total religious experience into a new spirituality for a new world longing to be born. Religious diversity is here to stay, and therefore religious differences must develop along new lines and lead to new attitudes. Unity is not a given; it has to grow and take shape over time. There is no religious tradition that can remain separate today and survive long into the future. That is why dialogue among religions is essential to the forward movement of life. As evolution continues and technology advances humankind, religions have to create new meaning together in the creation of a new global society of world citizens.

---

[68] Center for Religion in Public Life, "Nones on the Rise" (2012), pewforum.org website.

[69] Rabbi Rami, "The Nones among Us," sbnr.org website.

Religion is key to a new future of life. Despite doctrinal differences, religions can support one another and constitute a new unity out of their diverse doctrines. All religions call for a change of heart and preach the need for a profound transformation of self. Christianity, in particular, advocates a new creation, of making new wholes where there are existing fragments. It *is* a religion of evolution, because we believe in the power of new life at the heart of cosmic development, a new unity in God. Christians, however, must choose to evolve, to become conscious of what is yet unconscious and unwhole. Evolution is not driven by more information but by more being and consciousness. If we are concerned about the final things—death, judgment, heaven, and hell—we might consider that in a universe of infinite space-time these four things may be four dimensions of the one universal law of love.

Chapter 7

The Church as an Open System

Open Systems, Closed Systems

The path from Jesus of Nazareth to the institution of the Catholic Church is a long and complex one. There are many excellent theologians and historians to expound this story, so I won't try to do so here. My intention in this chapter is to ask if the insights from science can shed new light on the catholicity of the Church today in its institutional form. If so, what insights are helpful to the deepening of catholicity in an evolutionary universe? The Church is not an abstract idea or a static institution; it is a concrete reality. It began with the disciples of Jesus, formed under the pressures of radical Judaism, and, in the West, grew into a powerful political and cultural force. The Catholic Church with its rich intellectual tradition profoundly influenced Western civilization, including the arts, literature, science, and economics. As the Church influenced the culture, so too it was affected by culture. With the rise of modern science, the world machine became the dominant metaphor of the modern era, and the Church adapted its medieval cosmology to the new mechanistic paradigm. Danah Zohar writes:

> Classical physics transmuted the living cosmos of Greek and medieval times, a cosmos filled with purpose and intelligence and driven by the love of God for the benefit of humans into a dead, clockwork machine. . . . Things moved because they were fixed and determined; cold silence pervaded the

once-teeming heavens. Human beings and their struggles, the whole of consciousness, and life itself were irrelevant to the workings of the vast universal machine.[1]

Has the Church become mechanistic like so many other world systems? Is it "stuck in a rut," and if so, can it find its way out of the rut into a new future? Jesus lived with imagination, and he preached with imagination: "Imagine a small mustard seed," he said. "If you have faith as small as a mustard seed, you can say to this mulberry tree, 'Be uprooted and planted in the sea,' and it will obey you" (Lk 17:6). He aimed to instill imagination in his disciples so they could think the unthinkable and do the incredible. Similarly, it is helpful to imagine the Church in a new way that enkindles us to think the unthinkable and do the incredible. One way to reimagine the Church is by returning to nature and learning from nature how life can grow from a seed into a flowering tree. Rather than beginning with metaphors and symbols, I begin with an understanding of systems, since nature is based on organization and patterns of relatedness.

Physicist Fritjof Capra defines a system as "an integrated whole whose essential properties arise from the relationships between its parts."[2] Systems can be closed or open, and can be understood as mechanisms or holisms. Closed systems relate to the external environment as something stable and predictable; they assume that the environment will not intervene in or cause problems for the functioning of the system. A physical, closed system does not exchange any matter with its surroundings and is not subject to any force outside the system. It relies on internal processes and dynamics to account for the system's organization and function. Therefore, a closed system does not depend on the external environment and is best described as a machine that runs according to law and order; each part has its autonomy and particular function.[3]

---

[1] Danah Zohar, *The Quantum Self: Human Nature and Consciousness Defined by the New Physics* (New York: Quill/William Morrow, 1990), 18.

[2] Fritjob Capra, *The Web of Life: A New Scientific Understanding of Living Systems* (New York: Doubleday, 2006), 27.

[3] Jennifer M. Allen and Rajeev Sawhney, *Administration and Management in Criminal Justice: A Service Quality Approach* (Thousand Oaks, CA: Sage Publications, 2009), 27–64; Capra, *The Web of Life*, 46–50.

One of the best examples of a closed system, from my own experience, is traditional religious life. In 1984, I entered a discalced Carmelite Monastery in Sugarloaf, Pennsylvania. I had read Thomas Merton's *Seven Story Mountain* and wanted to pursue the type of contemplative life he described. I sought out the most ascetic way of life I could find. It was a newly established monastery on a sleepy farm-hill road in Pennsylvania, across the street from an inactive volcanic mountain called Sugarloaf. I entered the monastery with three other women (two from Canada and one from Ohio), and I was grateful for their presence. From the moment we crossed the threshold into the monastery, our independent lives became dependent on the prioress or superior of the community.[4] We were given clothes to wear, told where to sleep, where to eat, how to pray, and to do all these things under obedience in a routinized way. Our tasks were assigned to us each morning, and we were to do no other than the task we were given that day. Any infraction of obedience could encounter public reprimand. Our communal discussions were limited to the weather, the monastery pets, the bakery (we were self-supporting), and the vegetable garden (I must admit, we had winners; the prioress obtained a steroid-like spray for vegetables, and ours grew four times the normal size). We had no contact with the outside world, except a visit to the doctor or dentist. Visitors to the monastery were met by the portress (the sister who monitored the door and main entrance) and/or the prioress. The rest of the community was sealed off from the world and under the supreme command of the superior. It was a breeding ground for either profound dysfunction or profound holiness—there was little room for normal life in between. If the monastery was absolutely closed, however, I would not be writing this book. Every closed system has an aspect of openness within it. Nature is shot through with hope.

Holons and Organization

In the beginning of the twentieth century scientists began to realize that systems do not operate in closed, causal, deterministic ways, but rather in dynamic, nonlinear patterns or as open

---

[4] In the Carmelite monastic tradition, the superior of the community is referred to as prioress (for women) and prior (for men).

systems. Austrian biologist Ludwig von Bertalanffy challenged biology based on mechanistic, homeostatic (steady state) systems, emphasizing that real systems are open to and interact with their environments.[5] Bertalanffy took a bold step by saying that living organisms cannot be described by classical thermodynamics because they act as open systems and thus defy the second law of thermodynamics, which basically says that a closed system will eventually dissipate into disorder. By "open systems" Bertalanffy meant that systems feed on a continual flux of matter and energy from their environment: "The organism is not a static system closed to the outside and always containing the identical components; it is an open system . . . in which material continually enters from, and leaves into, the outside environment."[6] He set out to replace the mechanistic foundations of science with a holistic vision and developed the theory of general systems.

An open system allows interactions between the system's internal elements and the environment. The interaction can take the form of information, energy, or material transfers into or out of the system boundary, depending on the discipline that defines the concept. Open systems assume that supplies of energy cannot be depleted, since energy is supplied from some source in the surrounding environment. The organization of an open system is the

---

[5] Ludwig von Bertalanffy, "The Theory of Open Systems in Physics and Biology," *Science* 111 (January 13, 1950): 23–28. To appreciate the import of open systems, it is helpful to keep in mind the concept of change. Alicia Juarrero writes: "Western philosophy has for the most part explained change as a function of substance, a substrate that sustains and underlies change. For any given thing, its substance was not thought to change; only its superficial (accidental) attributes did." Juarrero goes on to say that "with the discovery of evolution, contemporary biology demonstrated that the notion of 'essences' is illusory. There is simply no such thing as an organism's 'invariable nature.' . . . Living organisms and their creations must instead be judged by their degree of resilience and flourishing . . . which in large measure is a function of connectivity and interdependence." See Alicia Juarrero, "Complex Dynamical Systems and the Problem of Identity," *Emergence* 4, nos. 1–2 (2002): 94–104.

[6] Ludwig von Bertalanffy, *General System Theory* (New York: Braziller, 1968), 121.

set of relations among its components; structure is the physical embodiment of its relational organization.

Whereas classical physics is based on parts making up wholes, physicist David Bohm took relationships between parts as primary. Each part is connected with every other part at the quantum level. Thus, the whole universe is the basic reality; primacy belongs to the whole, and each part is part of the whole. Arthur Koestler proposed the word *holon* to describe the hybrid nature of sub-wholes and parts in living systems. A *holon* is something that is simultaneously a whole and a part.[7] Holons exist simultaneously as self-contained wholes in relation to their subordinate parts, and dependent parts when considered from the inverse direction. In a closed system order is based on hierarchy or rank of importance, including responsibilities and power. In an open system hierarchy is related to the organization of the parts where each part is part of the whole or holons; hence, open-system organization is governed by holarchy or the integral organization of holons. A holarchy is a hierarchy of self-regulating holons in which each whole functions in supra-ordination to the parts, in relation to influences from higher organizational levels and in coordination with the local environment.[8] We might say there is an intrinsic wholeness embedded in nature reflected in its dynamic organizational systems. The activity involved is in the continual embodiment of the system's pattern of organization.[9] Nature is an interlocking network of systems. It is more flow than fixed, a choreographed ballet, a symphony, whereby an organism is dynamically engaged in its own self-organization, pursuing its own ends amid an ever-shifting context of relationships.

---

[7] For a discussion of holons see Judy Cannato, *Radical Amazement: Contemplative Lessons from Black Holes, Supernovas, and Other Wonders of the Universe* (Notre Dame, IN: Sorin Books, 2006), 94–102; idem, *Fields of Compassion: How the New Cosmology Is Transforming Spiritual Life* (Notre Dame, IN: Sorin Books, 2010); Ken Wilbur, *A Theory of Everything* (Boston: Shambala Publications, 2000).

[8] Mark Edwards, "A Brief History of Holons," integralworld.net website.

[9] Capra, *The Web of Life*, 161.

Vatican II as an Open System

Understanding open systems illuminates the changes in religious life after Vatican II. One way to grasp the import of the Second Vatican Council is to understand the Church waking up to its separation from the world. The call to "open the windows" of the Church to history, religious plurality, cultural complexity, and science was something of an ecclesial earthquake. One of the major points of radical change in the Church was in religious life. Women who had been cloistered and radically removed from the world now found themselves face to face with a world of richly varied experiences. The habit was exchanged for secular clothes, which caused major conflicts in communities, because religious identity was at stake. Sisters who had been in long habits with veils showed up at breakfast with slacks and leather boots. Instead of teaching grade-school children and quickly returning home for community prayer, now sisters could visit with students' parents or go out to a movie on a weekend. I experienced this shift personally when I left the monastery in 1988 and went to live with a community of German Franciscan Sisters in New Jersey. They were simple, kind women who ran a nursing home for women and a home for mentally disabled women. They entrusted me with a car and an education in theology at Fordham University, and for the first time in religious life I had the experience of freedom. I was able to come and go according to my university schedule, although I still had to work in the nursing home on weekends and in the summer, as well as participate in all community prayers and activities. From the German Sisters I learned the value of community celebrations and good beer, although the structure of the life was still under control of the superior and her council. It would take more time before I could embark on a new way of open-systems religious life.

Nature's Self-Organization

The discovery of systems biology led scientists in the twentieth century to ask how systems organize. Humberto Maturana and Francisco Varela wrote that "living systems are machines that cannot be shown by pointing to their components. Rather, one must show their organization in a manner such that the way in which all their peculiar properties arise becomes obvious."[10] They distinguished between "organization" and "structure" by saying that organization of a living system is the set of relations among its components that characterize the system as belonging to a particular class. The structure of a living system is constituted by the actual relations among the physical components; structure is the physical embodiment of its organization. They coined the term *autopoiesis* to describe "a network of production processes, in which the function of each component is to participate in the production or transformation of other components in the network. In this way the entire network continually 'makes itself' by producing its components and, in turn, is produced by its components."[11] In living systems "the product of its operation is its own organization."[12] The pattern of organization determines a system's essential characteristics.

Autopoietic systems are self-organizing systems that interact with the environment through continual exchange of energy and matter. Ilya Prigogine shed new light on dynamical systems when he described the structure of a living system as a dissipative structure, emphasizing openness of the structure to the flow of energy and matter. Prigogine's work on the evolution of dynamic systems demonstrated that *disequilibrium* is the necessary condition for a system's growth. He called these systems *dissipative* because they dissipate their energy in order to re-create themselves into new forms of organization. For this reason they are frequently called self-organizing or self-renewing systems. One of their distinguishing features is system *resiliency* rather than equilibrium.[13] Margaret Wheatley writes:

> Equilibrium is neither the goal nor the fate of living systems, simply because as open systems they are partners with their environment. . . . To stay viable, open systems

---

[10] Cited in Mark Taylor, *After God* (Chicago: University of Chicago Press, 2007), 318. See also Humberto Maturana and Francisco Varela, *Autopoiesis and Cognition* (Dordrecht: D. Reidel, 1980), 75.

[11] Capra, *The Web of Life*, 98.

[12] Maturana and Varela, *Autopoiesis and Cognition*, 82.

[13] Margaret J. Wheatley, *Leadership and the New Science: Learning about Organization from an Orderly Universe* (San Francisco: Berrett-Koehler, 1994), 88.

maintain a state of non-equilibrium, keeping the system off balance so that it can change and grow. They participate in an active exchange with their world, using what is there for their own renewal.[14]

Part of their viability comes from their internal capacity to create structures that fit the moment; when the needs change, so do the structures. Form and function engage in a fluid process where the system may maintain itself in its present form or evolve to a new order. The system possesses the capacity for spontaneously emerging new structures, depending on what is required. The autopoietic system focuses its activities on what is needed to maintain its own integrity and self-renewal. It changes by referring to itself; whatever future form it takes will be consistent with its already established identity. The system, according to Eric Jantsch, "keeps the memory of its evolutionary path."[15] Freedom and order are correlative in open systems. The more freedom in a self-organizing system, the more order.[16] Freedom is not opposed to order; rather, autonomy at the local level provides coherence and continuity.

Wholeness in nature works on the principles of self-organization, which include openness to the environment, a flow of energy, local autonomy, and freedom to self-organize. These principles provide the overall integrity and stability of an open system, whereby order emerges from patterns of information and energy. Open systems are nondeterministic systems and can undergo radical change. I suppose I knew this personally when I made the decision in 2007 to leave my German Franciscan community and to begin a new religious community in Washington, DC. The German sisters were still too closed to consider religious life in new ways. I had come to a point of inner freedom where I knew God was calling me to do new things; thus, I was impelled to step out of the comforts of institutional life and, with another Sister, take the risk of living religious life in a new way. I think the term *open system* best describes our way of life. We live in a

---

[14] Ibid., 78.
[15] Eric Jantsch, *The Self-Organizing Universe* (Oxford: Pergamon Press, 1980), 1, 49.
[16] Ibid., 40.

working-class neighborhood in DC and financially support our-selves (we pay taxes); if we don't work, we don't eat. We discuss the aims of the community together; we try to share responsibili-ties for the community as much as possible; we pray and play as community, but we respect the autonomy of each person and the work of the Spirit in each life. Each person is a holon who is conscious of being part of a larger whole. An open-systems way of life works best on shared vision and dialogue and least on control and lack of communication. Trust is an essential fac-tor, but trust requires kenosis, emptying oneself of control and power, and making space for the other to enter in. Where there is no trust, there is no real vision together because vision requires sharing in the same field of energy. An open-systems community, like the physical world itself, is based on relationships, not roles or duties but bonds of friendship, sisterhood (or brotherhood), respect, charity, forgiveness, and justice. Where these values are active and alive, life evolves toward richer, more creative forms, never losing sight that wholeness—catholicity—is at the heart of it.

Wise and Foolish

My varied experiences of religious life as both closed and open systems is consonant with the struggles of the Church today. The Church developed according to the models of nature known in the patristic and Middle Ages. These models were closed systems because, until recent times, this is how nature was understood. The hierarchical structure of the Church was (and still is) based on the three-tiered cosmological model of Ptolemy and the Neoplatonic structure of the fifth-century writer Pseudo-Dionysius. Pseudo-Dionysius developed the notion of hierarchy as sacred order and composed two main hierarchies that still frame the structure of the Church today. The Celestial Hierarchy of Angels, which is still recited by the priest at mass ("thrones, powers, principalities, cherubim, and seraphim") and the Eccle-siastical Hierarchy, which lists the members of the Church in their assigned roles (bishops, priests, deacons, monks, and laity). This hierarchy was given ontological status in the Middle Ages whereby the ordering of the hierarchy reflected graded levels of being; the top of the hierarchy had more perfect being compared to the lower rungs of the hierarchy, such as monks and laity, which had lesser being.[17] The Dionysian Hierarchy mirrored the Ptolemaic three-tiered, fixed universe. Wherever one stood in the hierarchy, one was to receive the divine light and be lifted up to God: "The goal of a hierarchy, then, is to enable beings to be as like as possible to God and to be at one with him."[18] Because the hierarchical order was established by God, one was not to seek any rank other than one's own, although one could be influenced by other ranks of order.[19]

The Dionysian Hierarchy was a beautifully ordered cosmology that sought to reflect the manifestation of God (theophany) in the cosmos. For Dionysius, the relationship between cosmology and theology was reflected in the Church. The development of the Church's hierarchy, from the pope to the laity, was shown in its clearly defined roles and responsibilities. Each role has a purpose and place in the institutional, hierarchical order: the pope and administrative hierarchy to govern; consecrated men and women to pray and serve; and the laity to obey and financially

---

[17] G. Geltner, "William of St. Amour's *De Periculis novissimorum temporum*: A False Start to Medieval Antifraternalism?" 35–36, academia.edu website. William of St. Amour, a secular master at the University of Paris in the thirteenth century, sought to exclude mendicant friars from university chairs by appealing to the Dionysian Ecclesiastical Hierarchy, in which the clergy occupy a higher rank than monks and thus are the only rightful holders of university positions.

[18] *Pseudo-Dionysius: The Complete Works*, trans. Colm Luibheid (New York: Paulist Press, 1987), 154. In his "Celestial Hierarchy" Dionysius describes the manifestation of God throughout all levels of creation: "If one talks then of hierarchy, what is meant is a certain perfect arrangement, an image of the beauty of God which sacredly works out the mysteries of its own enlightenment in the orders and levels of understanding of the hierarchy. . . . Indeed for every member of the hierarchy, perfection consists in this, that it is uplifted to imitate God as far as possible and, more wonderful still, that it becomes what scriptures calls a 'fellow workman for God' and a reflection of the workings of God" (154).

[19] Andrew Louth, *The Origins of the Christian Mystical Tradition: From Plato to Denys* (New York: Oxford University Press, 2007); idem, *Denys the Areopagite* (New York: Bloomsbury Academic, 2002).

support the Church. The well-known maxim of religious life held true for the Church itself: "Keep the Rule and the Rule will keep you." As the Church migrated from the world of Dionysius to the world of Newton, rules provided boundaries and created structures that secured things in a predictable and deterministic way of life.

Despite the discovery of Big Bang cosmology and evolution, the Catholic Church is still a closed system. It is virtually unchanged by the surrounding environment because the system is internally regulated by the separation of labor, roles, and responsibilities. The consolidation of the Church as a closed system—despite Vatican II—has prevented it from engaging a world of change and acting responsibly in history. Examples of a closed-system Church, especially in the last century, include the lack of resistance to the Nazi holocaust; the blind eye to the clerical culture of sexual abuse; the censoring of theologians who espouse religious pluralism and feminism; the excommunication of priests who support ordination of women; censoring public speakers (I once received a call from a bishop after a talk given by an auxiliary bishop to our theology students, asking if the bishop mentioned homosexuality or women's ordination in his talk); and the list goes on. A closed system, like my experience at the monastery, perceives everything outside the system as a potential threat to its function. Everything that does not have a role in the mechanized system is rejected. Even though Pope John XXIII wanted a pastoral Church open to the needs of the world, Vatican II failed to move the Church from a closed to an open system. Pundits ponder why, and scholars convene, but the reason is quite simple. A system closed to the environment will not change in tandem with the environment. A system open to the environment is affected by the environment; when the environment changes, so does the system, given a sufficient amount of time. The ability of a system to change in tandem with the environment *is* the viability of the system; that is, the mark of an open system is its ability to self-organize in relation to changes in the environment.

For centuries the Church has operated like a well-oiled machine, but the oil is running low and the machine is running down. The parable of the ten wise virgins can be read in view of closed and open systems:

Then the kingdom of heaven shall be likened to ten virgins who took their lamps and went out to meet the bridegroom. Now five of them were wise, and five were foolish. Those who were foolish took their lamps and took no oil with them, but the wise took oil in their vessels with their lamps. But while the bridegroom was delayed, they all slumbered and slept. And at midnight a cry was heard: "Behold, the bridegroom is coming; go out to meet him!" Then all those virgins arose and trimmed their lamps. And the foolish said to the wise, "Give us some of your oil, for our lamps are going out." But the wise answered, saying, "No, lest there should not be enough for us and you; but go rather to those who sell, and buy for yourselves." And while they went to buy oil, the bridegroom came, and those who were ready went in with him to the wedding; and the door was shut. Afterward the other virgins came also, saying, "Lord, Lord, open to us!" But he answered and said, "Assuredly, I say to you, I do not know you." Watch therefore, for you know neither the day nor the hour in which the Son of Man is coming. (Mt 25:1–13)

The foolish virgins were those not attentive to something new on the horizon; they assumed that life would continue unchanged and, if necessary, they would get their oil in time. They were like closed systems, not open to the environment. The wise virgins, on the other hand, were attuned to the possibility that something in the environment could change. They were like open systems, preparing themselves for the newness of the Lord to arrive. The wise virgins lived in the now; they did not presume anything, nor did they expect the machine of life to keep on humming. Rather, they lived in present moment, open to the impending arrival of the bridegroom. Thus, when the Lord appeared, they could let go of what they were doing and go out to meet him with open arms. The wise virgins lived into a new future, but the foolish virgins, blinded by the illusion of mechanistic life, were renounced and deprived of the banquet of life. Systems theorist Eric Jantsch once wrote, "To live with an evolutionary spirit is to let go when the right time comes and to engage new structures of relationship."[20]

---

[20] Jantsch, *The Self-Organizing Universe*, 40.

Openness to the environment means acquiring new patterns of relatedness that enable a system not only to survive but to remain open to more life. The only way for the Church to grow is to keep the oil burners filled, to let go when the right time comes, and to go out to the world anew.

Teilhard's Dream

Teilhard de Chardin described the Church as an open system, a new phylum of Christian amorization (from the Latin *amor,* "love") in the universe. *Phylum* is a (slightly dated) taxonomic term from biology that refers to the degree of relatedness or familial characteristics among the species or members. By speaking of the Church as a phylum, Teilhard imagined a new "christified" humanity, bonded by love, that would amorize the cosmos and kindle love in the evolving cosmos. In his view Christian love is the energy of evolution because love is at the heart of evolution. Anchored in the cosmic Christ, the Church bears witness to the living God as the life of the world and hence to its own life as an organic body in evolution. The Church exists, both in mission and as symbol, of the christification of the universe, the personalization of divine love incarnate at the heart of cosmic life. In other words, the Church does not exist for itself; it exists for the world. "God so loved the world that he sent the only Son . . . not to judge the world, but that the world might be saved through him" (Jn 3:16). In Teilhard's view, the Church is:

- the reflectively christified portion of the world
- the principal focus of inter-human affinities through super-charity
- the central axis of universal convergence
- the precise point of contact between the universe and the Omega Point

The risen Christ speaks to us of the personal unity of love at the heart of the universe, the invasion of the present by the power of what is yet to come: "In his great mercy he has given us new birth into a living hope through the resurrection of Jesus Christ from the dead" (1 Pt 1:3). Teilhard felt that traditional Christianity still lives too aloof from the world, too much at odds with "the natural religious current" of contemporary humanity, a closed system of routinized sameness. Like the ten wise virgins, Teilhard anticipated the changes of the world and the coming of Christ in new ways. He called for a new religion of the earth rather than a religion of heaven. Religion, in Teilhard's view, is primarily *on the level of human consciousness* and human action, rather than in institutions or belief systems, except insofar as these manifest and give direction to the former. He expressed his understanding of how religion is related to energy and evolution toward Omega by saying:

> Religion was not developed primarily as an easy way out [or] to provide shelter from the insoluble or intrusive difficulties met by the mind as it became active. In its real basis, it is biologically (we might almost say mechanically) the necessary counterpart to the release of the earth's spiritual energy: the human being by his appearance in nature, brings with him the emergence, ahead of him, of a divine pole to give him balance.[21]

In his final essay, *The Christic,* he writes: "In a system of cosmo-noogenesis, the comparative value of religious creeds may be measured by their respective power of evolutive activation."[22] This is a powerful insight. Does our profession of the faith, "I believe in one God, maker of heaven and earth," energize us for love? Does it inspire a higher consciousness of Christ in us? Does it impel us to go out and make wholes? We need an open-systems Church where patterns of relationship are woven into a christifying universe. In his talk to the United Nations Teilhard said:

---

[21] Ewert H. Cousins, "Teilhard and the Religious Phenomenon," UNESCO, International Symposium on the Occasion of the Centenary of the Birth of Teilhard de Chardin, Fordham University, New York, September 16–18, 1981.

[22] Pierre Teilhard de Chardin, "The Christic," users.globalnet.co.uk website.

The crises of our time are challenging the world religions to release a new spiritual force transcending religious, cultural and national boundaries into a new consciousness of the oneness of the human community and so putting into effect a spiritual dynamic toward the solutions of world problems. . . . We affirm a new spirituality, divested of insularity and directed toward a planetary consciousness.[23]

Faith in God and faith in this world are a source of great spiritual energy in human beings. We need people who will be passionately and simultaneously animated in both types of faith and so effect in themselves one heart, centered in God within and ahead. Human consciousness finds itself on the threshold of a new age that requires entirely new dimensions and values. The deepest beliefs of human beings must find new forms of expression.

Envisioning an Open-Systems Church

What might an open-systems Church look like? Pope Francis calls for a living Church in which the gospel is woven into our everyday lives and shared with others, as we meet people along the path of life. He writes in *Evangelii gaudium*: "If we allow doubts and fears to dampen our courage, instead of being creative we will remain comfortable and make no progress whatsoever. In this case we will not take an active part in historical processes, but become mere onlookers as the Church gradually stagnates" (no. 129). The pope bears a "catholic" spirit, open to the whole and a desire to create new christic wholes. However, his openness of gospel life in history cannot be supported by the closed, mechanistic structures of the Church. There is a passage in scripture that, I think, speaks to the gospel life as an open-systems life; it is the passage of the little child. One can imagine the motley group of disciples following Jesus, arguing over who was most important or his favorite disciple. Jesus pauses and calls a small child over to him. He then turns to the disciples and

---

[23] In Cousins, "Teilhard and the Religious Phenomenon."

says: "Truly, I tell you, unless you change and become like little children, you will never enter the kingdom of heaven" (Mt 18:3). On the human level, children are probably the best examples of open systems. They are enamored by the smallest things, like butterflies and maple leaves, and can creatively play by the ocean shoreline with a pail and shovel. They can be upset one moment and giggle wildly the next moment. They tend toward mimetic desire and want what their playmate has, but they also forgive more readily, forget past hurts, and play on. What did Jesus have in mind when he held up a small child as the model for gospel life? Simply, openness to life, and by this I mean playfulness, creativity, friendship, sharing, forgiveness, love, and a willingness to start anew. Heaven is where conflict, war, and mimetic desire are transformed into love and shared life. Christian life is intended to be an open-systems life; it is grounded in the openness of God, who shares life with us fully and completely.

I would like to highlight three aspects that can undergird the Church as an open system. First, the Church is grounded in the openness of God to something "other," to newness of life. The incarnation is deeply relational insofar as the Divine is embedded in materiality. Jesus was foremost about relationships and, in particular, the type of relationships that create wholeness and community. Second, the Church exists in history, which means it shares in the evolutionary story of the cosmos. It is organic, a living body; it emerges out of a long, evolutionary process and is part of this process. Third, and most important, the Church is about the life of Christ. It exists for the sake of this life, not simply to teach the gospel but to live the gospel in a way that life flows throughout the universe. An incarnational Church is, by definition, an open-systems Church, intended to be the living body of Christ growing into the fullness of cosmotheandric love—a Church that is not so much a teaching Church as a living one. What might a living Church look like?

Again, we can turn to scripture, where Jesus tells us that nature is a good teacher of living in the presence of God:

Who of you by being worried can add a single hour to his life? . . . Observe how the lilies of the field grow; they do not toil nor do they spin, yet I say to you that not even

Solomon in all his glory clothed himself like one of these.
(Mt 6:28)

When Jesus asked his disciples to "look at the lilies of the field,"
I think he was asking them to read the book of nature as the
book of God. To look is to contemplate, to ponder, to see what
God is doing in nature. The lilies do not simply reflect God;
rather, God is being God in the lilies—incarnation. So if we ask
how to live the incarnation as Church, we are asking how to live
like the lilies of the field. Modern science provides some lessons
from nature:

1. *Holons and holarchy mark living systems.* Everything
   in nature is a whole and part of a larger whole. Can we
   imagine the Church to consist of christified wholes, that
   is, those who have said "yes" to the public dimension of
   christifying love (baptism)? Can we recognize that holons are not gender specific, that every person is a whole
   and part of a larger whole that is the Church? Holons
   require a shift from seeing people as passive spectators,
   victims, or ignorant bystanders to seeing them as active
   participants in shaping reality, from reacting to what is
   handed down from on high to creating the future from
   below and within the relationships of daily life.[24] When
   the experience of being part of something is our own
   experience, we seek to create ourselves based on that
   experience. How we organize whole/parts locally and
   unify globally is the challenge of the Church's holarchy
   for the future.

2. *Morphogenetic fields.* Morphogenetic fields, as we discussed in Chapter 5, are unseen forces that preserve
   the *form* of self-organizing systems, maintaining order
   from within. That is, a morphogenetic field directs other
   members of the species toward the same form or behavior or what Sheldrake calls morphic resonance. What
   we do, how we think, how we act, and the choices we

---

[24] Peter Senge, *The Fifth Discipline: The Art and Practice of the
Learning Organization* (New York: Doubleday, 1990), 69.

make together for the sake of life create energy fields that strengthen the values of community. Canadian psychologist Donald Hebb (d. 1985) said that "Those who fire together, wire together."[25] Brain studies today show that working together actually causes the brains of individuals to fire together, as if there is one brain among them. The brain is an open system (composed of local systems) that functions in communication with the environment. It both is affected by the environment and affects the environment. A shared environment can give rise to a shared brain, so that becoming "one in heart and mind" is a reality. What if we consider the gospel life as a constellation of morphogenetic fields, realizing that common activity or shared thoughts can lead to new informational patterns in the world? Could we envision creating communities of gospel values such as peace, charity, and forgiveness based on interpersonal relationships in a way that can ripple and radiate throughout the universe? Can the Church see the sacramental life, especially the Eucharist, as a morphogenetic field of compassion, love, mercy, and forgiveness? Can this field be strengthened by conscious participation? If we could begin to think in these new ways, then we might consider how the Church could bring the faithful to a higher level of christic consciousness that energizes and excites us for the future.

3. *Open System.* I have already spoken about open systems but they are important enough to revisit in light of what nature can teach us about community. Letting go into new structures under shifting conditions in the environment is integral to open systems. Such systems change locally because they are autonomous and usually have local fluctuations; however, it is precisely the ability to change locally that provides the overall stability of the system. Change at the local level provides stability at the global level. Chaos theory tells us that local change can

---

[25] Donald O. Hebb, *The Organization of Behavior: A Neuropsychological Theory* (New York: Wiley, June 1949), 43–54.

have global effects. A butterfly flapping its wings on my geranium in Washington, DC, may disturb a weather pattern that can amplify over distance and initiate a storm in Thailand. Or, as physicist Paul Dirac says, "Pick a flower on earth and you move the farthest star." Perhaps local church communities have global effects as well. How we live and pray together can make a significant difference in the world. We can either help promote peace by our local relatedness or help catalyze war by our failure to relate. The roots of sin may lie in resisting new patterns of order because we insist on controlling the spontaneity of life.

The Church has had a difficult time letting go into new structures because a closed system does not have permeable boundaries. When the liturgical changes of Vatican II swept through local churches, there was a lot of confusion and misunderstanding around the changes. Within a short amount of time celebration of the mass went from Gregorian chant to guitar music, from solemn procession to dance, from the back of the priest on the high altar to the circle of the faithful around the altar; the faithful were shocked and confused because the mystery of God seemed to collapse in front of them, accompanied by a guitar strumming, bongos banging, and the priest meandering around the altar of sacrifice.

From an open-systems perspective, the difficulty of Vatican II was instituting change as a universal decision. Lessons from biology tell us that universal change is virtually impossible. In a self-organizing world of open systems, all change is local. An open-systems Church cannot function as a monarchy but as a holarchy. Rather than a monolithic structure trying to maintain universal sameness amid historical pluralism, an open-systems Church is a field of interlocking local communities, not unlike the early church that emerged after the death and resurrection of Jesus Christ. Local churches, empowered from within, can best discern their patterns of relationship and organization that vitalize a christic way of life. To be "church," in accordance with nature, is to "live local." Within the local milieu visions spread because of a reinforcing process. Increased clarity, enthusiasm, and commitment rub off on others in the community. Dialogue is essential to viable relationships and work best on the local level. "Dialogue is a conversation on a common subject between two or more persons with differing views, the primary purpose of which is for each participant to learn from the other so that he or she can change and grow," Leonard Swidler writes.[26] Dialogue is when a group "becomes open to the flow of a larger intelligence" and thought is approached largely as a collective phenomenon.[27] When dialogue and thinking are brought together in mutual relatedness, there is the possibility of creating a language more suited for dealing with complexity and of focusing on deep-seated structural issues and forces rather than being diverted by questions of personality and leadership style.

An open-systems Church requires a new view of leadership. The traditional view of leadership is based on assumptions of people's powerlessness, their lack of personal vision and knowledge of God, and their inability to master the forces of change. In an open-systems model leaders are designers, stewards, and teachers. They are responsible for creating the patterns where people continually expand their capabilities to understand complexity, clarify vision, think together, and learn together. Leadership is inspiring the whole to take responsibility for the whole. Can we see the Bishop of Rome and the College of Bishops as designers, stewards, and teachers? Can we see the example of Pope Francis as a christic fractal, a new pattern of order drawing others into new christic patterns? Are local, ecclesial communities lured by this "strange attractor" and, if so, how can they best reorganize in openness to this new pattern of order? Do we see the role of the bishops as empowering people to be "christifiers," helping people achieve more insight on the evolution of Christ? Do we see our leaders as teachers who empower a vision for the whole? This is the type of catholicity needed today, a renewal of life-energies inspiring a rise in consciousness and empowering participation in creating a whole earth community—peace among people and justice with nature—around the globe.

---

[26] Leonard Swidler, "The Dialogue Decalogue: Ground Rules for Interreligious Dialogue," *Journal of Ecumenical Studies* 20, no. 1 (Winter 1983).

[27] Senge, *The Fifth Discipline*, 226.

Toward an Open-Systems Theology

For the Church to vitalize the gospel in today's world, an understanding of Christ in evolution must spawn new ways of thinking and acting toward greater wholeness and unity; theology must change in accord with what we now know about the human person and the physical cosmos. Joel Pribam writes: "Perhaps progress in religion can occur as it does in science: without invalidating a theory, a greater myth may encompass it respectfully."[28] Or as Einstein noted, "Problems cannot be solved by the same level of thinking that created them." An open-systems Church requires an open-systems theology.

The International Theological Commission in a recent document affirmed that scripture is the "soul of theology." The commission clearly stated that the centrality of the divine word of God is essential to the task of doing theology: "The Scriptures are 'inspired' by God and committed to writing once and for all time; hence, they present God's own Word in an unalterable form, and they make the voice of the Holy Spirit sound again and again in the words of the prophets and apostles." The authors note that Christianity is the "religion of the Word of God," emphasizing that the incarnate and living word of God is spoken through the ages "in creation, through the prophets and sages, through the holy Scriptures and definitely through the life, death and resurrection of Jesus Christ, the Word made flesh." Although the document expounds the coherence of faith to culture, it does so noting the "ambivalence of human history." Striving to give a reasoned account for faith, the document seeks to show the Church's openness to culture, historicity, and the progress of the natural sciences. The strength of Catholic theology, according to the document, is "the strong relationship between faith and reason, first of all philosophical reason, so as to overcome both fideism and rationalism." The authors write: "Catholic theology recognizes the proper methods of other sciences and critically utilizes them in its own research. It does not isolate itself from critique and welcomes scientific dialogue."[29]

---

[28] Joel R. Primack, "Cosmology and Culture," physics.ucsc.edu website.

[29] International Theological Commission, "Theology Today: Perspectives, Principles and Criteria," nos. 4, 15, 20, 23.

But dialogue involves transcending the threshold that defines one world, entering into the world of another so as to return home with new insight and meaning. Does Catholic theology today enter into the world of science to return home with new insight and meaning? In a 1988 letter to George V. Coyne, SJ, director of the Vatican Observatory, Pope John Paul II stated that "science can purify religion from error and superstition; religion can purify science from idolatry and false absolutes. Each can draw the other into a wider world, a world in which both can flourish." Speaking to the Pontifical Academy of Sciences in 1996 he said that "theologians and those working on the exegesis of Scripture need to be well informed regarding the results of the latest scientific research."[30] Commenting on the findings of various sciences, from molecular biology to paleontology, he indicated that "the convergence in the results of these independent studies . . . constitutes in itself a significant argument in favor of the theory (of evolution)."[31] Openness to the modern sciences, according to Saint John Paul II, can help the Church remain on the path of truth and not wander off into error and superstition. While the late pope showed significant openness to modern science, the Church has not gone beyond hosting several excellent conferences on science and religion. Dialogue in a closed system is an external relationship; a system cannot be changed by the insights of dialogue unless the information is added to the system in order to change it. Dialogue in itself cannot impact a closed system. No true change can take place without transcendence of the dialogical partners and this means removing the boundaries. Real dialogue requires an open system.

Theology in itself is neither a closed nor an open system. How theology affects life and the life of the Church depends on how it is constructed. In his luminous Gifford Lectures the late Raimon Panikkar highlighted the integral relationship between cosmology and theology: "The conception of God has always been intimately connected with the reigning worldview of a particular epoch. Cosmology was part of theology as long as the cosmos

---

[30] Pope John Paul II, "Message to the Pontifical Academy of Sciences: On Evolution," October 22, 1996, in English on the ewtn.com website.
[31] Ibid.

was believed to be God's creation, the Divine intrinsically related to the universe." Panikkar states that "cosmology is that which discloses itself when Man (sic) is attentive to the disclosure of the cosmos, and deciphers, surmises, or understands what the cosmos is saying."[32] Theology, like philosophy, is not a particular science; rather, it is related to the whole. The very name of God is a cosmological notion; there is no cosmos without God and no God without cosmos. If theology is a function of cosmology, then knowledge of the sciences is *fundamental* to the task of theology. Although the relationship between faith and science results in a fragile sort of theology (for it is tied to what is a scientific view, which itself is subject to change), we too easily forget where earlier theological world-images came from. Zachary Hayes writes, "We have forgotten many of the details of the world as conceived by earlier theologies (for ex. the medieval concept of the planetary spheres)."[33] As a result we are often unaware of the extent to which such secular views have shaped our familiar religious language. He continues:

> If Augustine was able to speak theologically in a world conditioned by neo-Platonism, and if an Aquinas was able to construct a theology using Aristotelian categories to speak to a world wrestling with the Aristotelian world view, is it possible for contemporary theology to do a similar thing, taking a world view from the sciences?[34]

Despite the fact that modern science has progressed far beyond the insights of Aristotle and Ptolemy, the Church has yet to embrace a new metaphysical framework for doing theology. In *Fides et ratio*, John Paul II recalled that "the Church has been justified in consistently proposing St. Thomas as a master of thought and a model of the right way to do theology" (no. 43). Thomism is one system adequately mediating Christian truth.

---

[32] Raimon Panikkar, *The Rhythm of Being; The Gifford Lectures* (Maryknoll, NY: Orbis Books, 2010), 186.

[33] Zachary Hayes, OFM, *A Window to the Divine: Creation Theology* (Quincy, IL: Franciscan Press, 1997), 41.

[34] Hayes, *A Window to the Divine*, 87.

While central elements of Thomas's corpus remain essential, he admitted that a new conceptual framework is needed, one that acknowledges and incorporates advances in thought since the Middle Ages. Joseph Ratzinger (Pope Benedict XVI) advocated a similar position when he wrote:

> The church's preference for the work of Aquinas is primarily intended to provide, at a time of spiritual dissolution, a sound philosophy by which the abiding, naturally known antecedents of the faith are eminently validated; it is not aimed at forcing theology into a determined form. The church did not mean at all to put an impassable obstacle in the way of reshaping theology by the search of new philosophies.[35]

Both John Paul II and Pope Benedict XVI (Joseph Ratzinger) recognized that Thomism does not and should not exhaust the liberty of Christian thought, although few alternatives have been embraced. The Church continues to support the Thomistic-Aristotelian metaphysical framework for at least two reasons: first, it offers a stable, comprehensive explanation of God, humanity, and creation; and second, many theologians are not familiar with modern science and continue to do theology based on Greek metaphysics. Yet, in order for a more adequate philosophy to emerge from our present scientific understanding of reality, Catholic theology must relinquish the Greek philosophical and cosmological framework in which it is embedded. These forms have become inadequate for the continued life and development of the Christian faith.[36]

In *Fides et ratio* John Paul II called for a contemporary synthesis of faith and reason so that Scholasticism and modern thought would be able to fashion a new relationship (no. 85). But the encyclical rejects the historicist claim that what was true in one period may not be true in another (no. 87). Yet truth is embedded

---

[35] Joseph Ratzinger, "Theologia Perennis?" *Wort und Wahrheit* 15 (1960): 179–88; see also idem, *Theology Digest* 10 (1962): 71–76.

[36] Leslie Dewart, *Christianity and Revolution* (New York: Herder, 1963), 286.

in particular socio-cultural-linguistic worlds, in different cultures and religious expressions, and in the discoveries of science. If metaphysics speaks of the principles underlying reality, then insights from science must play a central role in the philosophical support of theology. We need a courageous assertion that the older, Scholastic type of theologizing is finished.

Teilhard's Philosophy

Teilhard de Chardin proposed a philosophy of love to support the principal features of evolution that include attraction, unity, complexity, and emergence—reflecting something deep and profound at the heart of nature. Love, he writes, is a passionate force at the heart of the Big Bang universe, the fire that breathes life into matter and unifies elements center to center; love is a cosmic unitive principle, a "cosmological force." Teilhard states, "Love is the most universal, the most tremendous and the most mysterious of the cosmic forces . . . the *physical* structure of the universe is love."[37] Love-energy is the history of the universe, present from the Big Bang onward. Love draws together and unites; in uniting, it differentiates. Love is the core energy of evolution—Omega. The fundamental energy of love in the universe means that, from a philosophical perspective, being is love-energy, an insight consonant with the quantum Big Bang universe. Teilhard writes: "What comes first in the world for our thought is not 'being' but 'the union which produces this being.'"[38] Love energy is intrinsically relational and undergirds relationality in the universe. Beings do not act toward a self-sufficient end in which relationship may or may not be important to that end; rather, union is the end toward which each being directs itself. Love is the affinity of being with being in a personal, centered way, a unity toward greater wholeness of being that marks all cosmic life. "If there was no internal propensity to unite, even

---

[37] Pierre Teilhard de Chardin, *Human Energy*, trans. J. M. Cohen (New York: William Collins, 1969), 72, 32.

[38] Pierre Teilhard de Chardin, *Christianity and Evolution*, trans. René Hague (New York: Harcourt Brace Jovanovich, 1971), 227.

at a rudimentary level—indeed in the molecule itself—it would be physically impossible for love to appear higher up, in a hominized form."[39]

The consistent evolutionary development toward more being underscores the primacy of energy in the universe and the intrinsic relationality of physical reality. Teilhard described the movement toward more being as *hyperphysics* to distinguish it from metaphysics. By *hyperphysics* he indicated that reality is unitive and dynamically oriented toward more being. He did not elaborate on the term *hyperphysics,* but the idea is invaluable because (1) it differentiates reality from a static, fixed metaphysics of sameness, (2) it is consonant with the energy of love as existential attractor, and (3) it undergirds the primacy of future since being is always directed toward more being. As the principle of attraction toward more being, love is the affinity of being with being and a general principle of all cosmic life. Teilhard writes that "love is the most universal, the most tremendous and the most mysterious of the cosmic forces."[40] The whole of reality from the lowest to the highest is covenanted, united in a bond of love.

Teilhard's philosophical *hyperphysics* turns theology toward the future; theology begins with reality as dynamically oriented toward more being (deeper relatedness) and increased consciousness. Evolution includes the fact that nature is open to the future, which makes the horizon of future the appropriate domain of redemption and fullness of being, as John Haught indicates.[41] A world opened to the future does not negate the present; rather it makes the present rich in possibilities to create something new. Theology does not aim to refine what has already been defined but to make wholes out of what is received (memory and tradition) insofar as the received empowers the present with new possibilities. Instead of neatly packaged concepts, the mind

---

[39] Teilhard de Chardin, *The Phenomenon of Man*, trans. Bernard Wall (New York: Harper and Row, 1959), 264.

[40] Teilhard de Chardin, *Human Energy*, 32.

[41] John F. Haught, *Deeper Than Darwin: The Prospect for Religion in the Age of Evolution* (Boulder, CO: Westview Press, 2003), 172–73; idem, "More Being: The Emergence of Teilhard de Chardin," *Commonweal* (June 5, 2009), 17–19.

is drawn to make sense of experience, even though it may not yet be explicit. Teilhard did not view mind apart from matter; rather, mind is the "withinness" of matter from the beginning of evolution. He considered matter and consciousness not as two substances or two different modes of existence, but as two aspects of the same cosmic stuff. The "within" is the mental aspect, and the "without" is the physical aspect of the same stuff: physical and psychic are co-related in the evolutionary movement of convergence and complexity. Knowledge progresses as we discover more about the world in which we live. When the mind can engage reality as a question rather than imposing prefabricated answers on reality, then one can begin to participate creatively in the future by bringing together scripture, tradition, and revelation in light of modern science.

God, the Power of the Future

Evolution impels us to think of God as drawing the world from up ahead, attracting it into a new future. Process theology maintains that God is neither simply an impersonal order nor simply the individual person who creates the universe. Rather, God and world are in process together; the world continually participates in God and God in the world. God, who is the primordial ground of order, embodies within Godself the order of possibilities, the potential forms of relationship that are not chaotic but orderly even before they are actualized. Nothing less than a transcendent force, radically distinct from matter but also incarnate in it, could ultimately explain evolution. Teilhard called this force God-Omega, the divine force of attraction that ultimately accounts for the world's restless tendency to move beyond any specific level of development. God is distinct from the world yet essential to it, just as the world is essential to God. Apart from God there would be nothing new in the world and no order in the world. God influences the world without determining it. This influence is the lure of ideals to be actualized, the persuasive vision of the good; it contributes to the self-creation of each entity, promoting the harmonious achievement of value. Between God and world there is genuine reciprocity, interdependence, and mutual immanence: "As God draws near to the world, the world explodes 'upwards into God,'" Teilhard wrote.[42]

Evolution brings with it the rise of consciousness, and as consciousness rises, so too does awareness of God. The human person is created to see God in every aspect of life, charged with divine energy, and to love what he or she sees. In this respect scripture is written daily in the supermarkets, nursing homes, playgrounds, post offices, cafes, bars, and in the scripts of home and community life. God is not hovering over us; God is the amazing depth, breadth, imagination, and creativity in culture, art, music, poetry, science, literature, film, gyms, and parks—all in some way speak the word of God. Every place is the place to find God, and God is in everything. "God is at the tip of my pen, my spade, my brush, my needle; of my heart and my thought," Teilhard wrote.[43] When theology reflects on the rich depths of everyday life as "God-talk" (theology) it expands the horizon of God and of life in God. It opens up life to more life in a way that new horizons form and life deepens. Theology that begins with the experience of life is "right brain" theology because it connects and enkindles passion; it is "open systems" theology because our understanding of God and the way God works in the world begins with our experiences of the world. Theology of the written text, without engaging life, is "left brain" theology. It focuses on specific questions, analyzes texts to address questions, and puts the answers into an abstract system of thought. Such theology neither connects to the living world of change nor enkindles new understandings of God, self, and creation. Theology that begins with the experiences of life gives more life to life. When theology does not connect with the whole of life or reflect on human experience, it becomes abstact, sawdust-dry theories—a tribal intellectual elitsm. Intellectual ideas can blind us to the trace of divine transcendence etched in the lines of the human face or in the veins of the maple leaf. Left-brain intellectual theology creates self-enclosed monads who are more preoccupied with their own ideas than evolutionary change. Open-systems theology is

---

[42] Pierre Teilhard de Chardin, *The Future of Man*, trans. Norman Denny (New York: Harper, 1964), 83.

[43] Pierre Teilhard de Chardin, *The Divine Milieu: An Essay on the Interior Life*, trans. Bernard Wall (New York: Harper, 1960), 64.

a type of "vernacular theology" that begins with experience of the world, attentive to new patterns of consciousness and new insights on the divine mystery, in relation to the evolution of culture and life.[44]

The Church can find new life in our age by refitting the gospel to a world in evolution and supporting open-systems theology, by which revelation is seen as process, relatedness, and patterns of organization. I propose that open-systems theology begin with the book of nature, that is, insights from modern science, as well as culture, economics, music, shopping malls, and Wall Street; a theology that begins with learning and experience rather than teaching; with creativity and imagination rather than a fixed set of principles; a theology where people continually expand their capacity to create the world they truly desire; where new and expansive patterns of thinking are nurtured; where collective aspiration is set free; and where people are encouraged to see the whole of life together, rather than as competing tribes. Studies have shown that in situations of rapid change, only those systems that are flexible, adaptive, and productive will excel. Commitment alone is not sufficient for the Church to grow into the future; thinking is essential, a type of thinking that makes greater wholes, thinking from the heart where the mind is attuned to the heart of the world.

---

[44] The term *vernacular theology* is borrowed from Bernard McGinn, who described a type of medieval religious thought arising out of religious experience in the Middle Ages and expressed in vernacular language. McGinn distinguished vernacular theology from Scholastic theology, which arose out of the university, and from monastic theology, which was rooted in religious monastic experience. Vernacular theology democratized and secularized theology by including the religious experience of all, men and women, and enabled the voices of those outside the elite educated circles, such as Francis of Assisi and Jacob Boehme, to be taken seriously. Thus a layperson was free to employ bold new forms of conceptualizing God and communicating the religious experience that simply would not occur to most professional theologians. Vernacular theology provided a new venue for all Christians to find God in the midst of the world. See Bernard McGinn, *The Flowering of Mysticism*, vol. 3, *The Presence of God: A History of Western Mysticism* (New York: Crossroad, 1998), 18–24; idem, *Meister Eckhart and the Beguine Mystics* (New York: Crossroad, 1994), 4–14.

Truth in Evolution

Teilhard saw an integral relationship among thinking, knowing, and loving as the matrix for human evolution. Knowledge must engage physical reality because this reality is the basis of who we are. To think is to unify, to make wholes where there are scattered fragments—"not merely to register it but to confer upon it a form of unity it would otherwise (that is, without thought) be without."[45] This calls for a certain attentiveness and intelligence brought to the level of encounter with physical reality. The mind creates by perceiving the phenomena of reality and in so doing continues the fundamental work of creation. Each time the mind comprehends something, it unites the world in a way that is new; it participates in the generation of the divine Word and creates a new unity through the Spirit. The knowing process, therefore, furthers evolution by uniting fragments of data or experience, creating new unities. For this reason knowledge is essential to the ongoing process of evolution. Teilhard said: "To discover and know is to actually extend the universe ahead and to complete it."[46] We pursue knowledge not to control life but to organize life for a greater unity, a deepening of being that is a deepening of love. Personal authenticity is built on fruitful dialogue, for it is in genuine understanding that knowledge expands being itself. This approach allows us to see the knowing process in a way that extricates us from the tethers of concepts. By conceptual preoccupation "we let concepts spawned by other minds do our thinking for us," John Haughey writes.[47] Knowledge that forms from the dynamism of the mind's thought processes is not information gathering or storing concepts in a mental warehouse; rather, knowledge is the energy of desire, the work of the Spirit, who is seeking to create anew.

---

[45] Teilhard de Chardin, *The Phenomenon of Man*, 249.

[46] Pierre Teilhard de Chardin, unpublished letter to Maurice-Irénée-Marie Gignoux, June 19, 1950, cited in Thomas M. King, *Teilhard's Mysticism of Knowing* (New York: Seabury, 1981), 35.

[47] John C. Haughey, SJ, *Where Is Knowing Going? The Horizons of the Knowing Subject* (Washington, DC: Georgetown University Press, 2009), 42–43.

Teilhard spoke of truth as part of the process of evolution; it is found in any comprehension that gives coherence to the present data and leads to further development. The two marks of truth, for Teilhard, are coherence and fecundity. Truth, like life itself, can be preserved only by being continually enlarged. To be engaged in the universe, to know, is to create new unities (and new horizons of insight) and thus to advance toward truth. The total coherence of the universe is that to which we are oriented, and this total coherence is truth in all its fullness. To retain its core identity, truth cannot be isolated or absolute but must be in dialogue with our experience in and of the world. Truth lives on the horizons of its immeasurable value and our experience of being in the world. It is meaningful not as an objective, abstract concept but as a concrete expression of living reality that deepens life. Its practical value is not so much that it preserves the past but that it illuminates the present. The best criterion of truth is its power to develop infinitely, which means truth is always a search and a discovery.

Evolution invites us to expand our consciousness of the divine mystery beyond the realm of human history and to see humankind within the process of an evolving cosmic history. We come from the whole and belong to the whole. As church, as theologians, as citizens of the universe, therefore, we need an "option for whole," and by this I mean we need a new consciousness that includes our Big Bang expanding universe and biological evolution as part of our intellectual search for truth. Theology must *begin with evolution* if it is to talk of a *living* God, and hence it must include physical, spiritual, and psychological change as fundamental to reality. Einstein's discovery of relativity means that space-time is a dimension of the unfinished, expanding universe; thus, whatever we say about God is bound up with the universe. By extending the knowing process into the furthest realms of cosmic relatedness, being acquires new depth. Knowledge cannot be satisfied with human history alone; it must reach into cosmic history, if it is in search of truth. To see evolution as revelatory of the divine Word means that we come to see the various forms and rhythms of nature as reflective of divine qualities. This means moving beyond the static images of God that are so familiar to us and that remain irretrievably tied to an archaic understanding of the cosmos. We are invited, through modern science, to widen our theological vision, to awaken to a dynamic cosmos in which we are deeply related, and to seek the divine Word expressing itself in the rich fecundity of cosmic life.

Chapter 8

Putting on the Mind of Christ

Quantum Consciousness

Our new universe story speaks to us of an evolutionary process of life out of which we humans emerge. Teilhard de Chardin did not see the human person lost or insignificant in light of evolution; rather, he saw the human person as the arrow of evolution, the self-conscious "mind" of evolution, one who influences the direction of evolution. We are integrally part of evolution in that we rise from the process but in reflecting on the process we stand apart from it. Inspired by Julian Huxley, Teilhard wrote that the human person "is nothing else than evolution become conscious of itself." That is, "the consciousness of each of us is evolution looking at itself and reflecting upon itself."[1] If we stop to reflect on this statement, we are taken aback by its cosmic breadth. What Teilhard indicates is that human consciousness is a Big Bang phenomenon, so that amid the complexities of human consciousness, there is a deep sense of belonging to a cosmic whole. The emergence of the human mind bears witness to the power of consciousness in evolution, not only as the ground of evolution, but as its future.

The notion of mind, on the human level, includes the brain as well as the body, the senses and emotions, as well as the environment of interaction. The mind is not so much an organ as a field or fields of informational flow. Today we know that

---

[1] Pierre Teilhard de Chardin, *The Phenomenon of Man*, trans. Bernard Wall (New York: Harper and Row, 1959), 221.

our bodies are *entangled* through a quantum field of electrical bio-photon resonance; thus, we are affected by others through wave/field interference. Our bodies, as well as our brains, appear to function like receivers/decoders within an information field that is in constant flux. We can refer to this field awareness as quantum-field consciousness or simply as *quantum consciousness* (because quantum implies non-local field effect). This field of consciousness (which has many subfields within it) is the realm of mind. All experiences have mind in common, and mind rests upon a field of consciousness that transcends the divide between the individual and the world, the human being and nature. The mind is where a sense of the whole—catholicity—becomes reality. We can think of mind as different levels of fields that include both hemispheres of the brain and the interaction of these spheres with each other. When the whole brain is enabling the whole person to connect to the whole environment, catholicity is alive. But our modern minds have been denied their right-brain full working and pulled into a tight left-brain rational functioning that operates as mechanical, linear, competitive, and narrow. The passionate right brain, with its magical world of creative visionary thinking, has been mostly sidelined. We have reduced mind to the mental analytical work of the left brain, depriving the world of conscious connectivity.

Rami Shapiro notes that Eastern European Jewish mystics of the eighteenth century (Hasidim) spoke of "spacious mind" *(mochin d'gadlut)* and "narrow mind" *(mochin d'katnut).*

Narrow mind imagines itself as separate from the world. It is isolated, often alienated, and sees the world as a zero-sum game in which success depends on another's failure. Scarcity defines the world of *mochin d'gadlut*: fear is its primary emotion, and anger is its most common expression.

Spacious mind, on the other hand, "sees the self as part of the Whole. . . . It engages life from a place of interdependence and compassion." We see a greater unity embracing and transcending diversity. The world is integral and interdependent.

Abundance is the hallmark of the world as *mochin d'gadlut* perceives it. As such, love rather than fear is its emotional foundation, and lovingkindness rather than anger is its defining characteristic. . . . Spacious mind does not negate narrow mind, but embraces and includes it in a larger vision. In this way your sense of self is freed from fear and anger, and you are empowered to engage the world with your own unique expression of lovingkindness.[2]

Training the Mind

The term *brain plasticity* refers to the fact that the brain is not a fixed set of neurons but is flexible. Gray matter can shrink or expand so that the brain is constantly giving birth to itself. The ability of the brain to generate new cells even in adult life is affected by the environment as well as genes. High levels of stress can decrease the number of new cells; so can being low in a dominance hierarchy. But the scars of stress can be healed. The plasticity of the brain means that the brain attends to what is most dominant in the system or, as Charlotte Tomaino says, "the brain is an organ that repeats what it knows."[3] The brain is not a closed mechanism or a fixed set of neurons but a constellation of open systems that operates at the edge of chaos. With one-hundred billion neurons and trillions of synapses, we are wired for novelty and creativity. Because the brain is constantly giving birth to itself, the mind is in a constant flux of connectivity; it can form new connections, expand its horizons, and achieve new levels of consciousness. Physicist Henry Stapp states that "our human thoughts are linked to nature by non-local connections: what a person chooses to do in one region seems immediately to affect what is true elsewhere in the universe. . . . *Our thoughts DO something.*"[4] Stapp thinks of the mind as a creative process: "Each creative act brings into existence something fundamentally

---

[2] Rabbi Rami Shapiro, *The Sacred Art of Lovingkindness: Preparing to Practice* (Woodstock, VT: SkyLight Paths Publishing, 2006), 5–6.

[3] Charlotte Tomaino, *Awakening the Brain* (New York: Atria Books, 2012), 60.

[4] Henry P. Stapp, "Quantum Physics and the Physicist's View of Nature," in *The World View of Contemporary Physics*, ed. Richard E. Kitchener (Albany: State University of New York Press, 1988); see also Larry Dossey, "Spirituality, Healing, and Science," huffingtonpost.com.

new: it creates a novel 'emergent' quality." He maintains that the brain can function on multiple levels of mind; in our day-to-day lives, we live with many minds. When I am imagining myself as a musician, a dancer, or a scientist, I am in the field of mind where the mind is the realm of many worlds. When I choose to act according to one of the ideas I have in mind, then the many worlds I live in collapse into *this* world that I choose at *this* moment.[5]

Meditation exercises the brain to establish the control of focused attention. Quieting the mind can strengthen the cingulate gyrus, the area of the brain associated with emotion formation and processing, learning and memory. Strengthening this brain area seems to be more effective in shifting the focus of the brain where one wants it. Tomaino writes: "An awakened brain and an awakened life means living from the inside vision of life desired, regardless of outside circumstances. When the inner reality is stronger and more real than the outer reality and you can act from your choice, you are entraining your brain and creating your life." She calls this process of focusing the brain on desired choice "neural focusing" or developing a "Buddha brain." Siddhartha underwent extreme fasts so that he would not be distracted by the cravings of the body: "This freed him and awakened his brain to an awareness of the inner peace that was possible if he let go of craving and desires."[6]

Developing a spacious mind, or "Buddha brain," however, is not easy for us because the complex human brain has multiple inputs of information together with a complex core awareness of self and built-in mechanisms of freedom and decision that are not conditioned by necessity. We tend to be egocentric, narrow-minded, mimetic creatures with a capacity for spacious mind but not a natural inclination to it; we must choose to strengthen our spacious mind. Siddhartha realized the transient nature of life and sought to expand the capacity of his mind, to move beyond suffering toward compassion and oneness with all sentient life. The first objective of the Buddhist meditator is to become

---

[5] Henry Stapp, "Quantum Theory and the Role of Mind in Nature," *Foundations of Physics* (March 8, 2001); Roger Penrose, Fred Kuttner, Bruce Rosenblum, and Henry Stapp, *Quantum Physics of Consciousness* (Cambridge: Cosmology Science Publishers, 2011).

[6] Tomaino, *Awakening the Brain*, 178, 52, 55–62.

detached from the thinking process itself. To attain this state is to reach *shamata* or "calm abiding."[7] This type of meditation calls for a willful self-emptying whereby the layers of ego fall away—all of one's false identities—and one arrives at the level of consciousness called *shunyata,* which is the level of the "unconditioned" or "emptiness." Emptiness is not nothingness but, paradoxically, "all-ness" or "oneness." It is the deepest core of oneself beyond thoughts, words and concept, the level at which there is no separate "I."[8] Only when we experience emptiness can our innate compassion arise.

In Theravâda Buddhism the cause of human existence and suffering is identified as craving, which carries with it the various defilements such as greed, hatred, and delusion. These are believed to be deeply rooted afflictions of the mind that create suffering and stress. To be free from suffering and stress is to be liberated from harmful attachments, permanently uprooting them by analyzing, experiencing, and understanding the true nature of such corruptions. The meditator is then led to realize the Four Noble Truths (the truth of suffering, the origins of suffering, the cessation of suffering, the path to overcome suffering) and attain enlightenment and nirvana.[9] According to Zen master Kosho Uchiyama, when thoughts and fixation on the little "I" are transcended, an awakening to a universal, non-dual self occurs: "When we let go of thoughts and wake up to the reality of life that is working beyond them, we discover the Self that is living universal non-dual life (before the separation into two) that pervades all living creatures and all existence."[10] Thinking and thoughts must not confine and bind us from true reality.

---

[7] Dalai Lama, "Generating the Mind for Enlightenment," dalailama.com website.

[8] Carol Flinders, *Enduring Lives: Living Portraits of Women and Faith in Action* (Maryknoll, NY: Orbis Books, 2013), 149.

[9] Huston Smith and Philip Novak, *Buddhism: A Concise Introduction* (New York: HarperCollins, 2003); Richard Gombrich, *Theravâda Buddhism: A Social History from Ancient Benares to Modern Colombo* (New York: Routledge, 1988), 159.

[10] Kosho Uchiyama, *Opening the Hand of Thought: Approach to Zen* (New York: Penguin Books, 1993), 98.

Buddhist monks and nuns undergo intense, ascetic discipline, becoming detached from all fleeting things and attaining oneness with all life. Tenzin Palmo, a British woman turned Buddhist nun, spent six years alone in a Himalayan cave, thirteen-thousand feet high, in a cell that was about six-by-six feet. She came down once a year to meet her master teacher, but otherwise she dedicated herself to meditation. Her example of monastic life shows us that one cannot attain enlightenment by will alone; rather, one must live into the path of the Buddha by choosing against self-separateness, by meditation and disciplining the mind, by following the teachings of the Buddha through a master, by sharing the same breadth of the master, and then by putting the teachings into practice.[11] Buddhist monasticism, like Christian monasticism, is based on the idea that solitary oneness is deep within the human person; *monachus* is the human capacity for oneness. For Christians, the monk dimension of human life is grounded in the image of God. With the awakening of reflective subjectivity, the individual takes a stand against the anonymous collectivity, becoming a distinct moral and spiritual self, and embarking on an individual spiritual journey.[12]

Putting on the Mind of Christ

While most of us live with many minds in multiple worlds at any given moment, the solitary one gathers the many levels of mind into a single-heartedness that might be described, in the

---

[11] Vickie Mackenzie, *Cave in the Snow: Tenzin Palmo's Quest for Enlightenment* (New York: Bloomsbury, 1998), 113–14.

[12] Ewert H. Cousins, "Teilhard's Concept of Religion and the Religious Phenomenon of Our Time," *Teilhard Studies* 49 (January 1, 2004): 11; Jean Gribmont suggests that "the spiritual life of monasticism is essentially hidden in the depth of human consciousness." I would say, quite simply, we are created for oneness. See Jean Gribmont, "Monasticism and Asceticism I. Eastern Christianity," trans. Marie Miklashevsky, in *Christian Spirituality: Origins to the Twelfth Century*, ed. Bernard McGinn, John Meyendorff, and Jean Leclercq, vol. 16, *World Spirituality: An Encyclopedic History of the Religious Quest*, ed. Ewert H. Cousins (New York: Crossroad, 1987), 89.

words of Mary Oliver, as "standing still, learning reverence from such astonishments as a phoebe, blue plums or a clam buried deep in speckled sand."[13] The lack of distractions and the concentration of attention on the present moment is itself creative of something new. As Danish novelist J. A. Larsen writes:

> I had been sitting in the garden working and had just finished. . . . It was still and peaceful—around me and within me. . . . Then it began to come, that infinite tenderness, which is purer and deeper than that of lovers, or of a father toward his child. It was in me, but it also came to me, as the air came to my lungs. . . . I inhaled the tenderness. The deep tenderness . . . extended further and further—it became all present. . . . This was my first actual meeting with Reality; . . . a *Now that is* and a *Now that happens*. . . . Time and space, characteristics of the *Now that happens,* were so to speak, "outside" . . . it is the continuously active creation with all its birth throes. I saw time and space as instruments of this creation. They come into existence with it and in the course of it, and with it they come to an end. The Newly Created stands in the *Now* [*that is*] and discards these tools. The freedom, the real *Being* begins.[14]

A "mind-fullness" of the *Now that is* is a mind that is not merely *in* creation but a mind that is creating, evolving the world into something new. Perhaps this is what Saint Paul had in mind when he wrote in the Letter to the Philippians: "Do nothing out of selfish ambition or vain conceit. Rather, in humility value others above yourselves, not looking to your own interests but each of you to the interests of the others. In your relationships with one another, have the same mindset as Christ Jesus" (2:3–5). To live the gospel life is to live on a new level of consciousness, a spacious mind, like Jesus, a deep awareness of oneness with God and neighbor, a consciousness of belonging to a whole.

---

[13] Mary Oliver, "Messenger," wisdomportal.com website.

[14] Johannes Anker-Larsen, "With the Door Open," in *The Protestant Mystics*, ed. Anne Fremantle (New York: New American Library, 1965), 253.

Christian monasticism developed out of this desire for a higher level of consciousness. Both anchoritic (solitary) and coenobitic (communal) monasticism called for long periods of solitude, focusing the mind on "higher things" through poverty, prayer, and meditation. The rigors of desert monastic life reflected the fact that gospel life is a gift, not a given. Baptism is not an insurance policy against hell but a commitment to a new level of relatedness with God and with the world being created by self and God. In the early church Christian asceticism was the liberation necessary to awaken a consciousness of self that would be truly human and Christian. This meant recasting the whole of existence in accord with the renewed consciousness of self. Solitude was, and still is, key to monastic life because solitude is the nourishing environment for liberation into oneness. Thomas Merton distinguishes solitude from isolation:

> He who isolates himself in order to enjoy a kind of independence in his egotistic and external self does not find unity at all, for he disintegrates into a multiplicity of conflicting passions and finally ends in confusion and total unreality. Solitude is not and can never be a narcissistic dialogue of the ego with itself. . . . Go into the desert not to escape other men but in order to find them in God.[15]

Solitude is not being alone; it is being alone with God. It is not an escape from people but a deepening of one's heart in God so as to be united with all that is of God. I was inspired by Merton's monastic solitude when I left academic research science and entered the Carmelite monastery. My great desire was union with God, to "put on the mind of Christ," although I had no real idea of what this desire entailed. While the monastery provided the environment for a higher consciousness of self-liberation, there was little instruction on the meaning of personal growth and development. Instead, I found myself on a rigorous schedule, baking several hundred loaves of bread a day, farming a large vegetable garden, mowing the lawn, cleaning the monastery, and

---

[15] Thomas Merton, *New Seeds of Contemplation* (New York: New Directions, 1961), 52, 53.

in between, trying to learn the art of prayer, for which we gathered for six hours a day. I realized I was in over my head when I fell asleep during quiet prayer one early morning only to awake and find myself hanging over the side of the chair. Everything about the life was censored and monitored, including community conversations, reading materials, and personal contacts. After a while I felt as though I was in a monastic prison, and I spent most of my prayer time either bitterly complaining or plotting my escape. When I eventually made my way to a Franciscan community, I found greater freedom in the organization of the life, but the emphasis was still on work. The community ran a nursing home to which the convent was annexed; hence, community life was intertwined with retired, frail, and aging women. I remember one old German sister, barely able to stand because of arthritis, pushing a mop. I said to her, "Sister, why are you doing this?" And she said, "If I don't work, I can't eat." The Germans had a strong work ethic, and the sisters worked around the clock no matter what their age or health condition. Retirement seemed like exclaustration; it was not an option.

It is no secret that Catholic religious women built the social arm of the Church, becoming educated and accomplished administrators of hospitals, nursing homes, schools, and orphanages, among other institutions. Work became genetically encoded into religious life. The regimen of work, prayer, and community, with few distractions in between, gave rise to successful Catholic institutions, but often at the expense of oneness of self in God and cosmos. I think many religious women have been exhausted for years and are just waking up to a new call for inner liberation and unity.

A New Mind for a New World

The gospel life is not a social agency of good works but a life of mindful presence or oneness in God. As such, the sacraments do not make one Christian; only a disciplining of the mind, following the way of Jesus, can truly form a christic life. Christian life, like Buddhist, Jewish, or Muslim life, requires personal responsibility. One must desire to put on the mind of Christ, one must *choose* to follow the way of the gospel with the guidance of a teacher or master, and then one must practice the gospel life in community. Going to church does not make one a Christian just as saying the Our Father does not make one a Christian. Rather, gospel life is *praxis*; it begins with awareness of God's presence and discernment of the inner mind or spirit. It is a life of awareness that something new is being formed and an invitation to be part of the creative process. Gospel life is receptivity to the gift of divine energy and a conscious "yes" to accept God's energy as the transformative energy of self and world. Thus, Christian life requires a conscious decision to shift the mind *(metanoia)* by training the mind to focus on the central values of the gospel and to dispense with all other things. Without the choice for a new level of consciousness, there can be no new reality or reign of God. Where our minds focus, there our treasure lies. As Rabbi Shapiro writes, "I made the choice for heaven and, having done so, I went in search of tools for living it."[16] When Teilhard said that we are evolution made conscious of itself, he indicated a basic lesson of modern science: there is no real "world" apart from us; rather, the world unfolds in and through our choices and actions. The concept of world is like a mirror; empty in itself, it can only reflect to the giver the values it receives. Rabbi Shapiro states:

> Will you engage this moment with kindness or with cruelty, with love or with fear, with generosity or scarcity, with a joyous heart or an embittered one? This is your choice and no one can make it for you. If you choose kindness, love, generosity, and joy, then you will discover in that choice the Kingdom of God, heaven, nirvana, this worldly salvation. If you choose cruelty, fear, scarcity, and bitterness, then you will discover in that choice the hellish states of which so many religions speak. These are not ontological realities tucked away somewhere in space—these are existential realities playing out in your own mind. Heaven and hell are both inside of you. It is your choice that determines just where you will reside.[17]

---

[16] Shapiro, "What Is Lovingkindness?" 6.
[17] Ibid., 5–6.

One might think, on face value, that the self-creation of heaven and hell conflicts with the scriptures, but in fact, the gospel message is based on invitation and choice, symbolized by the parable of the wedding feast: "'Tell those who have been invited that I have prepared my dinner: My oxen and fattened cattle have been butchered, and everything is ready. Come to the wedding banquet.' But they paid no attention and went off—one to his field, another to his business" (Mt 22:1–14). The question of heaven is not one of worthiness before God but accepting God's invitation for life: "I have set before you life and death, choose life" (Dt 30:15). By loving this creation into being, God endows it with freedom and becomes like a beggar before the power of the human capacity to decide what is worth living for and dying for.

The problems of our age—war, conflict, racial and religious injustice, economic greed, power, corruption, control and manipulation, lying and deceit—are human problems. We have literally lost our minds. We have untethered the human mind from any higher level of consciousness, allowing our minds to wander aimlessly amid fields of uncensored information, burdening the mind with emotional and psychological baggage, copious amounts of junk information, and dousing the mind with alcohol and drugs periodically. We have the equivalent of a fast-food problem with regard to the mind or, I would say, "junk-food minds." Our bodies may look trim and fit, but our minds are filled with "fatty information"; they are "flabby" and "out of shape" and unable to cope with evolutionary complexity; as such, we are headed for a "pancake world," turning into "pancake people," flat and fluffy, depleting our resources (both natural and spiritual) and, in short, devolving the cosmos. Just as the body cannot tolerate a steady diet of junk food indefinitely without eventually succumbing to a heart attack, so the mind cannot engage infinite unbridled information without becoming exhausted. Carol Flinders writes: "Desire is the human being's most precious resource. Spend it heedlessly and we are spiritually bankrupt."[18]

Gathering the mind into the presence of Omega is difficult in our modern age because we live in a world of distractions,

---

[18] Flinders, *Enduring Lives*, 47.

a world that weakens being by fragmenting and isolating relationships: "Our repeated behavior shapes our experience of
the world and triggers neural mechanisms for our reactions."[19]
Where is our mind at any given moment? How much do we
allow our minds to migrate into multiple worlds? The lack of
integrating our minds with our present reality and focusing
them on peace, justice, and compassion can lead us into dualistic
thinking. The distracted mind easily fragments into a thousand
unrelated thoughts and feelings. John Sack writes that dualistic
thinking is the root of all evil because it creates the illusion that
separateness is natural to existence:

> It is the radical rot behind every harmful thought or action,
> the source of all wars and violence, of nationalism, racism,
> claims of paranoia, insecurity, unhealthy competition, lack
> of cooperation and charity, hoarding and greed, abuse in all
> its devastating displays. . . . Only the human personality is
> capable of imagining and acting out of a division between
> God and us, between others and us. . . . If we would let
> creation be all things would teach us their common love
> of God. There is no escaping our unity with God and all
> things. The only way out is nothingness itself, for outside
> God there is nothing but nothing.[20]

Rémi Brague reminds us that "world" is not a given; it is an
outflow of the mind, a consciousness of the whole. Mind creates
a sense of the whole or catholicity. How we focus our minds and
shape our thoughts creates our world. For this reason "putting
on the mind of Christ" is not simply a spiritual exercise; rather, it
is integral to the world we create and the direction of the Church
in evolution. How do I experience God and world? What is my
relationship to the world? The Dominican mystic Meister Eckhart used the term *breakthrough* to describe the experience of a
unified consciousness with God, that is, a breaking through of
the ego's self-sense into a consciousness of oneness with God: "In

---

[19] Tomaino, *Awakening the Brain*, 60.
[20] John Richard Sack, *Mystic Mountain: The Ascent to Love* (Jacksonville, OR: CyberScribe Publications, 2014), 54–55.

this breakthrough I discover that God and I are one."[21] Similarly,
the Muslim mystic Mansur al-Hallaj writes:

> I am the One whom I love
> And the One whom I love is I—
> Two breaths and spirits sharing one body.
> When you see me, you see the One
> And when you see the One, you see us both.[22]

Eckhart knew God as the experience of Being itself. God does
not simply exist; God is existence itself. Thus God exists as the
Being of my being and my highest consciousness, my true self.
The self is entangled with God from all eternity. As the prophet
Jeremiah writes: "Before I formed you in the womb, I knew you"
(1:5). But if the self belongs to God, it belongs to all that God is
and is becoming; that is, the self does not simply belong to God
in this immediate moment, but it has always belonged to God in
the divine infinity of love. Thus the self that is still being created
in this space-time cosmic adventure belongs to God in the same
way that the world unfolding in and through us belongs to God;
and because God cannot stop loving and oneing, God is deeply
intwined with self and world. When Saint Paul states that we
are to have the "same mind as Christ Jesus," he means we are to
break through our individual egos and become one with God in
all our relationships so that, like Jesus, we create the world as a
reflection of the One we love, God.

To co-create with God is to gather the many fields of the mind
into a consciousness of love. Jesus said:

> You have heard it said that you must love your neighbor and
> hate your enemy, but I say this to you, love your enemies,

---

[21] Meister Eckhart, "Sermon 52," in *Meister Eckhart: The Essential Sermons, Commentaries, Treatises, and Defense*, trans. Edmunt Colledge, OSA, and Bernard McGinn (New York: Paulist Press, 1981), 199–203; see also Burkhard Mojsisch and Orrin F. Summerell, "Meister Eckhart," *Stanford Encyclopedia of Philosophy* (April 25, 2011).

[22] This version is cited in Sack, *Mystic Mountain*, 60. Mansur al-Hallaj (ninth century) was a widely known Sufi mystic, and his poetry is widely available.

do good to those who hate you, and pray for those who persecute you and treat you badly. In this way you will be children of your father in heaven, for he causes his sun to rise on the unjust as well as the just. (Mt 5:43–46)

A christic consciousness is a mind focused on one thing, the centrality of divine love. One modern, outstanding example of a person with christic consciousness is Saint Thérèse of Lisieux (d. 1926). As the youngest nun in her Carmelite monastery, Thérèse sought a direct route to God and found it in making love the center of her entire life: "I have found my vocation in the heart of the Church," she exclaimed.[23] This was no spiritual piety. The young Thérèse turned her entire will and efforts to the power of love, overcoming her natural inclination to anger, revolt, or animosity, and loving her Sisters, especially her enemies in community, with all she had. Seven hundred years before her it was said of Francis of Assisi that "he was always with Jesus: Jesus in his heart, Jesus in his mouth, Jesus in his ears, Jesus in his eyes, Jesus in his hands"; he bore Jesus always in his whole body.[24] Both Francis and Thérèse had a focused Christ consciousness, a deep entanglement with divine love that governed the direction of their lives. They show us that wholeness is holiness. The world becomes whole in love when we live in the oneness of love; training the brain for christic mindfulness means overcoming our dualisms. Non-dual consciousness is becoming aware of the larger whole of which we are a part. It involves overcoming the illusion of the separate self and recognizing one's connectedness to the whole of life. The only way into a sustainable future is to regain soul, both individual soul and world soul, by disciplining the mind, setting the mind on oneness or unity, and acting out of this oneness as part of a larger whole. Our thoughts are not neutral or private; they *do* something, and what they do is create the world.

---

[23] *Story of a Soul: The Autobiography of St. Thérèse of Lisieux,* trans. John Clarke, OCD (Washington, DC: ICS Publications, 1976), xiii.

[24] Thomas of Celano, "The Life of Saint Francis," in *Francis of Assisi: Early Documents,* vol. 1, *The Saint,* ed. Regis J. Armstrong, J. A. Wayne Hellmann, and William J. Short (New York: New City Press, 1999), 283.

Suffering and Unity

Francis of Assisi did not feel called to leave the world to find God but to find God in the world. Instead of going into the desert or living behind the walls of a monastery, he found the place of solitude within his own heart. The body is the cell, he said, and the soul is the hermit. What good is it to go to the monastery, he would tell his brothers, if we cannot find the treasure of God within us? Francis "put on the mind of Christ" by poverty, fasting, and long hours of solitary prayer in nature: "When he washed his hands, he chose a place where the water would not be trampled underfoot after the washing. Whenever he had to walk over rocks, he would walk with fear and reverence out of love for Him who is called 'the Rock.'"[25] His christic consciousness was a deep catholicity, a oneness of life that spoke to him of a cosmic family or community.

A year before he died, he was a physical wreck: leprosy, gastrointestinal disorders, and blindness marked his frailties. As he lay in a dark hut behind the San Damian monastery (where Clare and her sisters lived), he was torn between the struggles of earthly life and a desire for death, to be released from his body's miseries.

> "Lord," he prayed, "make haste to help me in my illnesses, so that I may be able to bear them patiently." And suddenly he was told in spirit: "Tell me, Brother, what if, in exchange for your illnesses and troubles, someone were to give you a treasure? And it would be so great and precious that, even if the whole earth were changed to pure gold, all stones to precious stones, and all water to balsam, you would still judge and hold all these things as nothing, as if they were earth, stones and water, in comparison to the great and precious treasure which was given you. Wouldn't you greatly rejoice?" "Lord," blessed Francis answered, "this treasure would indeed by great, worth seeking, very precious,

---

[25] "The Assisi Compilation," 88, in *Francis of Assisi: Early Documents*, vol. 2, *The Founder*, ed. Regis J. Armstrong, J. A. Wayne Hellmann, and William J. Short (New York: New City Press, 2000), 192.

greatly lovable, and desirable." "Then, Brother," he was told, "be glad and rejoice in your illnesses and troubles, because as of now, you are as secure as if you were already in my kingdom."[26]

Francis awakened to the reality that, despite his frail body and the conflicts of his community, heaven is in the *now*. He awoke and sang the "Canticle of Creatures":

> Most High, all-powerful, good Lord
> Yours are the praises, the glory, and the honor
>   and all blessing,
> To You alone, Most High, do they belong,
> And no human is worthy to mention Your
>   name.
> Praised be You, my Lord, with all Your crea-
>   tures,
> Especially Sir Brother Sun,
> Who is the day and through whom You give
>   us light.
> And he is beautiful and radiant with great
>   splendor;
> And bears a likeness of You, Most High One.
> Praised be You, my Lord, through Sister Moon
>   and the stars,
> In heaven You formed them clear and precious
>   and beautiful.
> Praised be You, my Lord, through Brother
>   Wind,
> And through the air, cloudy and serene, and
>   every kind of weather,
> Through whom You give sustenance to Your
>   creatures.
> Praised be You, my Lord, through Sister Water,
> Who is very useful and humble and precious
>   and chaste.

---

[26] "The Assisi Compilation," 83, in Armstrong, Hellmann, and Short, *Francis of Assisi: Early Documents*, 2:185.

Praised be You, my Lord, through Brother Fire,
Through whom You light the night,
And he is beautiful and playful and robust and
    strong.
Praised be You, my Lord, through our Sister
    Mother Earth,
Who sustains and governs us,
And who produces various fruit with colored
    flowers and herbs.
Praised be You, my Lord, through those who
    give pardon for Your love,
And bear infirmity and tribulation.
Blessed are those who endure in peace
For by You, Most High, shall they be crowned.
Praised be You, my Lord, through our Sister
    Bodily Death,
from whom no one living can escape.
Woe to those who die in mortal sin.
Blessed are those whom death will find in Your
    most holy will,
 for the second death shall do them no harm.
Praise and bless my Lord and give Him thanks
And serve Him with great humility.[27]

Francis's "Canticle of Creatures" reflects a new structure of reality. He used the words *brother* and *sister* to express his understanding of reality. Throughout his life he focused his mind on being a brother to all despite being rejected, misunderstood, and ridiculed. He experienced God's love in others and knew himself to be loved, and, therefore, he made love his vocation: "The love of him who loved us is greatly to be loved."[28] Through love he saw that nothing is independent; rather, everything is related. The "Canticle of Creatures" is his interior life projected onto the cosmos where love moves the Sun and other stars—christified

---

[27] Francis of Assisi, "The Canticle of Creatures," in Armstrong, Hellmann, and Short, *Francis of Assisi: Early Documents*, 1:113–14.

[28] Thomas of Celano, "The Remembrance of the Desire of a Soul," in Armstrong, Hellmann, and Short, *Francis of Assisi: Early Documents*, 2:373.

reality.[29] His canticle is a cosmic liturgy in which Christ is the high priest, although the name Jesus Christ is never mentioned, simply the words "Most High," "peace," and "humility." For Francis, God was not a thought or an idea but the experience of reality, a reality he experienced deep within himself.

The "Canticle of Creatures" is a vision of the whole that sees the self as part of the whole in the unity of love; it is the way the universe looks after the ego has disappeared. Francis's life was an ever-widening inner space through an ever-deepening christic consciousness. As he focused his mind on the love of God, he let go of life's many distractions. His neural-focused christic consciousness became a new experience of space and time. His mindfulness of Christ created for him a sense of slowed time and increased inner space. Francis lived in the now and focused his attention on each moment pregnant with divinity. There was no "clock time" for him. As he met the leper or heard the cries of the sick brother, he gave his whole being to loving God by loving his neighbor. From the depths of his Christ-consciousness, he saw a light shining through the most humble of creatures and, in this light, he saw a luminous thread of love binding his life to all others. Everything radiated divine love, and no element, no matter how small or insignificant, was left unloved. Out of a deep consciousness of inner love, Francis christified creation by seeing God in all things and all things in God.

A higher consciousness of love, putting on the mind of Christ, is not a trapeze act for saints; it is how we deal with human misunderstandings, conflicts, and death. Francis and Thérèse of Lisieux did not avoid suffering but leaned into it as part of their human growth in God. They trained themselves for a higher level of consciousness in the same way that athletes train themselves to win. Saint Paul saw his own road to holiness as one of discipline: "I discipline my body like an athlete, training it to do what it should. Otherwise, I fear that after preaching to others I myself might be disqualified" (1 Cor 9:27). Do we train our minds to create a new world? Can we find ways to evolve toward a higher level of consciousness?

---

[29] Eloi Leclerc, *The Canticle of Creatures: Symbols of Union*, trans. Matthew J. O'Connell (Chicago: Franciscan Herald Press, 1970), 222.

Etty Hillesum, a remarkable young Dutch, Jewish woman, was gassed at Auschwitz in 1943. During a period of several years she kept a diary, recording her inner life and struggles, revealing a young woman who loved life, literature, philosophy, and men. Etty put her finger on the pulse of the modern dilemma of suffering and aimed for a higher level of consciousness in the midst of the atrocity of the Holocaust. She gained the insight that lies at the core of contemplative traditions everywhere; namely, the mind is conditioned to go after pleasure and run away from pain. If we want stillness of mind, "so something of God can enter us," we must learn how to limit the conditioned responses. We must be able to experience something pleasurable without trying to hold onto it, and we must be able to experience the most intense forms of suffering without going to pieces or trying to pass it on to someone else. Carol Flinders writes: "What unifies her [Hillesum's] desires or integrates them is the necessity of finding her way to a depth where consciousness flows continuously back and forth between the poles of awareness of suffering on the one hand and unquenchable faith in meaning and beauty on the other."[30]

Etty came to believe that we are in error when we try to blame war or violence on others. She had a sense of inner-outer flow. Each of us moves things along in the direction of war, she said, every time we fail in love. She writes: "All disasters stem from us. Why is there war? Perhaps because now and then I might be inclined to snap at my neighbor. Because I and my neighbor and everyone else do not have enough love. . . . Yet there is love bound up inside us, and if we could release it into the world, a little each day, we would be fighting war and everything that comes with it."[31] She had to confront the chaos in her own undisciplined mind in order to confront directly the forces in human consciousness that had given rise to Nazism in the first place.[32] Flinders states: "To *release love* on a daily basis, and nourish the world with it, she would have to come to

---

[30] Flinders, *Enduring Lives*, 68.

[31] Etty Hillesum, *Etty: The Letters and Diaries of Etty Hillesum, 1941–1943* (Grand Rapids, MI: Eerdmans, 2002), 307.

[32] Flinders, *Enduring Lives*, 39.

grips with the way her mind worked. She would have to train attention itself, so that she could refocus it at will whenever it got stuck, whether it was stuck in desire, hatred, fear, or erotic daydreams."[33] In other words, Etty, like Francis and Thérèse, did not see the problem of violence outside herself but beginning with herself. She began to train her mind by distancing herself from the movements of her mind, cultivating moment-to-moment vigilance. Unlike Thérèse, she did not think that running off to a convent would accomplish anything. Rather, she had to find peace and clarity in the here and now: "I must fling myself into reality time and again . . . feed the outer world with my inner world and vice versa."[34]

Etty's mindful vigilance was living in the flow between immense suffering and daily moments of beauty. One moment she would tend to a dying mother lying on the cold, concrete prison floor with her children standing nearby, and in the next moment she would marvel at a small buttercup pressing through the cracks of the same prison floor. Instead of trying to push out suffering, she opened to it lovingly, leaning into it, because she realized that sadness too was part of her being. "Learning to accept even the parts of herself that she had wanted to excise became for her a kind of rehearsal for learning to accept other people as well, in all of their unloveliness. . . . She sought to be even-minded in pleasure or pain, and worked so hard at this that it became second nature."[35] Through a mindful vigilance of God's nearness, a tender desire to be one with God, and a resistance to the negative emotions of suffering and death, Etty consciously rooted herself in Omega love, tending to the needs of her suffering family and friends without succumbing to despair. Flinders writes:

> Because she learned how to let go of the merely personal, she could fully receive the sorrows of others without holding on to them—she knew in effect how to lift the gate and let the grief flow on out of her. . . . Everything could circulate *through* her. Joy, grief, anger, despair, and, of course,

---

[33] Ibid.
[34] Hillesum, *Etty*, 71.
[35] Flinders, *Enduring Lives*, 40.

love, above all, must be able to circulate through ourselves and one another and all of life.[36]

She perceived something new growing within her and she marveled at the contrast between the desolation that was happening all around her and the emergence of an altogether way of being in the world within her. She realized that the only way to prepare for the new age is "by living it even now in our hearts."[37] Etty put on the mind of Christ in the midst of human violence and destruction. She shows us that a new world is possible even in the face of war and suffering; for where the mind is, there lies one's treasure.

Mindful, Prayerful, Powerful

Our bodies are only as good as our minds; when the mind loses awareness of itself, it also loses awareness of its body. Mind and body form a unified whole. We need to factor into our daily lives times when we can slow down, shut out the noise and distractions, and focus our minds on the gospel values of a new world. Busyness has become a full-time occupation for the modern person. We fill our minds with all sorts of useless information, as if silence and stillness might threaten to extinguish us. Jesus knew the need to focus his mind on the God moment: He "often withdrew to lonely places and prayed" (Lk 5:16). Prayer is the awakening of the mind to God. To pray is not to parade around with prayer books and pious devotions (see Mt 6:6), but "to go into your room and pray"; that is, to retreat from the frenzy of life and to center the heart on God. Etty Hillesum writes: "Ultimately, we have just one moral duty: to reclaim large areas of peace in ourselves . . . and to reflect it toward others. And the more peace there is in us, the more peace there also will be in our troubled world."[38] Etty's remarkable oneness in God and

---

[36] Flinders, *Enduring Lives*, 67.

[37] Hillesum, *Etty*, 497; see also Meins G. S. Coetsier, *Etty Hillesum and the Flow of Presence: A Voegelinian Analysis* (Columbia: The University of Missouri Press, 2008), 174.

[38] *An Interrupted Life: The Diaries of Etty Hillesum 1941–1943* (New York: Washington Square Books, 1985), 229.

her realization that absolute love does not save us from suffering but empowers us to create life, even in the midst of suffering, is shown in the following passage:

> Tonight for the first time I lay in the dark with burning eyes as scene after scene of human suffering passed before me. I shall promise You one thing, God, just one very small thing: I shall never burden my today with cares about tomorrow, although that takes some practice. Each day is sufficient unto itself. . . . But one thing is becoming increasingly clear to me: that You cannot help us, that we help You to help ourselves. And that is all we can manage these days and also all that really matters: that we safeguard that little of You, God, in ourselves. And perhaps in others as well. Alas, there doesn't seem to be much You Yourself can do about our circumstances, about our lives. Neither do I hold You responsible. You cannot help us, but we must help You and defend your dwelling place inside us to the last.[39]

Saint Teresa of Avila, a woman of tremendous intellect and spiritual power, once wrote that "God alone suffices." Does God suffice? Or does "God sufficiency" seem too placating, too dismissive of our responsibility to act in the world? A closed-systems person might think so because sufficiency would mean following the rules, as in "keep the rule and God will bless you." But Teresa's insight reflects a person open to newness and creativity. The sufficiency of God means that in every new encounter, choice, or decision, God is there. Francis of Assisi had this kind of openness as well. One time when he and Brother Masseo were traveling, they came to a fork in the road. Masseo asked which way to go, and Francis told him to shut his eyes, turn around three times, and then open his eyes. After this strange request, Francis asked Masseo what direction he saw. That is the direction they would go. Our modern, left-brain closed-system thinking would analyze Brother Masseo's dilemma by asking numerous questions: Will this path take us where we need to go? What if we get lost? How will we know it is the right way? We seek to

---

[39] Etty Hillesum, *Essential Writings* (Maryknoll, NY: Orbis Books, 2009), 59.

control every aspect of life even though we know that, on the quantum level, life is uncertain and uncontrollable. In our left-brain efforts to control, we become unconscious of God and of our connectivity to the whole of life.

Teresa's "God alone suffices" means that God is in every direction. The direction itself is not important; it is oneness with God that makes the direction meaningful. Prayer becomes living prayer when our field of consciousness is not in a thousand different places but the one place of God; it kindles the consciousness that we are not alone, that we are loved, so that whatever we do and wherever we go, the people we encounter, the snow that we trudge through, the rain that soaks us, or the obstinate person at our table, are all part of God loving us. Our narrow, closed mindedness often leads us to think that life is parceled into good and bad, heaven and hell, love and hate, but a christic consciousness realizes that God alone suffices because in every direction and aspect of life, God is present; even in the most difficult circumstances we are being loved in a new way, into new being. Love is not something we do; love is what God does to us when we encounter each concrete moment of reality as gift. Teresa's "God alone suffices" is openness to the creative moment; it is about receptivity to divine love in the infinite moments of unfolding life.

Prayer is centering the mind on ultimate life-energy—God—through which we are connected to the entire universe. It opens the heart to a greater fullness of life and challenges us to surrender those parts of ourselves that we find unlovable or try to control or manipulate. Without "putting on the mind of Christ" or working toward a mindful oneness with God, life becomes an unending series of little distractions. We sit at meetings or in churches, but our minds are elsewhere, in other universes, living other lives. It is like a person who attends an opera, which he has waited months to see. He gets all dressed up, primes himself for a stupendous performance, arrives at the opera house on time, and in the middle of the opera realizes he has left his house key in the door at home. He spends the remainder of the performance wondering who he should call or if he should get up and go home. For all practical purposes he misses out on the rest of the performance. How many of us live in the midst of a thwarted opera? The infinite number of distractions through multitasking, multimedia, and multiple choices have rendered modern life an incalculable maze of dualisms; our bodies are often in one place while our minds are in another. We seem to be physically present, as we sit in a classroom or at a meeting, but our minds are circling the earth, especially as our electronic gadgets entertain us with multiple worlds of information and endless emails.

The scattering of our minds into multiple universes is the scattering of earth community into tribes and cults and diminished resources. Life is increasingly fragmented as we are doused with copious amounts of information in our wired world. We are restless, bored, impatient, and inattentive; for all practical purposes we are living in exile and are completely unaware of our disconnectedness. The modern mind-body dualism (physically present but wandering mind) persists because we lack focus and self-control. We are controlled instead by our electronic devices, by material things, by money, status, jobs, careers, and what other people think of us. Thus, we can no longer control what needs to be controlled, namely, ourselves. We think that by controlling the world and its creative impulses we can control suffering. But suffering finds us at every stage of life. John Sack writes:

> If we see our suffering as a demon, if our ego becomes addicted to it and allows it to become our newest identity, we only add to its power. If we see it as our father and mother, our loving teacher, if we can hear what it's trying to tell us, we can free ourselves from its grip. . . . We . . . emerge from suffering purified of ego, as gold tried in fire.[40]

The Franciscan way of poverty is to live *sine proprio*, not so much without things but without *possessing* things. Those who cling to things, not only material things but emotional things like anger, hurt, and power, or spiritual things like God or heaven, become lifeless because their minds are not focused on the now where divine love is bringing being into new being. Jesus said, "Let the dead bury the dead, you are to go and proclaim the kingdom of God" (Lk 9:60).

To put on the mind of Christ is to be present wherever Christ is emerging, whether it is in social media, at a baseball game,

---

[40] Sack, *Mystic Mountain*, 100–101.

or attending the local jazz concert. It requires us to let go of our expectations and preconceived ideas and reach out to others in the moments of life we are given. "In Native American terms, we must rediscover our *original medicine*. All that we are, whatever talents we have received, have been given so we might help those with whom we share creation and to further the evolution of this creation."[41] Putting on the mind of Christ is neuro-focusing on gospel values, such as love, peace, mercy, and compassion, not as abstract ideals but as relational values. Life is about relationships; justice is about relationships; peace is about relationships; love is about relationships. We are invited to let go of those things that prevent a deepening of relatedness to the whole of life and attend to the new patterns of relationships, the strange attractors in our midst. What are the new patterns we see or the new sounds we hear? Mindfulness of God opens the eyes and ears to one who can let go and live as an open system. One whose mind is centered in Christ knows that the present moment is all we have. The present is eternity in the now. We are to embrace this moment by emptying ourselves into it and surrendering to life's energy flow. Life unfolds in the now, in the fields of our choices. Every choice in the present creates the future. To put on the mind of Christ is to know the power within us to create the future, the power to evolve into a new unity, a new oneness in love through a unified, christic consciousness.

How to "unplug" and focus our attention on a higher level of consciousness is our challenge; it is as important today as minding the body. There is no blueprint for the kindom of God, no guarantee that daily prayer will bring about justice and peace. There is only fidelity to love, to God. To be conscious of the whole is to create the whole by renouncing the dualisms we insist on creating. Putting on the mind of Christ is living in the love energy of the now where there is no destination or final death; rather, every moment is God filled; and where God is filling the moment, something new is emerging, because God is ever newness in love. The death we fear or the final end we try to postpone by controlling our lives is an illusion. Death is in the now; the end is in the now; and the now is the invitation to create life and to experience the opera as fantastic.

----

[41] Ibid., 91.

Chapter 9

Conscious Catholicity

Revisiting Catholicity

When Plato came to the insight that the cosmos governs human action, he set off a new way of thinking about ethics, politics, and the human sphere. He could not have anticipated that just over two thousand years later scientific discoveries would show that we are the cosmos brought to self-consciousness. Catholicity is learning from the whole how to think about the whole; for Plato, the whole is our teacher; for Einstein and Bohm, the whole is ourselves writ large; for Bohr, the whole is an act of consciousness. *Catholicity* is the term that best describes consciousness of the whole. It does not define what someone is but what someone does. It is a virtue of ceaseless wonder whose spiritual dynamism cannot be controlled or manipulated. As an engagement of mind and heart, catholicity is bound up with personal authenticity, having a grasp of one's own self and self-consciousness. It is not conceptual or factual. Rather, it is the orientation of being itself toward more being, an awakening of consciousness to the reality of being incomplete and, yet, on the level of quantum reality, already one.

Throughout this book I have tried to show that catholicity does not begin on the human level and that it cannot be adequately grasped by institutional religion; rather, catholicity begins on the level of the Big Bang cosmos and the rise of consciousness. Nature has an intrinsic wholeness to it, a built-in catholicity. The process of evolution reflects the incompleteness of every whole; there is an impulse in nature toward greater wholeness and unity. Evolution discloses a dynamism of catholicity; every whole is part of a larger whole, and the whole process of evolution seems to yearn for ultimate wholeness. Life flows from a relational, nondeterministic world of quantum reality, yet in a direction of increasing complexity and consciousness. Throughout the unfolding of life we see that stasis, balance, and equilibrium are temporary states; what endures is dynamic, adaptive, and creative. Nature bears a capacity to self-organize and, at every stage, transcend itself toward more integral wholeness.

Teilhard suggested that multiplicity in nature is dependent on unity and on some final unity that does not need any principle beyond itself to unify it, since it is the already "One." He called this principle of absolute unity Omega, and he identified it with God. He indicated that in an evolutionary world, God is conceivable only within the context of evolution. He writes:

> While in the case of a static world, the creator is structurally independent of his work, in the case of an evolutive world, the contrary is true. God is not conceivable except in so far as he coincides with evolution but without being lost in (sort of a "formal" cause) the center of convergence of cosmogenesis.[1]

The God who is in evolution cannot be a God who creates from behind but from ahead, the prime mover who is the power of the future.[2] The presence of God-Omega is the presence of a central principle in evolution, which means that every aspect of life, from the smallest to the complex, is centered in Omega. This divine presence is divine Love, so that, we can say, divine Love empowers evolution through created energies. As love-energy combines disparate elements into new unities, consciousness rises; as love and consciousness rise in evolution, so too does unity or wholeness.

Teilhard described evolution as Christogenesis, whereby God within and God ahead is the same God (Omega) who is coming

---

[1] Pierre Teilhard de Chardin, *Christianity and Evolution*, trans. René Hague (New York: Harcourt Brace and Co., 1969), 239.

[2] Ibid., 240.

to birth in the physical universe; incarnation and evolution are united. Furthermore, he indicated that the rise of Christ is the rise of consciousness. From an incarnational stance, creaturely consciousness is entangled with divine consciousness. We can think of the divine Spirit as the consciousness of God bringing into being what is not yet conscious in a way that divinity rises up in and through created reality. Entangled divinity speaks to us of a deeply relational God. Divine energy and human energy, divine consciousness and created consciousness, mutually influence each other. The Spirit is the absolute freedom of God to love and to create anew in love. God, therefore, is freely in love with everything that comes to be and, as such, is the paradoxical mystery of love: emptiness and fullness. It is the deep, divine freedom in love that gives being to being (by becoming not-God in being) and, at the same time, draws being beyond itself, rising up as God in evolution. The Spirit "groaning in nature" (Rom 8:22) seeks to make new wholes, and it is the same Spirit who energizes our consciousness and directs our attention to wholeness—catholicity. The Spirit, who is the life-giving breath of God, breathes in us and throughout all creation as divine, unifying energy, drawing us onward toward universality.

Catholicity and the Human Person

While nature's intrinsic catholicity is shown in the organization of physical systems, catholicity becomes more challenging on the human level, where, I believe, it is in crisis today. The source of the crisis is threefold: First, we have no grasp of emerging from an evolutionary process and therefore of belonging to a cosmic whole; hence, we are unconscious of being in evolution. Second, we operate as closed systems with mechanistic mentalities. And third, we are stifled in our catholicity by religious doctrines based on an ancient cosmology. The human person, as Teilhard emphasized, is not distinct from creation, as if rising above it; rather, the human person is "evolution become conscious of itself."[3] Stated otherwise, the human person is "the

---

[3] Pierre Teilhard de Chardin, *The Phenomenon of Man*, trans. Bernard Wall (New York: Harper and Row, 1959), 221.

point of emergence in nature, at which this deep cosmic evolution culminates and declares itself."[4] So, if we are nature brought to self-consciousness, the only way to deepen life ahead is to live conscious of being in evolution, which means to strive for a consciousness of deep catholicity.

The way forward toward greater wholeness and unity must be inward, a deepening of mindful consciousness and focusing on love. Being must precede action; love over doing. We need to be attentive to our separate self-egos, locked into left-brain, mechanistic systems, shut off from passion and connectivity, and cloistered within the logic of our own thoughts. Closed off from the world, we have become inattentive to it. The world has become an object for our control and manipulation because we are unconscious of belonging to it; thus, we are prone to devolve it. Teilhard indicated that integrated thinking is a "particular actualizing of the whole."[5] Be attentive to your thoughts; they can change the universe.

In our digital age, when information is available at the touch of a button, we are losing the capacity to think. As we transfer the work of the brain to the computer, we are becoming increasingly mechanistic, less relational, and more forgetful. Our attention is away from organic, biological life toward virtual, cyber life. Mechanistic thinking belies nature, in which relationships are primary, and things that form from relationships are secondary. Catholicity requires that we renounce mechanistic thinking in all its forms and return to the primacy of relationality. To let go and surrender to life's ebb and flow is to live with an openness to life, to let go when the right time comes, and to engage new structures of relationship. Openness to new unities requires an inner freedom to evolve self and world. Karl Rahner writes: "It is a misunderstanding to assert that freedom is merely the capacity to do this or that, as if one decision has no bearing on the second decision. . . . Freedom is the capacity to do something definitive. Every act of freedom makes the achievement of one's

---

[4] Pierre Teilhard de Chardin, *Human Energy*, trans. J. M. Cohen (New York: William Collins, 1969), 23.

[5] Teilhard de Chardin, *Christianity and Evolution*, 100; Thomas M. King, *Teilhard's Mysticism of Knowing* (New York: The Seabury Press, 1981), 35.

life ever more final. Freedom is the capacity to achieve one's own self."[6] Heidi Russell writes: "We know our past but cannot know our future with certainty. The present is the interaction of our past and future; our past impacts the probability of current actions, our freedom plays a role in determining which future probabilities get actualized and how those actualizations impact our future probabilities."[7] Thus, freedom and catholicity belong together. The whole person is the creative person who explores and animates the universe out of an inner sense of freedom and participates in its evolution toward unity. As we strive toward wholeness through inner freedom, we are more open to truth in its many forms and to every value that deepens life. Catholicity, as wholemaking, then becomes a deepening of truth. Everything is ripe to reveal truth, so that truth is not an "either/or" but a "both/and" approach. Truth shines out in that which unifies and enriches; it is found in that which gives coherence to our experience and leads us to seek greater unity and depth. Truth, like catholicity itself, can only be preserved by being continually enlarged. An inner consciousness toward the deepening of truth means an inner freedom of radical openness to all truth and to every authentic value.

---

[6] Karl Rahner, "Theology of Freedom," *Theological Investigations*, vol. 6, trans. Karl and Boniface Kruger (Baltimore: Helicon, 1969), 182–84. See also Mark F. Fischer, *Karl Rahner: Foundations of Christian Faith* (New York: Crossroad, 2005), III.1.B, 95; cf. Karl Rahner, *Grace in Freedom*, trans. Hilda Graef (New York: Herder and Herder, 1969), 228: "Freedom is not the capacity for indefinite revision, for always doing something different, but the one capacity to create something final, irrevocable and eternal, the capacity of what by itself is everlasting. Freedom alone creates that which is final."

[7] Heidi Russell, "Quantum Anthropology: Reimaging the Human Person as Body/Spirit," *Theological Studies* 74 (2013): 951. Russell is basing her theological insights on quantum reality. Ian Barbour notes that for physicist Werner Heisenberg "tendencies in nature include *a range of possibilities*. The future is not simply unknown; it is 'not decided.' More than one alternative is open, and there is some opportunity for unpredictable novelty." See Ian Barbour, *When Science Meets Religion: Enemies, Strangers, or Partners?* (New York: Harper Collins, 2000), 69.

The Church and Catholicity

The life of Jesus and his consciousness of making greater wholes tells us that catholicity is not ideology; rather, it is the Spirit of love that resists ideology: "Where the Spirit of the Lord is, there is freedom" (2 Cor 3:17). The dynamism of catholicity is energized by the Spirit. God is the name of genuine unrestricted love bubbling up at the heart of life, attracting more insight, wonder, and creativity, which leads me briefly to examine catholicity and the institution of the Church. Yves Congar defined catholicity as "the integration of multiplicity with unity; or, more exactly, . . . unity as assimilating multiplicity. Unity comes first; and it is in relation to this unity that multiplicity must be understood and appraised."[8] How we interpret the relation between the many and the one, the cosmology in which catholicity is understood, and the role of the sacraments all influence how we understand catholicity in its institutional form today. Consider the following:

> The Church certainly has a crucial, even necessary, co-operative agency in liturgical acts of consecration, but most truly, supernaturally, and mystically, the Eucharist constitutes the Church. The Eucharist is the source and summit of Catholic Christian life, it is what gathers up all the fragments of truth, hope, and life into the mystical unity of Christ's Body, the Catholic One. . . . The presence of Christ to men of every time is actualized in his Body, which is the Church. That is a highly particularized and concrete embodiment of Christ gathering up the whole human race in the Eucharist. No other gathering practice, no other religion, whether it is liberal democracy, the global economy, or any other theopolitical vision of the whole, so the red-blooded claim goes, is as comprehensive as this Eucharistic gathering in the teaching of the Catholic Church. . . . The human race itself depends on the mystical body of Christ

---

[8] Yves Congar, "Catholicité," in *Catholicisme, Hier, Aujourd'hui, Demain, Encyclopédie en sept volumes*, vol. 2 (Paris: Letouzey et Ané, 1948), 724; idem, "Rome, Oxford and Edinburgh," *Blackfriars* 18 (September 1937): 657.

assembled in the Eucharist, extended through time so that the world might mature into redemption. The Eucharist that constitutes the Church enables fugitives from grace to become pilgrims of the promise in the fullness of time.[9]

There are many theologians, lay and religious, who hold to the position above. It encapsulates the Church's official position on what constitutes catholicity as described, for example, in the encyclical *Veritatis splendor* (no. 21). Is the Church equal to the Eucharist ("the Eucharist constitutes the Church")? Or does the Eucharist sacramentalize the heart of the Church's mission, the unfolding of the reign of God, to which the gospel bears witness? How we approach these questions, I believe, is how we understand catholicity in its institutional form. In a fixed, stable cosmology, the Eucharist is placed over and above the world as an object of adoration and worship, hence, the Church as center of the world. When the Eucharist is situated in the context of the world, undergirding a world in evolution, we are in an expanding cosmos. The first catholicity has a vertical direction and the second catholicity a horizontal one. Jesus of Nazareth lived the second catholicity.

For the viability of the Catholic Church today (and, indeed, of all religions), there must be a renewal of cosmology; by this I mean that catholicity must begin with the Big Bang and the development of cosmic, evolutionary life. We emerge out of a long history of interrelatedness, a history of emergence from the very small to the very large and complex. It is insufficient to talk about ecology or care for creation today without considering the big picture of the cosmos we now know to be our home. Our 13.8 billion-year-old cosmos began in a singularity, a point where space and time curved in on themselves, making it impossible to distinguish future from past. Scientists suggest that the singularity may form at the center of a black hole, and that our universe

---

[9] C. C. Pecknold, "The Catholicity of David Ford," *The Journal of Scriptural Reasoning* 7, no. 1 (2008), jsr.lib.virginia.edu website. The metaphysics of this passage is not to be overlooked. It is a classical metaphysical framework with a platonic structure of nature/supernature, heaven/earth, divine Being/created being, with an ontology of Eucharist based on Aristotelian notions of substance and form.

may have emerged out of a black hole, reflecting our embedded-ness in a supra or larger universe of four or more spatial dimensions.[10] The universe seems to be one giant whole within a larger whole; it is a cosmic holon all the way back and likely forward as well. From the point of faith we are saying that God is at the heart of this immense and mysterious cosmic process. Life and consciousness emerge from a mysterious beginning of wholeness and are moving toward greater wholeness, more consciousness, and life. Every act of cosmic unfolding is, from the point of faith, an act of creation and incarnation. God does not simply create; rather, every act of creation is a synthesizing union of God and created being. Jesus Christ emerges by way of evolution, just as each one of us is rooted in cosmic evolution. "The human person, and the quality of human life, is clearly interwined with the physical world in which it is so deeply rooted."[11] If we proclaim that Jesus is truly God and truly human, then we are also saying that what God does in Jesus is what God has been doing since the Big Bang. The whole evolutionary process is Big Bang christification; when Jesus appears, there is a fit between what God has been doing all along and what God does in the person of Jesus. Thus, every act of creation is an act of incarnation. What appears to the sciences as a process of cosmogenesis is seen from the perspective of faith to be a process of Christogenesis. Zachary Hayes writes:

> It is through this history of revelation that Christians come to perceive that the ground or source of the creative process is a limitless mystery of productive love. The creative ground is fruitful love; the mystery of the divine is love-community itself. . . . The entire process of history reflects the mystery of fruitful love in a variety of analogous ways. Science sees a process whereby, already at the level of basic chemical elements, individual elements with each other to form something new, as hydrogen and oxygen unite to

---

[10] For a discussion of the Big Bang and black holes, see Niayesh Afshordi, Robert B. Mann, and Razieh Pourhasan, "The Black Hole at the Beginning of Time," *Scientific American* (July 15, 2014), 41, 43.

[11] Zachary Hayes, OFM, *A Window to the Divine: Creation Theology* (Quincy, IL: Franciscan Press, 1997), 89.

become water. . . . Isolated, independent existence must be given up in order to enter into broader and potentially deeper levels of existence. It is when humanity enters upon the scene that this principle of unification for the sake of fuller existence takes on truly personal dimensions and is seen as love in the proper sense of the word. God's creative love freely calls forth within the world a created love that can freely respond to God's creative call . . . not to say that God creates a perfect world or the best possible world. . . . However, . . . in as far as God creates a good world, it is a world that is fit for the working out of the divine purpose . . . the ever-widening expansion of created persons in loving union among themselves and with God.[12]

If catholicity is a consciousness of belonging to the whole, then, as Hayes said, sin "is not a mere infringement of a law extrinsic to our nature. It is a failure to realize the potentiality of our nature itself. If our nature is fundamentally a potentiality to expand, sin is a contraction. . . . Sin is the resistance to expansion through union with others."[13] Perhaps we can say that sin is the failure of catholicity or the failure to become more whole, the failure of church to be more deeply personal and social through history.

The ministry of Jesus in the midst of community indicates that the Church exists for the world. If evolution is a movement whereby created reality becomes unified, more christic, the Catholic Church cannot be the contraction of humanity into an objective unity (symbolized by the Eucharist); rather, it recapitulates the movement of hominization or personalization of history in a constantly changing and evolutionary world. As Irenaeus of Lyons claimed: "The glory of God is the human person fully alive."[14] Thus, the Church exists for the christification of the world, that all may become one (universality), as Jesus is one

---

[12] Ibid., 90–91.

[13] Hayes, *A Window to the Divine*, 93.

[14] Irenaeus of Lyons, *Adversus Haereses*, bk. 4, ch. 20, sec. 7, in English *St. Irenaeus: Against the Heresies* (Book 3), trans. Matthew C. Steenberg and Dominic J. Unger, *Ancient Christian Writers: The Works of the Fathers in Translation* (Mawhah, NJ: Paulist Press, 2012).

with the Father in the Spirit. As humans become more conscious of the whole within them (God) and the whole in which they are embedded (the cosmos) and act according to the whole (catholicity), the isolated fragments of life are brought into greater unity (Christogenesis). The risen Christ, the cosmic Person, emerges as the world moves from imperfection to greater perfection, from immaturity to greater maturity, "so that humanity might learn to bear the mystery of its loving God and thus come to the fullness of life."[15] Sacramental life then becomes a public "yes" to the christification of the world (baptism); a willingness to be "membered" to Jesus in costly love and to create fields of compassion and peace (Eucharist); a choice to focus one's mind on the whole, to think according to the whole, and to act according to the whole (ethics). The consciousness of catholicity must be a consciousness of the whole; the Church exists not only as the body but as the consciousness of Christ, not simply bearing witness to but kindling evolution. To think of the Catholic Church as a new phylum in evolution (Teilhard's idea) is to see salvation as new creation, to find healing and wholeness in the grace of God, and, through the energy of divine love, to help heal and make whole a world of conflict and violence. In this way the Church stands as a sign of God's promise that every tear will be wiped away, that the wolf will lie down with the lamb, and that a deepening of our human-earth community is possible up ahead.

Models of Catholicity

What might a consciousness of catholicity look like, and who are the models of catholicity today? There is no greater visible model of catholicity at present than the Argentinian Bishop of Rome, Pope Francis. From the moment he was elected to the papacy and stepped out to greet the world by asking for prayer, Pope Francis has shown a new spirit of wholemaking, striving to move the Church from its static, inward-focused, legalistic mentality to a world-embracing church that lives on the margins. His awareness of the human person, especially the poor and the

---

[15] Hayes, *A Window to the Divine*, 74, 91.

suffering, has been inspirational. He has renounced pomp and circumstances, cufflinks and Audis, to embrace the poor, the marginalized, and the dispossessed. His charism is to bring the good news of God's love to all those who feel excluded from this love. He realizes that the law serves the Spirit and not the other way around. The law is not to stifle the Spirit of God but to liberate the Spirit to do new things. The example of Pope Francis's life and ministry is like a christic fractal, a new pattern of order that mirrors the life of Jesus. He lives in hope that this new energy of love will spread throughout the Church, and the Church throughout the world, so that Christ may become more visibly present in the world. He is remarkable in his zeal, energy, and freedom to self-actualize the gospel in a world grown weary of God, yet desperately seeking God.[16] If he could empower the Church to engage the new cosmology and, in particular, evolution, to link catholicity and cosmology, and thus to enkindle a new spirit of love-energy in the sacramental life of the Church, I think Pope Francis could help move the Church to a new level of consciousness and a new community of life for the world—an open-systems Church for an open-systems world.

While the Church has struggled with evolution and its implications for humanity, especially conscious evolution, Barbara Marx Hubbard, who is Jewish by birth, is deeply catholic in her efforts to raise conscious evolution to a new level of wholeness. As a teenager she was deeply disturbed by the human invention of the nuclear bomb, and she asked: "What is the purpose of humanity's power?" "What is my purpose?" Through much reading and deep spiritual experiences she realized that she is called to help humanity realize the fruitfulness of its creative power in God. In *The Revelation: Our Crisis Is a Birth*, Barbara explores what it means to be a co-creator in light of the Book of Revelation, which, in her view, shows the remarkable potential available to each individual to do new things.[17] She believes

---

[16] John Carr, "100 Days of Francis," *America* (2013); Leonardo Boff, *Francis of Rome and Francis of Assisi*, trans. Dinah Livingstone (Maryknoll, NY: Orbis Books, 2014).

[17] Barbara Marx Hubbard and Noel McInnis, *The Revelation: Our Crisis Is a Birth (Book of Co-Creation)* (Santa Barbara, CA: Foundation for Conscious Evolution, 1993).

that Jesus provides an example for us of what human beings can become. Her book reveals how humanity will evolve by using our vast creative power in harmony with the divine pattern. Like her other works, *The Revelation* is about our co-creation in cooperation with divine love. We have the power to become something new, but we must become conscious of this power and then act consciously according to this power for a greater unity. She states: "All people are born creative, endowed by our Creator with the inalienable right to realize our creativity, for the good of ourselves and the world."[18] Like Pope Francis, Barbara Marx Hubbard is a christic fractal and is generating new fields of conscious action for a more unified world.

A third example of catholicity is one that I see more broadly defined in the fourteenth Dalai Lama, who is the spiritual leader of Tibetan Buddhists. Like Pope Francis, his sheer energy to travel globally, bringing a message of peace and nonviolence to the world, and his respect for all life mark him as one with catholicity, a consciousness of the whole seeking to make a greater whole. In his remarkable book *The Universe in a Single Atom*, the Dalai Lama describes his own journey from a country boy to a world spiritual leader in a scientific age. He examines the place of science in the human realm and says that while science has revolutionized our knowledge of the physical, it has yet to provide a comprehensive understanding of reality and human existence. The Dalai Lama concludes that science cannot provide the wholeness we seek, that it must partner with religion and spirituality in the full flowering of life: "From the Buddhist perspective, a full human understanding must not only offer a coherent account of reality, our means of apprehending it, and the place of consciousness but also include a clear awareness of how we should act."[19] To have a consciousness of the whole, for the Dalai Lama, is to be attuned to modern science and to find ways of harmonizing science and spirituality to deepen wisdom

---

[18] "The Age of Co-Creation: An Interview with Barbara Marx Hubbard," *School of Metaphysics* (1993), som.org website; idem, *Conscious Evolution: Awakening the Power of Our Social Potential* (Novato, CA: New World Library, 1998), 57–87.

[19] Dalai Lama, *The Universe in a Single Atom: The Convergence of Science and Spirituality* (New York: Random House, 2005), 206.

and compassion. We are to live according to the highest possible values, the law of love and the law of compassion. In this respect I see the Dalai Lama as a christic fractal who is living out his own spiritual vocation as a co-creative participant in evolution and cosmic unity.

Finally, a model of catholicity that has become evident to me over the last few years is the Leadership Conference of Women Religious (LCWR). The LCWR has its history rooted in the spirit that led to Vatican II. In 1950 Pope Pius XII convened the First General Congress of the States of Perfection, calling to Rome the superiors general of religious orders throughout the world. Two years later the heads of men's and women's religious organizations met at the National Congress of Religious of the USA, where Reverend Arcadio Larraona, secretary of the Congregation for Religious, referred to a "movement" requiring change: "We must live in our times and according to the needs of our times."[20] What is fascinating about the history of LCWR is observing the efforts of religious women to be faithful to the gospel and attentive to the needs of the world. Their "life on the margins" defines, to the present day, the spirit of the conference. The prologue of a recent LCWR document states:

> Our foremothers and founders stepped into the chaos and the unknown of their day, trusting in God's good guidance and great providence. In our time, we are called to do the same. Inspired by the radical call of the Gospel, led by God's Spirit and companioned by one another, we embrace our time as holy, our leadership as gift, and our challenges as blessings.[21]

If catholicity is consciousness of the whole, catholicity best defines the mission of the LCWR. Religious women today, following Vatican II, strive to be more authentically human and christic, to participate fully in the evolution of self and world, to work toward a deepening of community where the poor, the earth, women and children are included in the banquet of shared life. Speaking to one of the LCWR sisters recently, I

---

[20] "LCWR History," lcwr.org website.
[21] "Prologue," "LCWR Call for 2010–15," lcwr.org website.

asked, "Where does this courageous, pioneer spirit to plow new frontiers and probe new horizons come from?" It was clearly the spirit of many women who founded religious congregations in the United States in the nineteenth and twentieth centuries, but what fires the spirit today? Her answer was brief and to the point: "Prayer is our power." As I reflected on her answer and my own experience of talking to many religious communities, I thought her insight was quite profound. Religious women have built the social arm of the twentieth-century church—the hospitals, schools, and social-welfare agencies—that have expressed the public face of the Catholic Church. At the same time they have been deeply committed to prayer, not just saying prayers, but long hours of deep, prayerful reflection on the scriptures and on listening to the Spirit of God. This obedience to prayer is the spirit of the LCWR, a consciousness nurtured by prayerful attentiveness to the reality of God in our midst and to the power of the Spirit drawing us beyond ourselves, to give ourselves to the more, so that life may become more abundant for all. The catholicity of the LCWR women is lived in openness to the future, as many communities strive to reorganize as open systems of shared energy for a new christic reality. Their prayerful spirit has ignited a consciousness of the whole, emerging out of a deep inner freedom in God; it is this inner freedom, held in contemplative space, that enables religious women to go forth despite the Church's efforts at times to stifle them.

What we see in the lives of the LCWR women, the Dalai Lama, Barbara Marx Hubbard, and Pope Francis is the unquenchable fire of the Spirit. The Spirit *is* the "trinitization" of God in history, the unmasking of divine love in the evolution of life, the deepening of relationality, and a consciousness of being part of a whole that empowers action toward unity. The Spirit is the life-giving force, entangled love-energy, luring evolution toward more being and love. As Saint Paul writes in his Letter to the Corinthians: "The Spirit searches all things, even the depths of God" (1 Cor 2:10). Where there is the Spirit, there is not only a consciousness of the whole but a movement of action toward the whole. A Sister wrote to me recently saying that Catholicism has too long ignored advances in the psychology of the self and its intertwining relationship with the Spirit (our holy oneness) in dynamic and creative interplay. If catholicity is having a sense of the whole, then prayer is the spiritual energy that weaves the Spirit of God and self into an integrated whole, kindling our thoughts and actions to make wholes out of the fragments of our experiences. Jesus's own prayerfulness was a deep, Spirit-filled energy of love, a "one-ing" with Omega-love. Catholicity requires persons of deep prayer who are conscious of belonging to a larger whole, orienting the entirety of their lives to the absolute whole that is God. There is no real transcendence toward wholeness without integration of self and God.

Waking Up

What does it mean to belong to the Catholic Church in a Big Bang cosmos and an age of consciousness? I think it means to wake up. Jesuit spiritual writer Anthony de Mello writes: "Most people don't know they are asleep. They're born asleep, they live asleep, they marry in their sleep, they breed children in their sleep, they die in their sleep without ever waking up. They never understand the loveliness and the beauty of this thing we call 'human existence.'" De Mello goes on to tell a story about a man who knocks on his son's door.

"Jaime," he says, "wake up!" Jaime answers, "I don't want to get up, Papa." The father shouts, "Get up, you have to go to school." Jamie says, "I don't want to go to school." "Why not?" asks the father. "Three reasons," says Jaime. "First, because it's so dull; second, the kids tease me; and third, I hate school." And the father says, "Well, I am going to give you three reasons why you must go to school. First because it is your duty; second, because you are forty-five years old; and third, because you are the headmaster." Wake up, wake up! You're grown up. You're too big to be asleep. Wake up! Stop playing with your toys.[22]

---

[22] Anthony De Mello, SJ, "Spirituality Means Waking Up," demellospirituality.com website.

Could we not transpose this story into the key of catholicity and the Church? We must wake up, all of us—laity, nuns, clergy, and bishops—and become conscious of the great call within us, the call to bring Christ to birth in the world. Get up! Go into the world and live in the flow of love. Forgive, show mercy, be compassionate, care for the poor, tend to the earth as family; find your inner wholeness in the love of God and create new wholes in your midst, in your communities, your workplaces, at shopping malls, and jazz fests. Live in the energy of the Spirit; let yourself be led into new patterns of wholeness, into new structures and languages that kindle life more abundantly. Stop playing with your toys, your electronic gadgets; stop creating books of laws and rules that lie on dusty shelves; do not lose yourselves to consumer products that blind your vision or distract your attention from the whole. Get up because you are too old to be asleep, lest you die in your sleep and the world dies of neglect. Grow up because it is time to move on. The world is begging for new and more abundant life. The life of the world is your life, and your life belongs to the whole of life. Stop trying to preserve yourself; lose yourself in something more than yourself because you have the power to christify life, to help unify it, to raise it to a new level of ultrahumanity. Live to the point of tears and don't be saddened by sin, misunderstanding, weakness, and hate. Omega love is in our midst, and this love is our power, our hope and our future. Remain in this love, because this love is the fire of life itself and will endure forever. Be the co-creator you are made to be: emblazon this world with the grandeur of God.

Chapter 10

Conclusion

There is a beautiful passage from the Psalms that evokes a sense of catholicity as ceaseless wonder:

> When I look at your heavens, the work of your
>   fingers,
>   the moon and stars that you have estab-
>   lished;
>   what are human beings that you are mindful
>   of them,
>   mortals that you care for them? (Ps 8:3)

It is indeed an awesome universe, this place we call home. Hidden within the dark energy of expanding life, there is a deep longing for unity. *Catholicity* is the word that best describes nature's craving for unity, the intrinsic capacity of being for wholeness. The new science, including Big Bang cosmology, evolution, and quantum physics, evokes a new understanding of catholicity. By tracing its roots from the Greek *cosmos* to our present day, I have tried to show that catholicity is fundamentally related to cosmology and consciousness. Cosmology, catholicity, and consciousness are intertwined. By coining the word *katholikos* the Greeks made sense of the human person in relation to the cosmos—one who stands under the stars, attentive to the stars and planets, learning how to live in harmony.

It is not surprising that the early Christians adopted this word to describe a new whole centered in Christ. Catholicity aptly described the early Christian disciples gathered around the bishop as teacher and shepherd of the gospel life, which they celebrated in the Eucharist. Inspired by the memory of Jesus and aware of his risen presence, the disciples had a consciousness of being gathered in the name of Jesus, signifying a new whole, a new creation—in a sense, a new cosmos. The Church became the sign and symbol of this new creation: "Where there is (consciousness of) Christ, there is the Church" marked this inclusive community. Those willing to dedicate their lives toward wholemaking in Christ became members of the Catholic Church.

The dynamic gathering power (and attractive power) of the early Church, however, did not last long. It was manipulated by Constantine the Great, who used the Church to consolidate his political power. The Arian controversy provided a great opportunity to amalgamate East and West under sole monarchical rule, making orthodoxy the litmus test of catholicity. Consciousness of the whole in Christ was replaced by allegiance to the truth of Christ. What was lost in the embroiled history of the Church's formation was the integral connection between catholicity and cosmology. Bitter disputes over doctrine and dogma depleted the gathering power of catholicity and replaced the meaning of catholicity with truth and salvation. The deep relationship between macrocosm and microcosm, integral to the Greek notion of catholicity, was marginalized. Orthopraxis was replaced by orthodoxy. In the modern period lawfulness and hierarchy defined the Catholic Church; emphasis was placed on sin, guilt, heaven, and hell, resulting in a dualistic and disconnected left-brain Church that functioned like a sturdy ship on the stormy seas of the world. To be "saved" was to be on board the ship. Vatican II sought to retrieve the connection between ship and sea, renewing the Church as the "people of God" on a journey toward the fullness of life in God. However, the loss of a dynamic consciousness of catholicity in the modern period was profound. This loss included (1) the loss of thinking in a way that unifies, (2) a lack of dynamic orientation toward making wholes through engaged action, and (3) reduction of catholicity to abstract truths. As a result catholicity became narrow and institutional, more divisive than inclusive. What I have tried to show on the various levels of nature, humankind, Jesus, and Church is that catholicity is a conscious movement *toward* universality, a wide expanse of consciousness that sees the world, as Gerard Manley Hopkins put it, "charged with the grandeur of God."

If the breadth and width of catholicity was lost after Nicea and collapsed in the modern period, it was also revived in the twentieth century by a lone Jesuit scientist writing from the deserts of China. Teilhard de Chardin was an observer, a paleontologist, and, like the Greeks, stood under the stars in awe at this marvelous universe we call our home. By bringing together evolution and Christianity in a single vision, Teilhard restored catholicity to its original meaning: consciousness of belonging to a whole and making new wholes by thinking and acting toward wholeness. His "deep catholicity" went hand in hand with his idea of "deep incarnation." God is deeply involved with evolutionary creation from the Big Bang onward. Divine love is the whole of every whole, empowering life toward greater wholeness and unity in love. This is the emergence of the Christ, who comes to explicit consciousness in Jesus of Nazareth, the wholemaker par excellence.

To find a new sense of catholicity in the twenty-first century is to discover the power of the spacious mind, the mind that gathers, ignites, fires, and wires together. What gathers us into new wholes in ways that God is more alive and present? What draws us inward and centers us so that life is seen in its depth and beauty? What kindles passion and connectivity? Teilhard de Chardin said that a new vision of the universe calls for a new form of worship and a new method of action.[1] To do so, however, the Church must reconcile itself with modern science; in particular, it must accept evolution as the narrative of biological and cosmic life. I think catholicity is bursting with life today, less within the Church and more outside the institution. I find a tremendous yearning among Nones and the millennial generation (born between 1982 and the early 2000s) for a more just and unified world. Many of the millennial generation are wholemakers involved in greening the earth, immigration reform, peace and nonviolence, economic justice, and environmental sustainability. They seek authentic community life, ways of meditation, and alternative gift economies; they believe that institutional religion

---

[1] Pierre Teilhard de Chardin, *Activation of Energy*, trans. René Hague (New York: William Collins, 1970), 267.

is out of touch with the world. Like transhumanists, the Nones long for religious ideals without the institution. Charles Taylor speaks of new social imaginaries in the postmodern milieu; God has not vanished but is being sought in the new terrain of a new social landscape.[2] How do we translate secular humanism into radical incarnationalism, whereby a consciousness of being drawn together is seen as the power of God pulling us toward something more whole and unified, a christified world emerging toward greater unity in love? Can we reimagine catholicity in an evolving universe in such a way that religion makes a difference to the world? Can we reimagine the Church as a system open to new thought patterns and structures that kindle the human spirit in its yearning for God? The Church of the future will depend on how we see ourselves in relation to the universe and how conscious we are of living in an evolving universe. The new series from Orbis Books, *Catholicity in an Evolving Universe* (of which this book is first), is intended to illuminate a new vision for the Church ahead. Catholicity, cosmology, and consciousness must be integrally connected if we are to forge a new path for the future.

The key to catholicity, orienting mind toward wholeness, is focusing the mind on the unity of God-Omega, on divine love. From a Christian perspective training the mind on love is awakening to the Spirit of God through prayer and meditation. The Spirit is divine love empowering life to evolve toward more wholeness and thus more unified consciousness. We see this empowering love in the life of Jesus, who showed a oneness of consciousness with God.

> When he came to Nazareth, where he had been brought up, he went to the synagogue on the sabbath day, as was his custom. He stood up to read, and the scroll of the prophet Isaiah was given to him. He unrolled the scroll and found the place where it was written:
>
>> "The Spirit of the Lord is upon me,
>>   because he has anointed me
>>   to bring good news to the poor.

---

[2] See Charles Taylor, *A Secular Age* (Cambridge, MA: Belknap Press/ Harvard University Press, 2007), 299.

He has sent me to proclaim release to the cap-
tives
 and recovery of sight to the blind,
  to let the oppressed go free,
 to proclaim the year of the Lord's favor."

And he rolled up the scroll, gave it back to the attendant, and sat down. The eyes of all in the synagogue were fixed on him. Then he began to say to them, "Today this scripture has been fulfilled in your hearing." (Lk 4:16–21)

Three words stand out in this passage—*Spirit, anointed,* and *today*—as if Jesus is saying, "The Spirit empowers me in this moment to do new things. Everything you have been praying for—liberation of the poor, sight to the blind, freedom of the oppressed—these things are now realized in and through my life because the Spirit of God is with me." How shocking! Can you imagine the rabbis and elders hearing this young man take the words of the prophet Isaiah as his own? In my view this is the beginning of a new cosmology, a new catholicity. Jesus, empowered by the Spirit, surrenders himself to the higher power of divine Love and dares to accept the Old Testament prophecy as his mission. From this point on the life of Jesus becomes a conscious commitment to love, mercy, and compassion, making wholes where there are fragments of human life and opening the eyes of the blind to the power of God in their midst: "Go and tell John what you have seen and heard: the blind receive their sight, the lame walk, lepers are cleansed, and the deaf hear, the dead are raised, the poor have good news brought to them" (Lk 7:22). Jesus does the unthinkable, the unimaginable, through the power of the Spirit. He would have loved the motto of Steve Jobs, "think different," but he would have added, "think new," because the power of God is yearning to do new things, to create more wholeness of life, to transform earth into the fullness of Christ, so that "they may all be one" (Jn 17:21).

Two thousand years later, and with insights from modern science, we can say that the Spirit of wisdom that filled the mind of Jesus was already present in the Big Bang. God-Omega is the love-energy empowering life from its beginning, one with unfolding life that comes to explicit consciousness in the life of Jesus. The Spirit that empowered the life of Jesus is the same Spirit released on the cross through the death of Jesus, empowering the disciples to gather into community, to continue the life of Christ in their own lives so that life on earth may flourish more abundantly and be transformed into the glory of God. The life of Jesus is about new creation, a new cosmos, a new oneness in God. To the extent we become, like Jesus, more unified in earthly life through the power of the Spirit, we too share in divine power in resurrected life, transforming all life into the fullness of Omega.

Teilhard felt that religion, Christianity in particular, had become too stale and static, too out of touch with the world, and too otherworldly. Religion, he said, is to harness the energies of the spirit; it is a technology of the human or created spirit by which the mind and heart are focused on new and deeper life. Hence, the drive for religion should be the same drive for technology; life in God should be increasing exponentially not arithmetically. To do so, however, religion must periodically redefine itself, undergo regeneration, because religion can get static or fixed. Religion is not something one arrives at; rather, it is the starting point for relationship with the absolute One—God. Religion, therefore, is always a genesis, a birthing of the Spirit toward greater unity. Without the dynamic energy of transcendence by which consciousness rises and relationships deepen, religion grows old and weary; it becomes rote, a mechanistic repetition of old ideas. To function out of an old cosmology with old ideas of matter and form, to think that God does not do new things, is to make an idol out of Jesus and to ignore the power of the Spirit.

In Teilhard's view humanity must understand itself as the arrow of evolution and actively prepare itself for the future it wants. If traditional religion focuses only on individuals and heaven, it is insufficient; people are looking for a religion of humankind and earth. Faith in God must now be lived with faith in the world, because God is creating the world into something new. The power of God creating anew unfolds in and through us. Thus, Teilhard said, we need people who will be passionately energized by faith in God and faith in the world, as two aspects of love energizing union toward wholeness. We need to "put on the mind of Christ" not as a spiritual exercise of imitating Jesus but as focusing our minds on the unity of love. We must become inwardly whole by training our minds to become more integrated, a higher consciousness of oneness; to unify the partials of our lives, in our communities and in our world; to make an "option for the whole." We need a new catholicity that integrates humankind's religious experience into a new spirituality for a new earth, yearning to breathe new life. Christianity is a religion of evolution, of making new wholes where there are fragments, a religion that demands a higher consciousness of unity in love. It is a religion of evolution because we believe in the power of God to do new things, symbolized by the risen Christ. Christians, however, must *choose* to evolve; to become conscious of what is yet unconscious and unwhole; to connect consciously to the whole planet, the whole earth community, and the universe. A conscious choice to evolve the christic underscores a new understanding of the sacraments, a new entanglement (baptism) and morphogenetic field (Eucharist) of oneness in Christ. Teilhard dared to reimagine Christianity as a religion of evolution. In light of Teilhard's vision, I offer the following points:

- Know earth as we know our own bodies. We are still too platonic and dualistic.
- Harness the spiritual energy of world religions whose global maturation is necessary for the completion of each person on earth.
- Believe in the forward march of thought, the physical reality of thought. To think is to unify; knowledge is about thinking, not information.
- See the evolving universe as both open and centered ahead with a new world soul emerging through the noosphere or global mind.
- Nurture a "zest for living" that is "dynamic, constructive and adventurous."
- Have a primal trust in life and an openness to the future; build on this trust, expand it, and consolidate it.

Nature tells us that within the inner dimension of every being there is a desire for more being; on every level of existence there is a yearning for greater unity or wholeness. Similarly, on the level of the human person there is an implicit faith in ultimate wholeness. I think this yearning for belonging and participating in something whole is what drives the passion of music fests, sports events, and social media. We are created for wholeness, and deep within we yearn to have a part in the whole. While cultural events placate our right-brain search for connectivity, cultural religion (venerating sports stars and music idols, for example) is simply indicative of our much deeper need for spiritual religion. We are religious beings to our core, and catholicity is the energy of life's core toward ultimate wholeness.

While transhumanists seek a posthuman future by becoming machine dependent, such dependence threatens to depersonalize and isolate us if we do not harness technology for a transcendent and unified goal. We are created for wholeness, and thus we are created for community. Technology can enhance or deepen life, but it depends on how we use it. The convergence of minds through the Internet can give rise to a new global heart, if we use technology for this purpose. But technology cannot replace religion. Religion has evolutionary importance as the direction of human energy and consciousness. Religious consciousness must evolve into global-collective consciousness. In the next stage of evolution world religions must come together for the sake of the world, because the whole earth is in desperate need of a spiritual center. We need to focus on finding this center rather than trying to fix the world's problems. The problems cannot be adequately resolved because they are rooted in the human, left-brain disconnect of unrelatedness. Hence, the problems of our age (and there are many) are not problems to be fixed but relationships to be healed. It is unfortunate that it takes situations of war or conflict to thrust people of different religions together, but it would be naive to think that we will evolve into a greater unity or world community without gathering together our religious energies and suffering through to something higher. A Sister of Saint Joseph once told me that she was working in a rundown hospital in Liberia, Africa, when the army invaded the town, rounded up all the people, and locked them in the Church. She recounted how Muslims and Christians hid under the pews, clutching one another for dear life. In the face of terror and suffering their left-brain control mechanisms dissolved. Empty of power, they held on to one another as brother and sister. They were released from the Church and told to walk. She said they walked hand in hand to the Ivory Coast, with only the shirts on their backs, and created a new life together—Muslims and Christians—forming a new whole in a new life.

Catholicity requires an integrated consciousness of the whole, a deep relationality, as well as a deepening of inner and outer wholeness. It calls us to recognize that connectedness is a basic reality of our existence. We are wholes within wholes. All we do affects all the other wholes of which we are a part and all the other parts that make us whole. Catholicity invites us to wake up and get up, to stretch our minds and hearts, and to reach for the stars. We are to think unto wholeness; love unto fullness; resist the forces of oppression, domination, and control by leaning into suffering and facing death as sister. Catholicity is an invitation to live in the present, open to the future and to the realm of infinite possibilities, which "eye has not seen, nor ear heard" (1 Cor 2:9); to give birth to God and glorify God by unifying life. Can we, as Church, creatively engage the work of the Spirit in our midst and think new? Can we dare to birth the life of Jesus in radically new ways in a world longing for unity? More so, can we liberate the Christ from institutional constraints and harness the energies of love for Christogenesis?

It is time for a new catholicity, a new religion of the world (to use Teilhard's idea), a liberated Church with the Spirit-filled Christ empowering us to become artisans of a new future. God is the power of unconditional love, the transcendent One who dwells in and authenticates our darkness. Transcendence does not loom over us; rather, we are its privileged bearer.[3] Thus, we are to think so as to unify and love with a grateful heart. To live in catholicity is to be conscious that each life breath that I call my own belongs to the stars, the galaxies, my neighbors and family, my enemies, past generations, and those to come. I am part of a whole, like you, and the whole is more than any one of us can grasp because the absolute wholeness of life is Love itself—God—the power of the future. We need to let go of trying

---

[3] Richard Kearny, *Anatheism: Return to God after God* (New York: Columbia University Press, 2011), 91.

to control life and wildly fling ourselves into the arms of divine Love. This is the only real way into the future of life. We have the power to create a new world, and we have the power to destroy this one. How we choose depends on how we grasp *this* moment as the kiss of God, impelling us to stand up and speak.

Select Bibliography

Abrams, Nancy Ellen, and Joel R. Primack. "Cosmology and Twenty-First Century Culture," http://physics.ucsc.edu/cosmo/primack_abrams/1769.pdf.

———. *The New Universe and the Human Future: How a Shared Cosmology Could Transform the World.* New Haven, CT: Yale University Press, 2011.

Brague, Rémi. *The Wisdom of the World: The Human Experience of the Universe in Western Thought.* Translated by Teresa Lavender Fagan. Chicago: University of Chicago Press, 2003.

Bohm, David. *Wholeness and the Implicate Order.* New York: Routledge and Kegan Paul, 1980.

Brown, Barbara Taylor. *The Luminous Web: Essays on Science and Religion.* Boston: Cowley Publications, 2000.

Bruteau, Beatrice. *The Grand Option: Personal Transformation and a New Creation.* Notre Dame, IN: University of Notre Dame Press, 2001.

Cannato, Judy. *Radical Amazement: Contemplative Lessons from Black Holes, Supernovas, and Other Wonders of the Universe.* Notre Dame, IN: Sorin Books, 2006.

Capra, Fritjof. *The Web of Life: A New Scientific Understanding of Living Systems.* New York: Doubleday, 2006.

Clayton, Philip. *Mind and Emergence: From Quantum to Consciousness.* New York: Oxford University Press, 2004.

Dalai Lama. *The Universe in a Single Atom.* New York: Broadway Books, 2005.

Delio, Ilia. *The Emergent Christ: Exploring the Meaning of Catholic in an Evolutionary Universe.* Maryknoll, NY: Orbis Books, 2011.

———, ed. *From Teilhard to Omega: Co-creating an Unfinished Universe.* Maryknoll, NY: Orbis Books, 2014.

———. *The Unbearable Wholeness of Being: God, Evolution, and the Power of Love.* Maryknoll, NY: Orbis Books, 2013.

Edwards, Denis. *Jesus and the Cosmos.* New York: Paulist Press, 1991.

Frank, Adam. *The Constant Fire: Beyond the Science vs. Religion Debate.* Berkeley and Los Angeles: University of California Press, 2009.

Flinders, Carol. *Enduring Lives: Living Portraits of Women and Faith in Action.* Maryknoll, NY: Orbis Books, 2006.

Haughey, John, SJ. *Where Is Knowing Going? The Horizons of the Knowing Subject.* Washington, DC: Georgetown University Press, 2009.

Hayes, Zachary. *A Window to the Divine.* Quincy, IL: Franciscan Press, 1997.

Hefner, Philip. *Technology and Human Becoming.* Minneapolis: Fortress Press, 2003.

Herbert, Nick. *Quantum Reality: Beyond the New Physics.* New York: Doubleday, 1985.

Goswami, Amit. *The Self-Aware Universe: How Consciousness Creates the Material World.* New York: G. P. Putnam's Sons, 1994.

Kasper, Walter. *The God of Jesus Christ.* Translated by Matthew O'Connell. New York: Crossroad, 1999.

King, Ursula. *Christ in All Things.* Maryknoll, NY: Orbis Books, 1997.

———. *The Spirit of One Earth: Reflections on Teilhard de Chardin and Global Spirituality.* New York: Paragon House, 1989.

Panikkar, Raimon. *The Rhythm of Being: The Gifford Lectures.* Maryknoll, NY: Orbis Books, 2010.

Pierre Teilhard de Chardin: Writings/Selected. Introduction by Ursula King. Maryknoll, NY: Orbis Books, 1999.

Rubenstein, Richard E. *When Jesus Became God: The Epic Fight over Christ's Divinity in the Last Days of Rome.* New York: Harcourt Brace and Company, 1999.

Marion, Jim. *Putting on the Mind of Christ.* Charlottesville, VA: Hampton Roads, 2000.

McGilchrist, Iain. *The Master and His Emissary: The Divided Brain and the Making of the Western World.* New Haven, CT: Yale University Press, 2009.

Sack, John Richard. *Mystic Mountain: The Ascent to Love.* Jacksonville, OR: CyberScribe Publications, 2014.

Schäfer, Lothar. *Infinite Potential: What Quantum Physics Reveals about How We Should Live.* New York: Deepak Chopra Books, 2013.

Sheldrake, Rupert. *A New Science of Life: The Hypothesis of Morphic Resonance.* Rochester, VT: Park Street Press, 1995.

Singh, Simon. *Big Bang: The Origin of the Universe.* New York: Harper Collins, 2004.

Teilhard de Chardin, Pierre. *Activation of Energy*. Translated by René Hague. New York: Harcourt Brace Jovanovich, 1971.

———. *Christianity and Evolution*. Translated by René Hague. New York: Harcourt Brace and Co., 1969.

———. *The Divine Milieu: An Essay on the Interior Life*. Translated by William Collins. New York: Harper and Row, 1969.

———. *The Future of Man*. Translated by Norman Denny. New York: Harper and Row, 1964.

———. *The Phenomenon of Man*. Translated by Bernard Wall. New York: Harper and Row, 1959.

———. *Science and Christ*. Translated by René Hague. New York: Harper and Row, 1968.

———. *Toward the Future*. Translated by René Hague. New York: Harcourt, 1975.

Thompson, William M. *Christ and Consciousness: Exploring Christ's Contribution to Human Consciousness: The Origins and Development of Christian Consciousness*. New York: Paulist Press, 1977.

Tomaino, Charlotte. *Awakening the Brain*. New York: Atria Books, 2012.

Zohar, Danah. *The Quantum Self: Human Nature and Consciousness Defined by the New Physics*. New York: Quill/William Morrow, 1990.

Wheatley, Margaret. *Leadership and the New Science: Discovering Order in a Chaotic World*. Berkeley, CA: Berrett Koehler, 1994.

Whitehead, Alfred North. *Process and Reality*. Edited by David Ray Griffin and Donald W. Sherburne. New York: Free Press, 1978.

Index